The British Economy

ECONOMICS HANDBOOK SERIES

SEYMOUR E. HARRIS, Editor

Burns—Social Security and Public Policy

Carlson—Economic Security in the United States

Coppock—International Economic Instability

Duesenberry—Business Cycles and Economic Growth

Hansen—The American Economy

Hansen—A Guide to Keynes

Hansen—Monetary Theory and Fiscal Policy

Hansen—Economic Issues of the 1960's

Harris—International and Interregional Economics

Harrod—The British Economy

Henderson and Quandt—Microeconomic Theory

Hoover—The Location of Economic Activity

Johnston—Statistical Cost Analysis

Kindleberger—Economic Development

Lerner—Economics of Employment

Taylor—A History of Economic Thought

Tinbergen and Bos—Mathematical Models of Economic Growth

Valavanis—Econometrics

The British Economy

ROY HARROD

Nuffield Reader in International Economics,
Oxford University

McGraw-Hill Book Company, Inc.
NEW YORK · SAN FRANCISCO
TORONTO · LONDON
1963

THE BRITISH ECONOMY

Library of Congress Catalog Card Number 63-14560

26855

PRINTED AND BOUND IN ENGLAND BY
HAZELL WATSON AND VINEY LTD
AYLESBURY, BUCKS

Editor's Introduction

Sir Roy Harrod, one of the outstanding economists in Europe and the official biographer of Lord Keynes, has written a book on the British economy which should be of great usefulness to American and British readers, and especially to students and the informed layman. This book offers not only an analysis of the British economy as it functions today, but Harrod also tells us how it came to be what it is today, and suggests what should be done in the future to provide maximum stability and growth.

On many issues Harrod throws a new and penetrating light. To what extent have the British recouped the losses of World War II, and notably in the export sector? How can an appropriate wage policy be achieved which would exclude inflation? How can the balance-of-payments problem be solved without at the same time deflating the economy? What is the relation and relative importance of demand- and cost-induced inflation? To what extent has the Labour government fundamentally changed the British system? What are the dangers of the Common Market for the British, the United States and for the under-developed countries? How can international liquidity be increased? What are the costs of high money rate policies? These are among the many questions to which Harrod applies himself, and no one, not even professional economists, can read this book without learning much. Yet it is all comprehensible to the student and the non-economist.

For the American public the book has special merit. Throughout, Harrod comments on the American version of the problems disturbing the British. The American economist is impressed by the similarity of problems facing the British and the Americans, and the alternative approaches to their solution.

Seymour E. Harris

Contents

CHAPTER 1

Introduction

In my endeavour to present a picture of the state of the British economy it has been my duty to stand back in order to get a general view and to summarize and assess the record, the potentialities and the forces underlying policy making. In the attempt to make such an assessment I have been surprised by the frequency with which the effects of the Second World War have had to be brought into the reckoning. The war was over eighteen years ago. It has been a tradition among economists that recovery from war is usually more rapid than had been expected. There is the solid economic fact that, although one may borrow money and leave behind a National Debt, one cannot mobilize the "real" resources of the future. One has to pay as one goes. Interest on a debt incurred at home is a mere transfer of income from one side of the balance to another. Thus, at the end of the war labour and other resources are available to supply current needs, and so recovery comes quickly. In the British case this has been only partly true. Even the existing situation cannot be rightly judged unless the effects of the war are borne in mind.

These considerations have forced a painful retrospect. The general tendency, on the whole a healthy one, was to try to forget about the harrowing incidents of war as soon as it was over. If one makes the effort of looking back one recalls that from the very beginning, in September 1939, a question mark was blazing in the sky—could the country survive? No doubt the British had partly themselves to blame for being in such a predicament, owing to preceding faults in diplomacy and the belated attention given to defencive strength. Be that as it might, the situation was as it was. It was a question of fighting on the beaches and in the streets. It was evidently to be a life and death struggle. All thoughts of matters unconnected with the war were swept aside. Every ounce of strength had to be engaged in a struggle lasting for six years.

The consequence was that the capital equipment of the country, except as required specifically for the war effort, went into disrepair, and fresh capital formation was non-existent. The bomb damage in the United Kingdom was not as serious as that in some countries. It would be an interesting statistical exercise to compare the value of what may be lost by bombardment with the value of what is lost by total abstinence from gross capital formation. More serious than the lack of capital formation at home was the deterioration of the capital and trade position of the United Kingdom on the external side. The British economy and way of living depended essentially on the position built up by the cultivation of overseas markets and the extension of overseas investments over many decades, and indeed over centuries. While physical capital at home can be rebuilt fairly quickly by a sufficient allocation of resources to that purpose, new overseas connections can be established only by a prolonged effort. Whatever the allocation of resources and whatever the policy, new overseas connections cannot be created at will. They have to be cultivated carefully over a fairly lengthy period of time. The financial losses overseas, whether by the destruction or sale of capital assets or by the incurring of liabilities, have been the central feature of the British post-war problem.

In the earlier period after the war what may be called the "siege economy" of war-time continued. This was marked by severe austerity and widespread controls. A Labour government was in power in this period. There were many misconceptions in the United States about what was happening in the United Kingdom. I have tried in the third chapter to disentangle the phenomena which pertained to a siege economy from the phenomena connected with regulations and measures that might be thought to be due to the socialism of the government then in power. I conceive that it is very important that there should be a clear understanding about these matters. It is not unlikely that a Labour government may be returned to power in the near or middle distant future. It would give rise to many cross purposes and frustrations in the relations between the United Kingdom and the United States if American citizens continued to have the kind of misconceptions about socialism in the United Kingdom that were prevalent fifteen years ago.

As regards the nationalized industries, the point is made rather strongly in the following pages that the main trouble that has arisen in this connection has not in general been from their lack of efficiency, about which there are differences of opinion, but from the fact that no proper provision was made for the finance of their capital requirements. This problem was not thought out. It seems to have been assumed that an all-powerful central government would find it easy enough to raise money for this purpose. This was due to very superficial thinking, or indeed to an absence of thought, and to a lack of appreciation of the magnitude of the problems involved. I have entered into the working of the monetary system in some detail, partly because this brings out a number of problems, not yet solved, which are common to the United States and to the United Kingdom, but also because it is impossible, without a rather close inspection, to understand why the nationalization of industries has caused such a fearful confusion in the sphere of finance. This in turn has been closely connected with the difficulties in grappling with the problem of inflation. These are problems that should be looked at very closely by any other countries which may contemplate large-scale nationalization.

As the years wore on, the manifest austerities of life became less severe. Pre-war standards were regained, except for certain classes of people, and surpassed. This may have caused an undue reaction and led to excessive optimism on the part of the British policy makers, especially in the later period of the nineteen fifties.

This book is avowedly critical of official policy making in recent years. In this criticism two themes recur.

First when, with the amelioration of conditions, the dislocations, manifestly caused by the war, began to fade out of sight, the authorities seemed apt to forget that there were still underlying dislocations. It was too quickly assumed that all could in future proceed by normal rules applicable to a peace-time economy. Thus one might have rules that in certain circumstances there should be deflation or reflation or devaluation, etc. Rules which may be properly applicable on the occasion of a deviation from normal when an economy is growing regularly, may be inappropriate when there is a large structural maladjustment that has to be cured. It is quite true that the expression "structural maladjustment" is too often dragged in to avoid the necessity for hard thinking or as an excuse for some fault or distortion that could quite well be corrected by normal procedures. The expression "structural maladjustment" should certainly not be used to describe every chance lapse from a position of equilibrium. It should be reserved for a distortion caused by something quite out of the ordinary. But the war was something quite out of the ordinary, and its effect in the British case was to leave behind a distortion that was quite out of the ordinary. It was a mistake to suppose that this could be corrected by credit squeezes or other devices for dealing with more transitory phenomena. A striking illustration of failure to pay sufficient attention to what remained of the structural maladjustment due to the war was the over-hasty abandonment of import restrictions in the later nineteen fifties.

The second line of criticism is related to a problem of more universal significance, which may continue to recur in all free enterprise countries. It is the problem that arises from the clash between the claims of a growth policy and the need to rectify an unfavourable external balance of payments in a way that best satisfies the principles of good-neighbourliness. It is becoming fairly clear that this clash of objectives has recently been present in the United States policy. It is also clear that in the United Kingdom in the recent period the claims of growth have been given second priority. There are signs at the time of writing that this situation may be changing. The recent appointment of a National Economic Development Council, with the duty of assessing growth potentialities and inferring what policies would be most conducive to their realization, may be a pointer to a change of view. Of course, such a Council could be appointed and yet have no important effect upon the course of events. But it is believed that thinking at the highest political level is itself undergoing some change. The reshuffle of the British Cabinet (July 1962) may be a symptom of this.

The clash between the requirement for growth and other policy objectives is surely a phenomenon liable to appear, and actually appearing in greater or less degree, in all free-enterprise countries. It has appeared in a rather acute form in the United Kingdom because in its case the conflicting objective was a markedly weak balance of payments; the need to put its balance of payments in good order cannot be neglected by any self-respecting country. The British balance of payments problem has been particularly acute owing to the war-time losses already mentioned. Accordingly the British position may constitute rather a good subject for a case study. It is for this reason that I have thought it useful to go into considerable detail in certain chapters that follow; unless the detail is understood the case study may be superficial, and generalizations that are plausible but not really tenable may be accepted.

In many respects policy making in the United States and the United Kingdom is confronted with similar problems; but in certain respects there are wide differences. American thinking about British problems and British thinking about American problems can yield more fruit in the way of deep economic diagnosis than can the thinking of economists when applied only to the problems of their own countries. Furthermore, we should be concerned not only with the problems of our own countries, but also with the economic viability and progress of the free world as a whole. The problems of its different parts interact, and it is incumbent on each country to seek solutions that are consistent with the general progress of the free world as well as with its own progress. Thus, it is hoped that this book may be a contribution to joint thinking about the common problems and the interlocking problems of the whole collection of free countries.

CHAPTER 2

Progress Since the War

I. PRODUCTION

No economy ever stands still. One may take a snapshot of it at a given moment, but one gets a better understanding of it if one reviews its progress over a certain space of time. We are becoming accustomed to think in terms of "growth rates", and are indeed formulating economic policies for the countries of the free world in terms of these. Accordingly the United Kingdom is here described in terms of the recent growth of the different parts of its economy.

First it is necessary to establish a starting year, and 1948 has been chosen. This is the year in which the worst dislocations immediately consequent upon the war had been remedied. According to the statistics, as recently readjusted, total consumption was then 1 per cent below the level of 1938.[1] As the population had increased by about 5 per cent, this meant a cut back of more than 1 per cent in the standard of living of each person. Furthermore, the individual was oppressed by a lack of freedom of consumer choice. Some articles were rationed and many others were still not available for purchase.

On the other hand, more was being spent on industrial investment and by the government than in 1938. To provide for this, it seems that total national output must have been about 3 per cent higher than in the pre-war year. Thus the United Kingdom had recovered a little from the set-back of the war, and was in advance of certain other countries. But her position should be contrasted with that of the United States.

[1] Statistical sources: Bank of England, Statistical Summaries (to 1939); Central Statistical Office, annual white papers and blue books on National Income and Expenditure; Central Statistical Office Monthly Digests of Statistics; twice yearly white papers (H.M. Treasury) on the U.K. Balance of Payments; H.M. Treasury, U.K. Balance of Payments, 1946–1957; annual Economic Reports of the President (U.S.) and of the Council of Economic Advisers; U.S. Department of Commerce, monthly Surveys of Current Business.

According to official figures, its National Income at "constant prices" (i.e., after adjusting for the rise in dollar values due to inflation) was 67.8 per cent above the level of 1938, while its consumption was 53.5 per cent up. This presents a very striking contrast with the British case. The difference was partly due to much greater unemployment and underemployment of resources in the United States than in the United Kingdom in the years immediately preceding 1939. Something must also be explained by the energy and vitality of American industry. But it also appears that the British economy was more damaged by the strains of war. At the outset, when the United Kingdom was caught napping without adequate preparation, everything had to be done in great haste, and in the later stages the proportion of resources going to the war effort was very great indeed.

An increase of production of only 3 per cent over a ten-year period is, of course, a very small one, and it is against the background of this severe set-back that subsequent events must be reviewed. The damage on the side of the external balance of payments was even greater.

Rates of progress since 1948 are set out in Tables 1, 2 and 3. Since a figure means little in isolation, it has been thought well to place the rates of progress in the United States alongside, as a yardstick.

TABLE 1

AVERAGE ANNUAL INCREASE OF PRODUCTION SINCE 1948*

	Percentage rates	
	U.K.	U.S.
Gross National Product (constant prices) . .	+ 2.7	+ 3.5
Industrial production .	+ 3.7	+ 4.0

* U.K. to year ending September 1961; U.S. to 1960.

It is to be noted that, for the United Kingdom, the increase in industrial production exceeds that in total National Income by more than in the United States. This was the natural consequence of efforts by the United Kingdom to remedy the shortage of material goods, which was still prevalent in 1948.

As the population of the United States was growing somewhat more rapidly, it is well to set out rates of growth per head (Table 2).

TABLE 2

AVERAGE ANNUAL INCREASES PER PERSON SINCE 1948

	Percentage rates	
	U.K.	U.S.
Gross National Product per person of working population* . .	+ 2.1	+ 2.2
Gross National Product per person of employed population . .	+ 2.0	+ 2.4
Industrial production per person employed in industry . .	+ 2.7	+ 3.4

* Working population and employment relate to Great Britain, viz., United Kingdom excluding Northern Ireland. The exclusion of Northern Irish labour could involve a statistical error but only a small one.

When allowance is made for population increase, the rates of growth of National Income come very near together. On the other hand the comparative performance in industrial production by the United Kingdom is seen to be less good.

Next we may consider the main sectors of the economy (Table 3).

TABLE 3

AVERAGE ANNUAL INCREASES BY PRINCIPAL SECTORS SINCE 1948

	Percentage rates	
	U.K.	U.S.
Consumption	+ 2.4	+ 3.4
Gross fixed capital formation .	+ 5.5	+ 2.0
Net fixed capital formation .	+ 7.7	
Government	+ 2.4	+ 5.1
Gross National Income . .	+ 2.7	+ 3.5

The increase of consumption in the United States is substantially closer to its increase in total income. In the United Kingdom government expenditure marched with consumption, the rising margin between consumption and total output being devoted to the much larger increase in gross fixed capital formation. In the United States, on the other hand, the increase in gross fixed capital formation fell considerably below the increases in consumption and total National Income, while governmental expenditure grew more rapidly. A figure has not been inserted for *net* capital formation in the United States, since the statistical methods of computing capital consumption may not be the same in the two countries. The higher growth rate of fixed capital formation in the United Kingdom may be attributed to the greater set-back caused by the war.

In 1960 the United Kingdom was appropriating a substantially higher proportion of the Gross National Product to capital formation, especially to industrial capital formation (Table 4).

TABLE 4

GROSS FIXED CAPITAL FORMATION IN 1960 AS PERCENTAGE OF GROSS NATIONAL PRODUCT

	U.K.	U.S.
Total . . .	16.3	13.8
Residential . .	3.0	4.2
Industrial. . .	13.3	9.6

The greater rise in governmental expenditures in the United States (Table 3) was in part due to its heroic efforts in providing for the defence of the free world. But it will surprise many to learn that non-defence governmental expenditures on goods and services constitute a slightly larger fraction of the Gross National Product in the United States than they do in the United Kingdom (Table 5).

TABLE 5

GOVERNMENTAL PURCHASES OF GOODS AND SERVICES IN 1960 AS PERCENTAGES OF GROSS NATIONAL PRODUCT

	U.K.	U.S.
Total . . .	16.6	19.8
Defence . . .	6.3	8.8
Non-defence . .	10.3	11.0

The United Kingdom has had the reputation of being rather lavish with governmental expenditures on behalf of the welfare of its citizens; these include the provision of a free health service. It may, however, be appropriate for the United States, as a much richer country, to devote a higher proportion of its income to non-defence governmental expenditures, as in fact it does.

Throughout the period the level of employment in the United Kingdom has been high, although the differences between the two countries may not be so great as it would appear owing to questions of definition. In the period 1951–1960 the average unemployment for Great Britain was 1.6 per cent compared with 4.2 per cent in the United States.

In both countries there has been a desire to maintain employment at a high level. The higher level actually achieved in the United Kingdom may be attributed to the urgent need to make good ground lost during the war in the fields of consumption, investment and the external balance of payments.

The incidence of cyclical recessions in the United States has been well charted. Those of 1948, 1953–1954, 1957–1958 and the minor one of 1960–1961 are generally recognized. The position in the United Kingdom has not been so clear. Production mounted uninterruptedly until the winter of 1951–1952. Thus the 1948 recession in the United States was missed in the United Kingdom. This may be taken to be the natural consequence of the low levels prevailing in 1948, by comparison with the United States, as stated above.

There was, however, a British recession lasting from the fourth quarter of 1951 to the fourth quarter of 1952. In this the United Kingdom was out of phase with the United States, but in phase with the other countries of Europe and the rest of the world generally. The reason for this is not far to seek. In 1952 the American economy was boosted by its huge defence programme. Although the United Kingdom stepped up its defence expenditures considerably in that year, this was not sufficient to offset the other forces making for recession at home and abroad. On the other hand, the United Kingdom and other European countries, having recovered from their own 1952–1953 recession, thereafter pushed forward, being unaffected by the recession of 1953–1954 in the United States.

This lack of coincidence in the timing of the American business cycle and that in the other industrial countries was a very important factor in the economic history of the early nineteen fifties. It was a helpful factor, since it prevented any cumulative external effects of the American recession gathering momentum in the world as a whole.

The United Kingdom entered upon a very strong investment boom in 1954–1955. Thereafter its history becomes irregular and fails to conform to any traditional business-cycle pattern. Strong damping measures, of kinds that will be described in later chapters, were taken during 1955 and led to a slight recession in 1956, which put the United Kingdom out of phase both with the rest of Europe and with the United States. There was a slight recovery in 1957, when further damping measures were taken, leading to a more substantial recession in 1958, the United Kingdom thus coming again into phase with the United States and the world generally. There was a strong recovery from the last quarter of 1958 to the first of 1960, which was due to vigorous expansionist measures that were taken by the government. In the early part of 1960 damping measures were again adopted, leading to a slight recession; in 1961 there was a very mild recovery, but further damping measures were taken leading to a deeper recession.

From the foregoing it appears that since 1955 there have been rather frequent bouts of measures in restraint of demand in the United Kingdom. Indeed in seven years there was a gap of only about twenty months in which the economy was not subject to rather severe restraints. Many think that it was due to these that its rate of growth was substantially less in the later than in the earlier part of the post-war period (Table 6).

Table 6

Average Annual Increase in Gross Domestic Product (Factor Cost) at Constant Prices as Percentages in the United Kingdom

1948 to 1955	+ 3.5
1955 to the year October 1960—September 1961	+ 2.2

The alternative view, which may have been the official view, has been that the lower growth rate was due to factors on the supply side, viz., the lack of productive resources.

Table 7 does not appear to bear out this view.

TABLE 7

WORKING POPULATION AND FIXED CAPITAL IN THE UNITED KINGDOM

Year	(a)		(b)
	Average annual increases in working population* (Great Britain)‡ as percentage	Average annual amount of net fixed capital formation,† industrial only, in £ million	Industrial net fixed capital formation as percentage of net Domestic Product§
1948 to 1955 . .	+ 0.7	652	1948 3.5
1955 to the year October 1960—September 1961 . .	+ 0.7	1106	1954 4.5 1960 6.9

* Less those in armed forces.
† Valued at constant prices (1954).
‡ See footnote to Table 2.
§ Market prices.

The supply of labour increased as much in the second period as it did in the first. The supply of capital equipment available for industry increased much more rapidly. The increase was fairly continuous throughout the whole period, accelerating markedly in the later part of it. It is to be noted that net capital formation (relative to National Income) was twice as high in 1960 as it was in 1948. The figures in Table 7 exclude residential construction.

It may be that the "law of diminishing returns" has been operating in relation to the higher rate of industrial investment. But its operation would not explain the phenomena. For the increase in the labour force in the second period, which was as great as that in the first period, should have been able to sustain as high a growth in the second period as in the first, if it had been provided with no more extra equipment than was provided in the first. It was, in fact, provided with much more extra equipment in the second period. Therefore, even if there were "diminishing returns" to extra equipment, the labour force in the second period ought to have been able to increase output by more than in the first period.

From this it seems reasonable to infer that the lower growth rate was due to forces operating on the demand side, viz., to official measures for damping down the economy. These were manifest enough.

Commentators have pointed out that there was a similar falling off of growth in the United States in the later part of the period. No exact comparison with the United Kingdom is possible. If one were to choose a year to constitute the turning point in the United States, that would probably be 1953. But this might not give the right basis for diagnosis, since there can be no doubt that growth was much increased in the years immediately before 1953 by the huge defence programme. While from time to time restraints on demand have been imposed by the Federal Reserve System, on the whole restraints deliberately imposed by policy makers have been far less severe in the United States than in the United Kingdom in the last seven years. It may be that the weakening in growth in the United States has been due to more deep-seated causes, such as the much higher standard of living in the United States, which may entail a weakening in demand for additional material goods. In the United Kingdom, by contrast, no one could deny that there is still plenty of scope for the production of a much larger amount of material goods, which would be greatly welcomed by its citizens. Our further study of the British economy may throw some light on the comparative position of the two countries in this regard.

II. INFLATION

Like the United States, the United Kingdom has been afflicted with a continuing inflation since the end of the war. There has been disappointment that inflation did not come to an end when the greater part of the readjustments required at the end of the war had been completed. In the British case, a factor of major importance was the excessive devaluation of sterling in 1949. This was a driving force making for inflation, which continued in operation for a number of years after the event.

First it may be well to look at the period as a whole, from a pre-war year to 1960. In Table 8, United Kingdom prices are expressed in dollars as well as sterling, to show how the two sets of prices are related to each other at the existing rate of exchange between sterling and the dollar. The devaluation of 1939 has to be taken into the reckoning, as well as that of 1949.

TABLE 8

CONSUMER PRICES IN 1960
1938 = 100

U.K. expressed in sterling	U.K. expressed in dollars	U.S.
287.9	168.9	209.6

It can be seen that consumer prices in the United States have risen substantially more than consumer prices in the United Kingdom, when translated into dollars. This does not necessarily mean that the dollar is overvalued relatively to sterling. It is a general rule, although somewhat paradoxical, that a more efficient country has a higher cost of living. As the productivity of those engaged in producing goods that enter into world trade rises, their wages, etc., rise in proportion. The wages of those engaged in the distributive trades have to be put up, more or less in sympathy; but offsetting increases in efficiency in the distributive trades cannot always be realized. Accordingly the margin between the ex-factory price and the price in the shop tends to increase.

Productivity in manufacture and agriculture rose more in the United States than in the United Kingdom during the period as a whole; and so, therefore, have American wages. One would expect, in consequence, a certain upward shift in consumer prices in the United States relatively to the United Kingdom, but not, perhaps, one quite so great as that shown.

A better idea of relativities may be gained from export prices (Table 9).

TABLE 9

EXPORT PRICES IN 1960
1937–1938 (AVERAGE) = 100

U.K. expressed in sterling	U.K. expressed in dollars	U.S.
348.5	198.6	217.7

Here again it can be seen that American prices have risen somewhat more than United Kingdom dollar prices. This might suggest on the face of it that there is a small overvaluation of the dollar, but it may be that certain factors in the world situation that have become unfavourable to the United Kingdom make it necessary for the United Kingdom to have somewhat lower export prices, in order to enlarge her exports sufficiently to balance her accounts. It is reported that in a number of lines British exporters are working at very narrow margins. Furthermore it cannot be assumed that relative United States and United Kingdom prices were in equilibrium in any particular year before the war. The average of 1937 and 1938 has been taken, since there was a considerable drop in American export prices in the latter year. The devaluation of 1949 was so important in relation to British inflation that it is worth while to look at the situation in that year (Table 10).

TABLE 10

CONSUMER AND EXPORT PRICES 1949
1938 = 100

	U.K. expressed in sterling	U.K. expressed in dollars	U.S.
Consumer prices 1949 .	200	164.8	168.8
Export prices 1949 (January–August) .	251.9	207.9	187.6

According to consumer prices, the degree of inflation in the two countries in terms of dollars, i.e., allowing for the British devaluation of 1939, appears to have been almost identical. But, as has already been explained, it is probable that, for equilibrium, consumer prices should have risen less in the United Kingdom. A comparison of export prices does suggest that sterling had begun to lose value relatively to the dollar. It cannot be taken to be certain that a devaluation was required in 1949, but the figures suggest scope for a moderate one. If we base a calculation on the export price figures, although these give only a rough and ready criterion, the devaluation should have been from $4.03=£1 to $3.64=£1. Actually the pound was devalued to $2.80. It was suggested at the time that an overdevaluation was required in order to stimulate British exports. This argument was not very convincing, as British exports had been pursuing a strongly upward course since the end of the war. A much more powerful motive in the minds of the authorities responsible for devaluation was to have one so big that it would terminate all future speculation against sterling. In the early part of 1949 there had been heavy adverse speculation, and this forced the hands of the British authorities, who did not desire devaluation. They were determined that such a situation should not arise again, and so they decided to have so large a devaluation as to make all speculators feel that there was not likely to be another one. This, however, was a wrong principle on which to operate, since the devaluation had far-reaching effects on the course of trade and prices, some of them of an undesirable kind. It is a most important maxim that economic policy makers should never assess the degree of devaluation (or upward valuation) required by reference to its probable impact on the minds of speculators; rather they should endeavour to assess what the fundamental disequilibrium in trade and prices requires. This maxim still has great relevance for future policy making.

Table 11 has been constructed to show how the rate of inflation of consumer prices in the United Kingdom varied from time to time within

TABLE 11

AVERAGE ANNUAL PERCENTAGE RATE OF PRICE INCREASES

Year	Import prices per cent	Consumer prices per cent
1946–mid 1948	+ 13.1	+ 8.3
Mid 1948–Sept. 1949	− 5.5	+ 0.8
Sept. 1949–mid 1951	+ 33.8	+ 6.4
1951–1960	− 2.1	+ 2.7

the post-war period, and notably the important effect of the devaluation.

We begin with the period of immediate post-war reconstruction, when the inflationary pressure of demand was very strong. British import prices, although not consumer prices, had already begun to rise rapidly between 1945 and 1946. It is thought that the large upsurge in world (dollar) prices in the period immediately after the war was partly due to the rapidity with which the American authorities relaxed wartime controls over the internal economy in 1946. It may be that if the American authorities had proceeded more slowly, the inflation of dollar prices could have been better contained.

Then a period of fifteen months is shown in which British import prices actually fell. Consumer prices, which had not yet caught up on the previous rise of import prices, rose very slowly; at this time a "wages pause" was in successful operation in Britain.

Then came the great devaluation after which import prices in the United Kingdom rose by no less than 66.3 per cent in the course of twenty-one months. This rise was not wholly due to the devaluation, but was inflamed by the Korean war; but the rise in United Kingdom import prices started before the Korean war; the rise in United Kingdom import prices from September 1949 to mid-1951 was about 17 per cent greater than that in American import prices; and then, when world prices began to come down, the fall in United Kingdom import prices was 4 per cent less.

It is clear that by mid-1951 consumer prices had by no means been adjusted to the rise in import prices consequent upon the devaluation of sterling. There has been argument about how far the post-1951 inflation in the United Kingdom was due to the delayed effects of devaluation and how far to independent causes of inflation arising within the economy. Economic science will probably never be able to furnish an answer to this question. The process of adjustment to an upsurge of import prices was a slow-working one. In the first place, it took time for the increases in the prices of imported materials to be reflected in the prices of goods in the shops. The British have on the whole shown themselves rather conservative in adjusting prices. Furthermore, the devaluation came upon Britain at a time when, as already noted, a wages pause was in successful operation. This continued for a time. Despite the rise in the cost of living, which began to operate in the winter of 1949–1950, there was no significant upward movement of wages for another year. The upward adjustment of wages naturally necessitated a further increase in the cost of living; and so a vicious spiral was set up. But in the case of some administered prices there was a lapse of six years or more before the inevitable adjustment of prices to domestic costs was made. Then this belated adjustment, being reflected in a further rise in the cost of living, provoked further wage demands. It is doubtful whether even in 1960 the full effect of the devaluation had worked through the whole economy; in the period September 1949–1960 while import prices rose by 56.8 per cent, the increase of consumer prices rose by only 40.9 per cent.

III. BALANCE OF PAYMENTS

Much the largest set-back for the United Kingdom resulting from the war was in the balance of payments. Very large external losses occurred, and, to redress the situation, it was necessary to have a big structural readjustment in the economy. This determined the course of events. Furthermore, economic policy makers have had recurrent anxieties about the balance of payments throughout the post-war period, and these have caused them to take measures calculated to restrain activity in the domestic economy at times when these were not strictly appropriate from the point of view of the business cycle. This may be taken to be the principal cause of the rather weak growth rate manifested by the United Kingdom in the period.

Before the war, the United Kingdom's external balance on current account depended to a large extent on the receipt of payments for what are known as "invisible" items, notably interest and dividends on overseas investments. This was a position that had been built up over many generations. As population grew rapidly in the nineteenth century, it became evident that the United Kingdom would come to depend more and more on imported food; the growth of industry also entailed the import of many materials. Thus the thickly populated islands intensified the policy, inherited from earlier times, of establishing world-wide trading connections. By successive stages a policy of complete Free Trade was put into full operation. Part and parcel of this policy was investment overseas. The remission back of interest and profit on these investments was not a burden on the balances of payments of the developing countries, since the United Kingdom was hospitable to a rising quantity of imports; thus the servicing of the investments could be rendered in goods without any strain. The arrangement was mutually advantageous. The developing countries received the investments, for infrastructure, etc., and thus made progress which would otherwise have been impossible. British overseas investment came to be on a scale that constituted a far higher proportion of her national income than anything that has been attempted by the advanced countries since the Second World War.

Meanwhile the British came to rely on these receipts to balance off part of her rising requirements for imports. She was thus relieved of the task of raising her exports to match. Rather, she cast her bread upon the waters, and, although losses were incurred, on the whole the system worked well and seemed to be a sensible one.

In the four years from 1935 to 1938 net service receipts on current account paid for 33.6 per cent of British imports f.o.b. (free on board). In addition to this, the figures show a deficit amounting to 3.8 per cent of imports; but this was probably unreal. It was thought at the time that the Board of Trade estimates of the services items were unduly conservative.

Immediately after the war the net services items became heavily negative, mainly owing to overseas military expenditures. Thereafter there was some recovery, but only to a small fraction of the pre-war proportion. In 1960 net services paid for only 1.5 per cent of imports.

The principal items of change may undoubtedly be attributed to the war. Foreign investments had to be sold, and debt was incurred. In 1938 net investment income from overseas paid for 26.9 per cent of all United Kingdom imports (f.o.b.). In 1960 it paid for 5.8 per cent only. Also in consequence of the war, overseas government expenditures —a negative item in the balance—increased from 1.7 per cent of imports in 1938 to 6.9 per cent in 1960. There was also a loss of net shipping receipts from a plus item amounting to 3.9 per cent of imports in 1938 to a negative item amounting to 1.4 per cent of imports in 1960.

That this heavy loss had occurred was well known at the end of the war, although its magnitude could not be precisely determined. We may now base ourselves on the recorded figures for 1960. Experts do not think there is any immediate prospect of improvement in services. In order to fill the gap created by the loss on services items, it was necessary for exports to rise over imports by 57.4 per cent. This means, of course, that exports would have to rise by much more than 57.4 per cent, since some increase of imports was inevitable. Thus if imports rose from 100 to 200, exports would have to rise from 100 to 314.8. The essence of the British problem was how to get so large an increase of exports without any countervailing increase of imports. Other countries have succeeded in raising exports by more than the United Kingdom, but in many cases these have been able to avail themselves of a corresponding increase of imports. It is naturally much easier to increase exports if one can increase imports at the same time by a corresponding amount, since the additional imports release domestic productive resources that can be made available for producing the exports. The scale of the loss and of the structural readjustment required was greater than that of any other country. It may be noted, however, that France also had a heavy task in this respect. Germany and Italy, by contrast, had no such problem; their imports have risen more than their exports. The United States has increased its exports more than its imports, not to make good war-time losses, but in order to effectuate a generous and far-sighted policy of extending aid to the free world. But the proportionate rise of American exports over imports was not so great as the British; and in relation to the American National Income, this excess rise of exports was very small indeed by comparison with the excess rise in the United Kingdom in proportion to the British National Income. Thus in this respect the United Kingdom has had a truly formidable task.

In order to get a figure to fix in mind, it is expedient to add something for long-term capital outflow, which had been small in the pre-war period of world depression. An absolute minimum for this may be taken to be £200 million a year, part of which is required for the re-payment of debts, also a consequence of the war. The remaining part may be taken to be the bare minimum for grants and loans to developing countries and *net* direct investment overseas. The British authorities have from time to time rightly thought that the United Kingdom should aim at a higher figure than this. If we include the figure of £200 million a year, as a requirement, then it has been necessary for exports to rise over imports by 65.7 per cent, and this may be taken to be the key figure in the consideration of what follows.

In 1961 the actual rise in the volume of exports over imports was 55.6 per cent, and the rise in the value of exports over the value of imports f.o.b. was 55.1 per cent. Comparing these figures with the requirement of 65.7 per cent, we find that more than five-sixths of the great task of structural readjustment had been achieved.

The close correspondence between the volume and value figures indicates that the "terms of trade" were roughly the same in 1961 as in the four pre-war years. But from the end of the war until quite recently the terms of trade were heavily against the United Kingdom, as was also the case with other industrial countries. In the worst year, 1951, the deterioration in the terms of trade amounted to 31 per cent.

A rather longer table of figures is set out, with an apology for burdening the reader, but in the hope that, if he studies them carefully, he will find more thrill in them than could be conveyed by words.

The first table (Table 12) gives *volume* figures. A subsequent table (Table 13) gives *value* figures. From the point of view of solvency it is, of course, the value figures that count. In the last year the volume and value figures come together, but, during the passage, when the terms of trade were so adverse to the United Kingdom, the table showing the value figures is less favourable. The interest of the volume figures is that they show what was achieved by sweat and toil on the one side and by austerity on the other. In the nineteen twenties men of good-will rightly took the view that it was a wrong policy to ask Germany to make heavy reparation payments. But the burden that it was proposed to place on Germany then, which many thought to be harsh and inhuman, would—except for some extreme figures mentioned at the Paris Peace Conference, which everyone knew to be unrealistic—have involved a much smaller outflow of exports not balanced by imports, and therefore a much smaller burden than the United Kingdom has had to suffer since the war.

The target requirement of 65.7 per cent is set at the head of Table 12. It will be seen that, in terms of volume, this was achieved very quickly,

TABLE 12

Required RISE OF EXPORTS IN EXCESS OF IMPORTS:—65.7 PER CENT
1935–1938 (FOUR-YEAR AVERAGE) = 100

Year	*Volume* figures		
	Exports	Imports	Rise of exports over imports per cent
1946	94.71	68.87	40.3
1947	103.3	78.39	36.3
1948	131.3	82.64	65.3
1949	143.2	89.00	69.8
1950	165.4	86.64	90.8
1951	162.2	97.23	66.8
1952	152.9	89.54	70.7
1953	156.0	96.27	62.0
1954	162.2	97.23	66.8
1955	174.7	108.7	60.6
1956	185.7	107.8	72.2
1957	188.8	111.7	69.0
1958	180.9	111.7	62.0
1959	188.8	119.3	58.1
1960	199.6	134.8	48.1
1961	204.8	131.9	55.4

namely in 1948, and sustained thereafter, with ups and downs, until 1959. There were two sides to this quick achievement. During the war exports had been allowed to fall to as low as one-third, in the worst phase, of their pre-war level. This was due, not only to the cutting off of certain markets, but also to the deliberate policy of the British government, which prohibited exports, except those strictly required to sustain the economies of countries, whether allied or neutral, which by their own exports were helping the war effort.

By 1948 exports had regained and risen substantially above their pre-war level. But the achievement of the target in that year was as much due to the restriction of imports to a level below pre-war. This low level of imports was secured by very strict controls, and was the counterpart of a policy of extreme austerity on the domestic front. It will be seen that imports did not regain their pre-war level until 1955, no less than ten years after the end of the war. As exports were then running at 74·7 per cent above their pre-war level, and as many of these exports had an important import content, the austerity required of British citizens was correspondingly greater.

During the course of the nineteen fifties those controls over imports, which had served to compress them to so low a level, were progressively removed. The effect of the removal of the import controls is seen in the second half of the nineteen fifties, and more notably in the years following 1958.

The figures, showing as they do a substantial decline from the target achievement in the last three years for the first time, suggest that the pace at which import controls were removed was too great. It may be thought that it was rather unsatisfactory that any controls should still be needed at a date so far removed from the end of the war. This is certainly unsatisfactory, but in extenuation it must be urged that the United Kingdom had the hardest task, on foreign trade account, of any country in the world, and that the structural readjustment required by so great a rise of exports without a countervailing increase of imports has been a very difficult one, especially for a country which was initially devoting so large a proportion of its output to exports.

The table brings out strikingly the effect of the devaluation of sterling in 1949 both in the rise of exports in 1950 and in the rise of exports over imports in that year. It also suggests, first, that since exports had been rising well up to 1949 the devaluation was not clearly needed, and, secondly, that the beneficent effect of it was entirely shortlived. Furthermore, the value table (Table 13) will show that this beneficent effect as regards the volume of exports, which entailed much sweat and toil for British producers, was largely lost by the deterioration in the terms of trade that was the consequence of devaluation.

The value figures in Table 13 tell a story which is, naturally, similar to that of the volume figures; but the United Kingdom's attempt to achieve the target is seen to be not so good. This was owing to the

TABLE 13

Required RISE OF EXPORTS OVER IMPORTS:—65.7 PER CENT
1935–1938 (FOUR-YEAR AVERAGE) = 100

Year	*Value* figures		
	Exports	Imports	Rise of exports over imports per cent
1946	187.2	139.0	34.7
1947	233.7	202.2	15.7
1948	331.3	233.0	42.2
1949	385.0	258.6	48.8
1950	466.8	310.5	50.3
1951	564.8	454.4	24.3
1952	578.1	379.2	52.0
1953	553.4	378.9	46.0
1954	586.1	393.1	49.0
1955	636.2	446.3	42.6
1956	702.8	447.1	57.1
1957	728.8	463.8	57.1
1958	699.3	433.1	61.4
1959	726.8	468.5	55.2
1960	768.3	534.5	43.7
1961	792.1	511.9	54.7

severe worsening of her terms of trade that occurred after the war. This was a burden that the United Kingdom shared with other industrial countries. While the volume figures give the correct picture in terms of effort and austerity, it is the value figures that are relevant to solvency. The value figures show that the target set out at the head of the table was never quite gained.

It is to be noted that the great, but entirely temporary, gain in 1950, in consequence of the devaluation in 1949, which is seen in the volume table, hardly appears at all in the value table. The gain in volume was offset by a worsening in the terms of trade. Thus, while the volume figures show a rather spectacular gain for one year, but do not suggest any permanent strengthening in the position as a result of devaluation, the value figures suggest that there was no gain at all. This is rather important in relation to the whole question of the usefulness of devaluation.

In the volume table, 1951 was not notably worse than the surrounding years, apart from the freak year of 1950. In the value table, on the other hand, it stands out as much the worst year since 1947. This was due to the exceptionally bad terms of trade consequent upon the Korean War, which is to be distinguished from the general worsening in the terms of trade which ran for more than a decade and was due in part to the devaluation of sterling and in part to general post-war conditions.

In the value table the falling off since 1957 is shown to be not so bad as in the volume table. The upsurge of the volume of imports was partly offset by improved terms of trade.

Both tables show that in 1962 the United Kingdom was still faced with part of the task of improving her merchandise balance, to make good the financial losses of the war. More than five-sixths of that task had already been achieved; but the remaining one-sixth was something that could not be dismissed lightly; it meant a rise of exports of about £250 million, without any countervailing rise of imports, i.e., in addition to any rise of exports that might be needed to balance further increases of imports.

When the ideas underlying British policy have been discussed, it will appear that the United Kingdom began to adopt too complacent an attitude during the course of the nineteen fifties. It was not sufficiently appreciated that such success as had been achieved was partly due to the effect, or after-effect, of import restrictions. Thus the authorities appeared to have ceased to think of balance-of-payment difficulties as essentially arising from the financial losses of the war. The structural readjustment required in consequence of these was not one which the ordinary process of monetary and fiscal policies could be relied on to achieve.

It still appears that some special "artificial" measures are needed to stimulate exports or retard imports before final equilibrium is reached. The general view is that such artificial measures should be applied particularly to exports, although anything in the way of export subsidies might be worse, from the point of view of the objectives of the GATT and of the United Kingdom itself, for establishing good international canons of behaviour in commercial policy. The actual figures, however, do not suggest that, from the point of view of balanced growth, the emphasis should be laid upon stimulating exports. Table 14 shows that the rise of imports has been more nearly in line with, although below,

TABLE 14

VOLUME INCREASES BETWEEN 1935–1938 (FOUR-YEAR AVERAGE) AND 1961

Volume of exports	+ 105.9 per cent
Gross Domestic Product at constant prices .	+ 47.9 per cent
Volume of imports	+ 31.9 per cent

the rise in the Gross Domestic Product, than the rise in exports. This table (Table 14) suggests that, if artificial measures are necessary, they should be applied to imports rather than to exports.

CHAPTER 3

Socialism

I. THE BACKGROUND

The United Kingdom was ruled by a Labour government formally wedded to the doctrines of socialism from 1945 to 1951. This fact has left its imprint on the structure of the economy. The possibility, and, in the long run, likelihood of the Labour Party being returned to power has its relevance to what may be considered feasible or desirable in current economic policy. Opinions differ about how important is the change since 1951 in the outlook of Labour leaders who would be likely to be responsible for policy.

Exaggerated ideas were entertained in certain quarters abroad about the significance of Labour rule, which might be expressed in such a phrase as "Britain has gone Socialist". A milder alternative, which was, however, also misleading, was that the Labour government was responsible for a new kind of régime in Britain, called the "Welfare State". The changes wrought by the Labour government, although significant, were much less far-reaching than is implied in such a summing up.

It would be a mistake, however, on the other side, to think of the Labour Party as nothing more than a party popular with the wage-earning population, having kinship, for instance, with the more "progressive" elements in the Democratic Party. It is dangerous to ignore origins, and it may be expedient to take a brief look at these.

Socialism in Britain was antecedent to Marx, being represented in the early nineteenth century by such writers as Robert Owen, William Thompson and Thomas Hodgskin; but there is no doubt that Marx, who lived for most of his adult life in London, revived these earlier ideas and made specific contributions to British thinking. He had a strong influence on such diverse minds as Hyndman and George Bernard Shaw (the playwright[1]). The latter, it is true, joined with others in founding the Fabian Society, which was supposed to represent a watered-down kind of socialism. But this is not really a correct view of the matter. What distinguished the Fabians was their opinion about wise tactics, namely a gradual step-by-step approach (the Society being named after Fabius *Cunctator*), and they in no sense abandoned the ultimate objective of socialism, which is the "nationalization of the means of production, distribution and exchange". This was thoroughgoing doctrinal socialism.

The British Labour Movement had already gathered significant strength in the middle of the nineteenth century, and at that time its leaders were not socialist, but radical, in the British, *not* American, sense of that word, i.e., they were strong democratic individualists. The conversion of the main mass of labour to socialism towards the end of the century was probably due, more than anything else, to the extreme form in which the doctrine of *laissez faire* was held, even by the more progressive elements in the Liberal Party, so that urgently needed reforms for dealing with the problems of dire poverty in those days were ruled out as being "contrary to the laws of political economy". In the early part of the twentieth century British socialists were not to be distinguished from communists by reference to the final economic objective, which was the same for both, but by the fact that the objective was to be achieved by the constitutional methods of democracy and that individual liberties would be safeguarded in full under the new régime. That was the ideological background of the British Labour Party.

It is important to bear in mind that the Trades Union Congress was a co-founder of the political Labour Party. On certain occasions it has exerted a crucial influence on policy, and it has sometimes been supposed that this was an unwarrantable incursion by an organization, designed to look after the industrial interests of its members, into matters that were none of its business. Such a view is not in accord with the facts of history. The Trades Union Congress, as co-founder, is morally entitled to make its views felt. Its main stress is naturally on matters likely to affect the daily lives and economic interests of its

[1] It is interesting to recall that all the lights on Broadway (New York) were extinguished on the evening of the death of this great pioneer of socialism in Britain.

members; it would tend to be opposed to airy-fairy schemes that might endanger solid work-a-day interests; but this does not mean that it has abandoned its attachment to the doctrines of socialism.

It does not follow that all members of the Trade Unions that are affiliated to the Trades Union Congress have to be socialists. Their political freedom of choice is safeguarded by the division of Trade Union funds into those for political and those for non-political purposes, and by the right of members to "contract out" of subscribing to the political section.

Before the Labour Party became the second party in the State, its members did much to support and co-operate with the Liberal Party, despite the fact that the latter was ideologically at the opposite pole. The two groups could make common cause in such proximate aims as social reform, the Liberals having already departed somewhat from their adhesion to *laissez faire*, and in other issues of a more strictly political character (e.g., Irish Home Rule, the reform of the House of Lords). This period of *de facto* co-operation may have done something to soften the rigidity of socialist doctrine in the Labour Party.

During the last twelve years there have not been plans for extensive nationalization in the short-term Labour Party programmes. It is not considered likely that they will reappear. On the other hand the ideological background might predispose a Labour government to more active economic planning and to state intervention in economic processes at a greater number of points than is the case with the Conservative government.

There were two periods before 1945 when the Labour Party was in office as the government of the United Kingdom, namely for a few months in 1923 and for a longer period from 1929 to 1931. In neither period did the Labour Party have the power to do what it liked, since it was dependent on Liberal votes. The second period ended in a fiasco, which had certain paradoxical features that are worth noting. The Labour Party was for a number of years greatly discredited by this fiasco.

It occurred at a time when the world slump, following the Wall Street crash of 1929, was at its worst. The United Kingdom suffered, like other countries, and unemployment was approaching 30 per cent.

The Budget was in heavy deficit, as was also the Unemployment Insurance Fund. All experts, with the exception of the late Lord Keynes, held that an essential prerequisite for the recovery of the economy was to eliminate these two deficits. The Labour government, as represented both by the Prime Minister (Ramsay Macdonald) and the Chancellor of the Exchequer (Philip Snowden), did not disagree with this view of the experts, and wished to take steps accordingly. But it was impracticable to get a balance in the Unemployment Insurance Fund without reducing unemployment benefits, and at this point the Trades Union Congress, with its primary anxiety for the actual welfare of its members, put its foot down. The manifest inability of the government to carry into practice what it thought to be right and necessary severely shook foreign confidence in the United Kingdom, causing the overthrow of the Labour government and, incidentally, the fall of the gold standard in this country, which has had such far-reaching consequences ever since. The paradox is that according to modern ideas, in the United States no less than in the United Kingdom, these deficits would be regarded as helpful in what was the worst slump of all time, namely as "built-in stabilizers".

It was in 1945 that the Labour Party for the first time gained power as well as office. The causes of this great change, which surprised many, owing to the nation-wide popularity of Winston Churchill, cannot be specified with certainty. Some stress that the General Election of 1945 was the first chance that voters had had of expressing their censure of an appeasement policy, vis-à-vis Hitler, which both left the country ill-prepared for war and yet did not succeed in staving off the war. Memory of the very heavy unemployment in the inter-war period may have had its influence. It is true that this had not secured a Labour victory in the General Election of 1935, but at that date the fiasco of 1931 was more keenly remembered than it was in 1945. The stirring up of feelings and thoughts caused by the war may have enhanced the readiness of the average voter to take a risk and try out something new. It may have been just that regular swing of opinion by which the British electorate seeks a change of government from time to time.

The performance of the Labour government may be reviewed under three main headings: (1) the Welfare State, (2) an economic policy operated by a widespread network of controls and (3) the nationalization of certain industries.

II. THE WELFARE STATE

There have been greatly exaggerated ideas abroad both about the amount of change involved in the setting up of the so-called "Welfare State" and also in regard to its being in some way specifically an emanation of socialist principles. In any meaningful use of this expression one should say that the Welfare State was introduced by the Liberal government of 1906 to 1914. This included the principle of compulsory social insurance for health and unemployment, with employers, employees and the government all contributing to the necessary funds; the outright provision by the taxpayer of aid for the needy, such as by old age pensions; and assistance for the lowest paid groups of workers through the statutory fixing of minimum wages by tribunals ("Trade Boards"). The scope of these various measures was greatly extended after the end of the First World War by the Coalition government under Lloyd George. It would be a nice point whether or not the extension of the Welfare State after the First World War was greater than that which occurred after the Second.

The following elements may be distinguished in what was done by the Labour government.

1. It was universally recognized by all concerned that the time had come for a general overhaul of the whole complex of social security payments. There were various gaps that needed filling in. It was desirable to make the insurance schemes more actuarially sound, a matter which had given recurrent trouble throughout the inter-war period. Scales of contributions and benefits would have to be adapted to the changed value of money. There was a general feeling that family allowances, long since adopted in France and some other countries, should be incorporated. This may have represented some change of ideology from the days when they might have been condemned as undermining parental responsibility; but a change in the population position may have had some marginal influence, as births since

1921 had been below the level required in the long run to sustain a stationary population.

Reforms along all these lines would certainly have been undertaken by a Conservative government, had it been returned to power in 1945; there was nothing specifically socialist about them. Whether the Labour government was more generous in certain respects is a matter of doubt. Nothing can be said with certainty.

2. Something has to be attributed to the specific influence of Lord Beveridge, who was a Liberal member of Parliament in the closing years of the war, but defeated in his constituency in the General Election of 1945. He had played a part from time to time in the development of social security in Britain from the very beginning (1908) and was chairman of the Unemployment Insurance Fund from 1932 to 1943. During the war Churchill's government assigned him the task of making recommendations for post-war action on all the technical matters referred to above. During the course of discharging this task, he took the bit between his teeth and made a sort of breakaway. It is not easy to define exactly what this breakaway consisted of.

Lord Beveridge had the idea that he should take advantage of his position in order to write a report, which would be an inspiring document, and hold out the hope to a war-weary population, both in the Forces and at home, that the post-war world would be a better place to live in. Living in the years before the war had been harsh for many people owing to the heavy unemployment. While his report was not immediately concerned with that—he wrote another one on that topic later, in his private capacity—he thought that it could be made a vehicle for giving people the idea that they had something to look forward to and would be better cared for. But it is not clear that the substance of his proposals was anything very revolutionary, save in regard to one or two points to be mentioned shortly.

When it became known what he was doing, there was great irritation in political circles. Perhaps the politicians felt that he was stealing their thunder, or, since the precise range of his proposals could not yet be known as a whole, that he was committing them, by writing a potentially popular document, to positions that they would not necessarily be willing to accept. It is believed that originally his report was intended to be confidential to the Cabinet, but Ministers had fobbed off so many questioners in Parliament about post-war conditions by telling them that Beveridge was reporting on all these matters that it became clear that the report would have to be published. Originally he had been appointed to be chairman of an interdepartmental committee; he himself then had the status of a war-time Civil Servant. Accordingly a note was sent round instructing departmental representatives to disassociate themselves and explaining that it would be published as the personal report of Beveridge, as assisted by representives of the departments.

There is at least one respect in which the public owes him a great debt of gratitude. The attitude of uplift, which coloured the whole report, enabled him to propose enormous increases in the contributions of employees, as required for actuarial purposes. Because of the uplift, these were accepted by public opinion and by those who would have to pay the contributions, without serious question. It is doubtful if any government would have dared to initiate proposals for such large increases had they not had the authority of the Beveridge Report, which, by its spirited and challenging idealism, supplied the momentum for imposing these onerous charges. Thus he should have the credit for having put the Insurance Funds on a thoroughly sound actuarial basis.

The main specific feature of his report was the proposal to universalize the insurance systems. Hitherto, although the majority of people belonged, the comparatively well-to-do had not participated. The idea doubtless was that the exempted classes were well able to look after themselves, whether by taking out their own insurance policies or otherwise. Beveridge argued that it was right in principle that all should be included. There was something undemocratic, even patronizing, about the previous system. There was the feeling that these funds, to which, of course, the State contributed, were intended for the "servant" class, not for the "masters", who were above such things. Since all were liable to the evils to be insured against—ill-health, old age, etc.—there was no reason in principle why this system should not apply to all.

The Labour government adopted the Beveridge principle. It is just possible that the extension of the system to those not personally participating (a minority) was the cause of there being so much talk about the "Welfare State", as though it was something new. But the extension, while interesting from the point of view of principle, can clearly not be thought of as constituting a social revolution.

Beveridge also proposed a free national health service.

3. The Labour government adopted the free national health service. This has to be set down as an important departure. Although there has been some friction from time to time with sections of the medical profession, on the whole the free health service has been a great success and remains very popular.

4. A great campaign for house building had to be undertaken after the war. The local authorities were given the duty of proceeding with this; subsidies were provided; rent restriction was imposed on the pre-existing houses. Basically this complex of measures was the necessary aftermath of the war, during which house building had been almost entirely suspended. This had been a form of "investment" which it was rightly thought had to be suppressed during the war, to release resources for other purposes. Thus, when the war was over, there was a vast shortage. Had there been no rent restrictions, rents would have soared up. While other needed goods might become available for consumers after a fairly short interval, it was evident that it would take a long time to bring the provision of houses up to the required level. Owing to the nature of housing, it is clear that special measures were needed.

The strict logic of subsidizing house building may be called in question. In the abstract it can be argued that there was no reason why this particular form of consumer need should be favoured. This issue was tangled with the wider question of preventing a "cost inflation", which crops up in many connections. It is doubtful whether a Conservative government would have dealt with the problem very differently. When it later resumed power, it conducted an even more vigorous campaign for house building, but laid greater stress on private enterprise. But it might well have thought that, in the early stages, the main brunt of the work would have to be undertaken by the local authorities.

5. In one sense food subsidies may be regarded as one element in the new "Welfare State". It is probably incorrect so to regard them. They originated in the war, and they constitute the most striking example of the contrast and conflict between cost inflation and demand inflation,

too often thought to be two aspects of the same thing. The food subsidies, granted during the war, were unquestionably demand inflationary. During that time the government screwed taxation up to what it regarded as the highest feasible level. Beyond a certain point, a further increase of taxation is bound to cause acute inequity as between one individual and another at a given income, since some have numerous responsibilities while others have not. Thus, having got as much as it can by taxation, a war-time government has to borrow the rest. Every effort was made to raise the level of personal savings. Given the level of taxation, and given the level of personal savings, any extra expenditure by the government is demand inflationary. Thus the food subsidies, rising to the high figure of £500 million per annum towards the end of the war, were undoubtedly demand inflationary. And the government was doing all it could to limit inflation. The food subsidies were given as an antidote to cost inflation. While demand inflation is limited, being measured by the quantity of excess demand, and while its effects can be in part repressed—by rationing, material allocations, price controls, etc.—, cost inflation is less easy to deal with ; it could lead to a vicious spiralling of wages and prices and eventually galloping inflation. During the war it was decided to take the risk involved in this extra bit of demand inflation, in order to secure the cost-deflationary effect of food subsidies. An informal understanding was reached with labour that, if the cost of living was held down—and it was for this that the food subsidies were required—they would not ask for wage increases. All this was successfully put through : wages rose very little after the first two years of the war.

Similar arguments applied when the war was over. The food subsidies entailed higher government expenditure, and, when the Budget came to be balanced, a higher level of taxation. But to remove the food subsidies would inevitably entail corresponding wage increases, since the standard of living was anyhow being held at a minimal level in the years immediately after the war. Thus a spiralling between wages and prices, greater than that which actually obtained, might have been generated.

Although the food subsidies have been somewhat reduced, the problem remains alive until the time of writing. It affects negotiations regarding the Common Market. The British allow free imports for food, but sustain farming production at home by giving subsidies. The continental countries prefer to impose tariffs on imports and have a higher level of internal prices. The British have been making great efforts, of which more will be said hereafter, to check the vicious spiral of cost inflation, with excessive wage increases pushing up prices and prices pushing up wages. Too rapid an abandonment of the food subsidies might make this task more difficult.

It may be that members of the Labour government regarded food subsidies as part of their general policy of helping the less well-to-do. It is doubtful if this is correct, since the well-to-do also gained by the food subsidies. Their maintenance has been mainly governed by the desire to prevent cost inflation.

Whereas Labour should be given credit for enthusiasm and efficiency in putting through the necessary measures, it is not clear that there is much in the items, as listed above—apart, perhaps, from the free health service—that either constitutes a radical departure from pre-war British policy or is widely different from what the Conservatives would have done. Foreign ideas about all this have been very much out of balance.

III. CONTROLS

It is very difficult to know how to place policy under the head of "Controls" in relation to the "socialism" of the post-war government. It took over the whole panoply of war-time controls and kept them in being. It may safely be said that a Conservative government would have done the same, anyhow for a number of years.

It is true that the United States largely got rid of controls in 1946. It is not clear whether, even from the most anti-socialist and anti-planning point of view, this was a good thing. Had controls been kept in being a little longer, the great upsurge of dollar prices, which had a world-wide effect, might have been avoided. There was much less inflation during the Second World War than there was during the First World War, although the former was a much greater economic effort for both the United Kingdom and the United States than the latter; but after the Second World War there was a much larger bout of inflation than there was after the First; this has always seemed rather a disappointing outcome.

Whatever may have been the rights and wrongs of the matter for the United States, there is no doubt that a further period of control was essential for the United Kingdom. The latter country was confronted with a vast balance-of-payments problem, as shown in the last chapter, and also with an enormous pressure of domestic demand. The mere fact that British consumption was running some 1 per cent below the pre-war level at a time when United States consumption was up 53.3 per cent, entailed that there was bound to be a far greater pressure of demand on consumer account. The same was true of demand on capital account, since the run-down was also much greater in the United Kingdom. The loss on services items on external account meant that artificial measures would have to be taken to stimulate exports, while imports would have to be rigidly controlled and held well below the pre-war level. But such a control of imports could not be undertaken in isolation, since it was bound to increase internal inflationary pressures still further. As well as total exchange control and the strict control of imports, the internal economy was regulated by the requirement for licences for new building and plant and equipment, by the allocation of materials, by rationing and by price controls. In fact the United Kingdom had to go through a further period of "siege economy".

This policy was christened at the time by the word "austerity", for which Britain became well known. Travellers observed that in many countries on the Continent of Europe the amenity of living increased much more rapidly after the war than it did in the United Kingdom.

In a book published at the time,[2] I argued that the United Kingdom was "trying to do too much", namely by way of investment, especially in the basic industries, and that more resources should be devoted to the building up of stocks, to exports and to consumption, the last mentioned to give a stronger incentive to workers and to raise morale. I argued that the market mechanism should be allowed to function more freely. But this would have entailed, as I fully recognized, an even stricter control over investment. I held that some of the fixed investment then proceeding should be postponed in favour of other uses of our

[2] R. Harrod, *Are These Hardships Necessary?*, Rupert Hart-Davis, London, 1947.

resources. This was a question of economic judgement, and Conservatives, as well as Socialists, dissented from my views.

We have to consider how the maintenance of the régime of controls has to be interpreted in relation to the socialism of the government of the day. Did the Labour government regard the controls as temporary expedients that would, in due course, be dismantled, or did it regard them as part of the permanent machinery of regulation in a socialist State? Who knows? Probably different individual Ministers looked at the matter in different ways. Some may have thought that the controls would be continued in perpetuity. Some may not have thought the matter through, giving their attention only to day-to-day necessities. Politicians do not usually revert continually to questions of underlying social philosophy, unless compelled to do so. Before the end of the term of socialist government, a good many controls were in fact relaxed. One day a newspaper carried the headline "Holocaust of Controls".

The fact is that no one knows how far a Labour government, if returned to power in the autumn of 1951, would have gone towards liberalization within the private enterprise sector of the economy. Since it is unlikely that a Conservative government would have taken a different attitude towards the régime of controls in the nineteen forties, and, indeed, on its assumption of power (1951) it actually intensified certain restrictions, this aspect of socialism, if it is right so to regard it, cannot be said to have made any lasting imprint on the British economy.

The maintenance of easy money during this period has been a subject of controversy. Dr. Dalton, an able Chancellor of the Exchequer, has since been much vilified in this connection. It is not, however, certain if his critics are correct.

Both the United Kingdom and the United States financed the war at low rates of interest. In this respect they both created a new landmark in the history of finance. In all previous wars, including the First World War, the authorities had assumed that, since the government would have to borrow vast sums of money, it would have to acquiesce in paying higher interest to lenders. In the Second World War techniques were evolved, notably through the creation of plenty of liquidity in the community, whereby large borrowing was carried through smoothly without any upward movement in interest rates. There were two very powerful arguments in favour of this policy. First, since in conditions of modern total war it was evident that all unnecessary investment must be stopped by legal prohibition, and since the main economic purpose of a high interest rate is to discourage investment, it followed that high interest rates would not achieve their main purpose. Their normal work of discouraging investment would be more effectively achieved by outright prohibition. Secondly, since there was heavy governmental borrowing, low interest rates saved the taxpayers of the future a vast amount of money. It is interesting to observe that at the end of the First World War the United Kingdom, having a National Debt of some £8,000 million, had to face an annual interest charge on it of about £320 million; after the Second World War the National Debt had risen to about £26,000 million, but the interest charge on it to about £500 million only. Had the interest charge been running at the same rate at the end of the Second World War as it did at the end of the First, this would have meant that about £500 million extra would have had to be found in taxation—a burden that in 1946–1947 would have been crushing. Indeed it would have been necessary to consider some large-scale capital levy, or, even worse, some "currency reform".

Similar arguments were applied after the war. Further borrowing was in sight; also, maturities were impending, and, with rising interest rates, conversion loans would have had to be offered on terms less favourable to the taxpayer; and there was a vast mass of floating debt, all carrying a minimal rate of interest. If, indeed, controls over capital investment were inevitable for a further term of years, then they could take the place of a high interest rate in its capacity of discouraging investment, and it would be unnecessary to burden the taxpayer with additional interest charges. If all did not proceed quite according to this plan and inflationary pressures were in fact generated, it must be said that this was because the authorities were not strict enough in holding investment projects down to the resources available.

It is to be noted that the United States pursued exactly the same policy as the United Kingdom during this period, namely one of cheap money. The logic of the United States policy is, however, less clear, since their investment was not being checked by direct controls. In both countries bill rates were held at minimal levels until 1951. It is interesting to observe that this side of the policy was terminated at about the same time in the two countries; apparently this was for different reasons, although the philosophers of history may be able to find some deep-laid common cause. The termination in the United States was marked by the "accord" between the Treasury and the Federal Reserve System in March 1951. This was due to the fact that American opinion was reluctant to acquiesce in the need for the revival of the whole panoply of war-time controls, in order to finance the Korean war and the huge defence programme then in prospect, and held that inflationary tendencies should be kept in check by the indirect method of monetary and fiscal policies. But how could the Federal Reserve System pursue an anti-inflationary monetary policy if it was committed to holding the bill rate at a minimal level and holding 2½ per cent United States bond at par? This gave the Federal Reserve authorities the arguing matter to secure the "accord". In the British case the change of policy was due to the accession to power of the Conservative government and the occurrence at the same time of a rather severe balance-of-payments crisis.

As regards the longer-term interest rate (bond rate), the British authorities did not succeed in holding the line until 1951. The policy began to break down in the spring of 1947. This was an example of the victory of public opinion over the government. In the autumn of 1946 there was a crisis of fuel shortage of major dimensions, followed in the spring of 1947 by a cold spell of unprecedented severity and length. Meanwhile inflationary pressure was getting more intense, and people refused to believe that the authorities could hold a 2½ per cent bond rate in such circumstances. It was this scepticism which made the authorities unable to persevere in the low long-term rate of interest.

It has been suggested that Dr. Dalton might have succeeded had he been content with the 3 per cent that had been shown to be maintainable through all the exigencies of the war, and that where he made his mistake was in trying to push on to 2½ per cent. Once his policy was seen to break down, the rate advanced to well above 3 per cent.

In an interesting article[3] Mr. Nicholas Davenport, who is a good

[3] N. Davenport, *The Spectator*, February 23, 1962.

authority on these matters, brought evidence for the view that the attempt to go too far was due, not to the exuberance of Dr. Dalton himself, but to the advice of Treasury officials. This may be evidence of a certain tendency in the Treasury to be doctrinaire and a little out of date, which has been manifested in very different directions in recent years.

A final point may be made about controls. These, along with the austerity consequent upon them, led to the Labour Party becoming unpopular. The citizen cannot always distinguish nicely between the needs of the case and the culpability of the government. In certain respects the Labour government was certainly wanting in regard for the feelings of consumers. For instance, bread rationing was introduced in peace-time although it had not been found necessary during the war. Many other items, including petrol, continued to be rationed, and many goods were unavailable in the shops. This, rightly or wrongly, damaged the image of the Labour Party.

IV. THE NATIONALIZATION OF INDUSTRY

The nationalization of a number of industries was the most distinctive manifestation of the socialism of the government. Recent utterances by leading Labour spokesmen suggest that the Labour Party is no longer wedded to the policy of further nationalization, although this used to be so central a feature of the socialist programme. Nationalization is certainly no longer popular, except among stalwart Labour members. It would be dangerous, however, to assume that this aspect of British socialism is altogether a thing of the past. An attempt to rescind the clause which puts the nationalization of the means of production, distribution and exchange as the final objective was defeated at a Labour Party conference in 1961.

A limited number of industries only were nationalized. This leaves the United Kingdom as what is sometimes called a "mixed economy". One might regard the present *status quo* as more or less permanent, even should the Labour Party be again returned. On the other hand, the mere fact that the nationalization stopped short at a certain point does not afford evidence either way, since what was done was quite sufficient to occupy the six years available.

Although the sphere of nationalization was rather extensive, there may be danger of exaggerating the degree to which this was a departure in the direction of socialism. It is quite possible that a Conservative government would have nationalized some of the industries affected. It may be useful to take a brief glance at those concerned.

One may ask whether there was any principle governing the selection of industries to be nationalized. The concept of "public utilities" may have some significance, although it does not cover the whole range; so may the concept of "monopoly". In some cases these coincide, as with electricity and gas, where an invasion of public domain is involved, and the local authorities are not likely to be willing to give a number of competing companies the right to take up the pavements of the same town. There has also been the idea that "basic industries" ought to be nationalized. This is rather a vague concept. Such expressions are often used as "industries on which the whole economy depends". But depends in what way? In these days of specialization the area of mutual dependence is very wide indeed. Some members of the Labour Party may have been influenced by the thought of Keynes. He held that, in order to iron out the business cycle and maintain a high level of employment, it might be necessary for economic policy makers to have some control over the amount of investment in certain important industries. It is to be noted that the nationalized industries are very big capital users; although they employ only about a quarter of the labour force, they have at times approached the point of being responsible for nearly half of all investment in productive industry (including transport). Control of investment did not necessarily imply nationalization in Keynes's mind; that in his view need only be looked upon as a weapon of last resort if one could not get the control in any other way. Yet, if such control was judged expedient, this might work in the mind of a socialist as a good reason for nationalization. There is also the point that an industry could be thought suitable for nationalization where, in any case, it could be best administered by some standard rules, like the Post Office, over the country as a whole.

A. Coal

We may begin with coal. On the face of it this is not a very suitable industry for nationalization. The United Kingdom has a great multiplicity of producing units, conditions in which are widely different from one part of the country to another. One would expect a great diversity of techniques to be required, in accordance with the richness or structure of the seams. It does not at all partake in the quality of being a natural monopoly. And yet, paradoxically, of all the industries within the group, this is the one that it is *most* likely that the Conservatives would have nationalized at that time. The root cause of this was the intense desire of the operatives themselves that their industry should be nationalized. If this desire were frustrated, it would be difficult to get co-operation for increasing productivity. Coal mining is not a pleasant occupation, and, with the growing amenities of modern factories, recruitment was bound to be difficult, as indeed it has continued to be. One may look at the matter in simple human terms and ask whether what a vast mass of people earnestly desire—there were until recently almost as many mine workers as farm workers in Britain—should be denied them on the ground of an abstract political or economic ideology.

What has been the root cause of this attitude among the operatives? It has been suggested that it was due to bad management on the side of labour relations. This is an allegation difficult to check. The mine workers certainly *believed* their troubles (heavy unemployment, etc.) to be due to managerial shortcomings. There were doubtless deeper reasons, to which I shall return.

Meanwhile it should be added that there have continued to be more far-reaching allegations concerning the inefficiency of pre-war management in the coal-mining industry. It is alleged that operating efficiency continued to deteriorate and that nothing was done to introduce up-to-date equipment and modernized methods. In this regard there were wide differences as between the various important regions. For instance, many of the mines in Derbyshire and Nottinghamshire were thoroughly modernized and could indeed claim to be as efficient as any in the world. But in other parts of the country, e.g., Yorkshire and South Wales, there was a running down. This raises an important point of principle. The mines in Derbyshire and Nottinghamshire were rich, and it was worth sinking capital in them. If similar amounts of capital were not sunk in other parts of the country, this may not have been because the managements were inefficient, but simply because it was known that they were not worth these expenditures. Economic efficiency does not consist in always introducing the most up-to-date equipment that an engineer can think of, but rather in a correct adaptation of the amount of new capital sunk to the earning capacity of the old asset. In not introducing new equipment, the managements may have been wise, not only from the point of view of their own interest, but from that of national interest, which requires the most profitable application of available capital disposal.

This brings us to the point of principle. It has often been argued by socialists that the profits of good mines should be used to offset the losses of inferior ones, and has even been adduced as an argument in favour of nationalization which would enable the offsetting process to be carried out. It would suffice for the national interest if the coal-mining industry as a whole paid its way. The fact that it has not done so since nationalization may be evidence that the old managements were wise in their generation. It is not, of course, the right principle that the profits of good mines should be used to recoup losses on others. Rather it is right that as much should be extracted from the inferior mines as can be done by old-fashioned methods, and that they should gradually go out of action.

Of course, there may be a social objective, such as preventing the decline of certain villages or regions, or for having regard to the welfare of the middle-aged mine workers, for whom it might be a hardship to change their occupations. To cover these there might be a case for giving subsidies, to keep the old mines at work. But at the same time thought would have to be given to whether public funds could not be used more advantageously, e.g., by subsidizing new "infant" industries in the coal-mining areas and to training mine workers in new skills.

The idea that by centralizing and pooling the finances of a whole industry its unprofitable sections can be sustained, crops up in other connections also when the advantages of nationalization are considered.

The administrator is not always alive to the economic unsoundness of this procedure; indeed this is one of the greatest dangers inherent in the doctrine of nationalization.

To return to the attitude of the mine workers and their keen desire for nationalization, the most fundamental reason of all is probably that, until recently at any rate, labour was far the highest element in cost (about 85 per cent in the nineteen twenties), so that it was more exposed to bearing the brunt of trade oscillations than labour in other industries. The most striking example of this was in the prolonged strike of 1926. By returning to the pre-war gold parity in 1925, largely for prestige reasons—this was a classical episode in the inter-war history of the United Kingdom—the authorities somewhat overvalued the pound and thus put all export trades into difficulties. A high proportion of coal output was then exported; and there was accordingly an immediate demand for a reduction of wages and a lengthening of the working week. Other industries, in which wages were a smaller element in cost, might manage to get along; but in coal mining it was impossible to mark down export prices by some 10 per cent without adjusting the wage-cost structure. The strike caused the most intense bitterness. Why should mine workers be victimized while other members of the community were not having their incomes reduced? Another cause that perhaps tended to harden the views of mine workers was their local concentration in townships or villages, where the Party doctrine was cherished and not softened by a mixing with other types of wage-earners, who might not be so much addicted to it.

The coal-mining industry had, from a distant date, been more subjected to state interference than others. Naturally enough, it drew the early attention of humanitarian reformers in the first half of the nineteenth century, who got parliamentary legislation to enforce minimum conditions. It was the first industry, apart from a very limited number of "sweated" trades, to have a statutory wages minimum (1912). In 1919 the majority report of the Sankey Commission recommended nationalization. When the Labour Party gained office, but not power, in 1929, it was bound by its pledges to reverse the lengthening of the working day from 7 to 8 hours which took place after the 1926 strike. Actually it gave the workers only a half-hour back. And even this was represented as making the industry unpayable, should nothing more be done. To meet the producers' case, the government imposed by statute a very rigid cartel system, giving the producers fixed quotas, which they could buy and sell, and the power to fix prices. Thus, although coal mining is not a natural monopoly, it was made a rigid artificial monopoly in 1930. The Conservatives, when returned to power shortly afterwards, did not reverse this. Official thinking in those days of acute depression was rather favourably inclined to the cartel idea. In 1938 coal itself, as distinct from the operating units, was nationalized.

Thus, there was a long history of bad labour relations, state interference and compulsory cartelization behind the decision of the Labour government to nationalize. The situation was a tangled one. It is difficult to see what any other government could have done.

B. Electricity and Gas

Secondly, there is electricity and gas. Here we are at the opposite extreme, with industries which, by normal criteria, would be considered suitable for unified control and management. These fall into the category of "public utilities", and are by their nature monopolies. Certain general principles should presumably be applicable to their administration on a national scale. Substantial sections of these industries were already owned and managed by local authorities, so that, to that extent, the issue was not one between public and private ownership, but between centralization and localization. But in the case of electricity, centralization had already come in. As early as 1926 a Central Electricity Board had been set up to organize the national "grid" for the nation-wide distribution of electricity in accordance with a single plan.

The principle, already referred to under coal, of subsidizing certain regions out of the profits of others, reappears. There has been the idea that the various areas, some remote, are entitled to their electricity, and should not have to pay the full economic cost of the service. In the case of electricity, unlike that of coal, the principle could be defended on the ground that the provision of a supply yielded "external economies" for other industries, which are of real economic benefit to the nation, although not capable of being credited to the accounts of the suppliers of electricity.

C. Transport

The railways have been subject to public control from the outset, owing to the monopoly position implicit in the compulsory purchase of land. It is true that in the early days the authorities allowed compulsory purchase by competing lines, but this could only be done to a limited extent and did not entail competition in the full sense in the provision of railway services. In the inter-war period the railways, whose capacity to earn profit in the late nineteenth century had been considered so safe that their stock was given trustee status, went into the doldrums, owing to the growth of road competition. A whole series of official committees was set up to investigate the resulting problems. It might be thought desirable to release the railways from the restrictions, e.g., as regards uniform non-discriminatory freight charges, which had been originally imposed as a safeguard against their abuse of monopoly power. They were monopolists no longer! Not much progress was made on those lines. To help them, restrictions were put on road haulage by a system of licensing. Despite many attempts, the correct principle for imposing charges (cost of service, what the traffic will bear, etc.), so as to get the most economic distribution of traffic as between the railways and the roads, has never been successfully worked out. Here again we have a tangled situation.

Railways have been considered an appropriate industry for nationalization in other countries not addicted to socialism. The inclusion of road haulage under the nationalization of transport was much more controversial and more sharply opposed. Apart from the general predilection for nationalization by the government, there was the idea that both sides of the transport industry should be nationalized in order to get a proper "co-ordination" between rail and road services. But this idea of co-ordination has proved to be an elusive one. The fault may be that of the professional economists, who have been unable to state clear general principles.

It is to be noted that there was a precedent for combining rail and road services under one public department, in the form of the London Passenger Transport Board, established in 1933. This was recognized to have been a great success; but it must be added that this rested on the magnificent work for unification which had been antecedently accomplished by private enterprise.

Air services were also brought within the net. Here the fact that subsidization had been required before the war could be considered relevant. The BOAC had already been established as a public corporation in 1939.

D. Iron and Steel

The nationalization of iron and steel was a much more specifically socialist measure than the other nationalizations, all of which could be reasonably defended within the ideology of private enterprise, and was much more fiercely opposed. This was not a public utility and had no tangled problems; it was by admission an efficient industry. Here the idea seems to have been uppermost that it was desirable to nationalize an industry on which the whole economy was vitally dependent.

But the monopoly argument could also be used. For several decades the industry had contained a number of trade associations, some of which adopted price fixing and other cartel practices. When Britain departed from its age-old policy of Free Trade in 1932, an Import Duties Advisory Committee was set up, which recommended protection for the iron and steel industry, subject to its making its network of trade associations more comprehensive and complete. This was another example of the predilection of official thinking for cartelization in those days of acute depression. (There was surely something analogous in the early years of the New Deal.)

The industry took the hint. There were complaints, whether well founded or not, that, by this system of "administered" prices, it kept prices too high. One cannot but be reminded of recent complaints of administered prices in the American steel industry. Thus the iron and steel industry did not have quite a clean record in 1945 as being a fully competitive industry. It had been highly cartelized with the encouragement of, and under the protection of, the government.

E. Bank of England

Most of what has to be said about the Bank of England is reserved for another chapter. Once again we have a case where past history seemed to point towards nationalization. And in the world generally the doctrine that it was highly desirable for a central bank to be entirely independent of the government had begun to weaken.

From 1694 the Bank of England had operated under its charter, revised from time to time, and until 1932 had, in fact, been largely independent of the government. It kept the government account, managed the National Debt and, since 1844, had had, subject to exceptions, a monopoly of the note issue. Its central duty was to maintain the convertibility of its notes, and, to this end, it was free to use its discretion, subject to limitations imposed by the Charter, in the conduct of monetary policy. On the occasion of two wars (Napoleonic and First World War), when it was relieved of the obligation to convert its notes into gold, it was understood that it was its prime duty to render its notes convertible once more as soon as possible after the war was over, and, during the war, to bring all its influence to bear upon the government in limiting inflation to the greatest possible extent.

But in 1932 the scene changed. Owing to the world slump, the German moratorium, and some vacillations by the Labour government, which have already been referred to, the United Kingdom was driven off the gold standard in September 1931. What then was the prime duty of the Bank? To restore the gold standard at the previous parity at the earliest possible moment? No. There was a widespread belief, probably out of date by 1931—widespread public opinion on economic matters is so often out of date—that the pound was overvalued and that it would not be desirable to return to the previous parity, and probably not desirable, anyhow for the time being, to return to any parity at all. What, then, was the Bank to do? It had shareholders and depositors to whom it was responsible. It was all very well to say that it must maintain the convertibility of its notes at a fixed parity; that was a clearly defined and readily intelligible obligation. But now the situation seemed to be that it was no longer required to do this. It was hoped that it would use its normal powers to prevent undue oscillations in the foreign exchange market. It should not allow sterling to sink too far, but nor, on the other hand, should it allow it to rise too much, e.g., to its previous parity; it must, while preventing excessive oscillations, allow it to find some level (undefined) which could be considered as an equilibrium, and in the best interests of the country in relation to its balance of payments and to the situation of heavy unemployment which existed. All this was very vague. In the honest pursuit of this objective, it might do things open to criticism. And what about the interests of its shareholders and depositors?

With the situation so fluid and undefined, it was perfectly obvious that the Chancellor of the Exchequer, no less, must have the responsibility for the British foreign exchange policy. Accordingly the Exchange Equalization Account was set up as part of the Treasury. It was operated by the Bank of England, and the motions carried out by that institution were much the same as the Bank would have executed had the change not been made.

But it was necessary to put the Chancellor in a position in which he could bear the brunt of criticism and not be able to say, "That is the business of the Bank of England, in which I have no right to interfere". For instance, towards the close of 1932 the pound was allowed to drop somewhat, and the Americans complained that this had frustrated action previously taken by the Federal Reserve System during the summer to get some lift of prices and of business activity in the United States. This was before the final climax of the slump in the United States, when banks had to close, in the winter of 1932–1933. The position would have been intolerable for the Americans, and for everyone else, if the Chancellor had been able to say, "That is none of my business".

Accordingly, from that day forward the Treasury and the Bank of England had to be in constant mutual consultation about policy regarding sterling on the external side. This was *de facto* a partial nationalization, and a more important event than the formal nationalization of 1945. Whether the Bank of England or the Treasury had the predominant influence in what was actually done between 1932 and 1939 will probably always be difficult to determine. One may think that in all technical matters the Bank remained supreme, and that on general policy there need have been little difference of viewpoint between the two bodies. And the position in this respect may not have altered much since the formal nationalization in 1945.

One further point may be made in regard to the historical antecedents of this particular nationalization. During the crucial years of the world slump between 1929 and 1932, it was thought that the Bank had exerted its influence on the side of deflation. (This was also true, but to a lesser extent, in relation to the previous decade.) In fact the Bank was probably no more deflationist than the Labour Chancellor of the Exchequer, Snowden. Keynes was a lone voice on the other side. But in the following years there was a great change of opinion about the evils of deflation and the appropriate action to be taken in the event of slump. Furthermore, there were delicate negotiations in 1931 between the Bank of England and the Federal Reserve System (from which, along with the Bank of France, temporary loans were obtained prior to the suspension of the gold standard), and it was believed that out of these negotiations might have come the suggestion, so hateful to Labour, that the deficit of the Unemployment Insurance Fund should be removed by reducing benefits paid out. Did the Bank of England maintain that such an idea was anathema, or did it, on the contrary, express the opinion, with the Labour government still in office, that it was a useful one?

The detailed history of this matter is not yet established. What is an undoubted fact is that great bitterness was generated in Labour Party circles about the alleged deflationism of the Bank of England. There were fears that, if it was left independent, it might put its deflationist spoke in the wheel of socialist planning for full employment.

From that time forward there was no doubt that, if the Labour Party ever gained power, one of its first actions would be to nationalize the Bank of England.

If we take the whole picture, it appears that the Labour government from 1945 to 1951 did not take the country much further towards the national ownership and control of industry than might have been thought expedient by middle-of-the-road people, who were not deeply wedded to the doctrine of *laissez faire*.

When the Conservatives came into power, they de-nationalized the iron and steel industry and, to a considerable degree, road haulage. They also allowed some competition with the two great state corporations, BOAC and BEA, in civil aviation.

The nationalized industries were not run, like the Post Office, as government departments. "Corporations" were set up and given a certain independence of status. In the law courts they are not regarded as emanations of the Crown, i.e., of the executive arm of the government, but are treated as independent bodies. The employees of the corporations do not rank as civil servants. What distinguishes the corporations particularly is that they do not work for profit. Ultimately the Minister, within whose domain the operations of each corporation lies, is answerable for them in Parliament; but he refuses to answer questions relative to their day-to-day work. The exact borderline has naturally been a matter of much discussion. The problems of the appropriate degree of centralization have also been discussed and investigated by committees. By a paradox, the Fleck Committee—Sir Alexander Fleck was a most experienced industrialist, being at that time chairman of Imperial Chemical Industries Ltd.—held that the organization of the coal industry was too de-centralized, while the Herbert Committee held that the electricity industry was too centralized. In consequence of the latter report the Central Electricity Authority was broken up into a Central Electricity Generating Board and a number of area boards.

As regards the dividing line between ministerial responsibility and corporation independence, the topic that has provoked most discussion has been that of wage and price policy. In this area there are many vexed questions still to be settled. The general view is, even among those who regret that so much nationalization was undertaken, that these corporations have been working with reasonable efficiency, and that, the step having been taken and there being an inevitable monopoly element in most cases, no good purpose would be served at this stage in trying to unscramble the omelettes.

There is, however, one great gap in the arrangements that were made for nationalization—namely, the right method for financing new capital outlay in these industries. Discussion of this must be left to a later chapter, where the British financial mechanisms will be examined. This problem of the finance of these industries is crucial for the whole question of the management of the National Debt, which has become so central a feature of general monetary policy. This problem stretches out, and at certain periods has been the cause of weakness in the international position of sterling itself.

V. SOCIAL CHANGE

Can it be said that there was a "social revolution" in those six years in which the Labour government, wedded to socialist doctrines, was in power? If we consider the feelings of the main rank and file of people, it is doubtful if they had any joyful sense that a new and better régime had been ushered in. For them the great improvement, as compared with the pre-war period, was the fact of full employment. But this arose from the fundamental post-war economic conditions and had nothing to do with the specifically socializing measures of the government. On the other side, there was a régime of austerity and rationing, so that life was in many ways hard.

The idea that a great social change had occurred was more prominent in the minds of those in the upper and middle income groups. They experienced a relative deterioration in their conditions, and many, who did not look too deeply into causes, may have attributed this to the Labour government.

In fact, the social change that they felt, as a matter of direct personal experience, had somewhat different causes, of which the two principal ones may be mentioned.

First there was a new crushing burden of taxation. This could be rightly attributed to the Labour government only to the extent that it had gone further in the public provision for a Welfare State than a Conservative government would have done. It must be remembered that part of the requirement for higher taxation was due to higher defence expenditures, part to the larger interest charges involved by the National Debt and part to those extensions of the system of social security which were overdue and which any government would have felt bound to implement at the end of the war. The extra frills that we may think were added by the Labour government increased the tax burden in only a minor degree. Furthermore, it was inevitable that a large part of the extra taxation required should fall on the upper and middle income groups. It is to be recalled that those were years of austerity in which hardly any rise in general consumption could be allowed. In such circumstances it would have been very difficult to impose further burdens on the lower income groups. One had to apply the taxes where there were margins of expenditure not strictly necessary.

The heavy rates of taxation had effects other than their immediate oppressiveness. It became impossible for people of substantial income to set aside savings. In former times, for instance, a lawyer in good practice expected to be able to save enough to acquire an independent investment income; thus he might decide to enter public life on an income acquired previously by his own efforts. This inability to save out of income affected other occupations also, including industry. There has been a tendency, much criticized in certain quarters, for business men to regain some of the amenities of life by charging expenditures to business account. This, however, cannot have much effect on home life. There has also been some tendency for property owners, in their resistance to a depression in their standards of living to which they had previously been accustomed, to live on capital. It is also believed by some that rich people have been able to evade the burden of very high income taxation by living on "capital gains". This, however, is fallacious, if applied as a generalization to property owners. Doubtless a limited number, who have been exceptionally able or lucky, have been in a position to do so. But, by and large, there have been no net capital gains. The value of property has probably not on the whole risen more than the cost of living; it has in fact barely kept pace with inflation. Of course, those who regard an increment in the money value of their capital as a capital gain, may increase their consumer expenditure accordingly; but, unless that increment is more than in proportion to the rise in the cost of living, they are really not living on "capital gains" but on the original corpus of their capital, to the detriment of their future incomes. Statistics on capital values are inadequate. There has probably been an overall increase in the value of real estate. But against this has to be set losses in real terms, i.e., in their goods value, of capital assets on other accounts.

The Americans have also had the experience of crushing rates of taxation in the higher income brackets. But, in the British case, the steep progression in tax rates began at a lower level. Thus, the surtax, superimposed upon the standard rate of income tax, began at £2,000 a year (=$5,600 after 1949), until the reform by the Conservative government in 1961 which raised the lower limit to $14,000 a year. The Americans have been able to bear less harshly on the middle group of incomes, because the margins available for tax collection in the higher groups were of greater absolute amount.

The second change, which made the upper and middle income groups have the most acute sense that there had been a "social revolution" after the war, may surprise Americans, since they had already experienced this change long before. This was the disappearance from the market of domestic servants in any substantial numbers. The reason for this disappearance accounts also for its earlier occurrence in the United States. It is the increasing value of labour, as such, owing to rising productivity in industry. It is not possible to have a continuing increase in the wages of those industrially employed, as determined by their rising output, without having a corresponding change in the wages at which domestic service is available. It is a matter of common observation that the poorer a country, the larger the amount of the domestic service available for those whose incomes are above the average. In fact progress in the methods used in the output of material goods inevitably alters the relation between the value of a given material object and the value of human labour, whether it be labour engaged in industrial production or in a service of any kind. And thus, as a community grows rich, its pattern of spending shifts towards the relatively cheap material goods and away from the relatively expensive personal services.

This trend had, of course, been proceeding in the United Kingdom for many years before the Second World War. If one looks back to the period before the First World War, one would expect to find a family with no more than £300 (=*c.* $1,500) a year having one living-in servant, and for incomes above this it soon rose to the level of two or more. Between the wars the position was much tighter than this. But a factor that retarded the tendency against domestic service was the heavy unemployment between the wars. Then came a lapse of six years in which all available man-power was swept into the war effort. Doubtless many expected that, after the Second World War was over, there would be a return to conditions similar to those that prevailed between the wars. But this did not happen. In due course life was adapted to this change, as it had been in the United States so many years before. But it took many by surprise, and they may have attributed their troubles to the socialist government.

In summary, it may be said that the two main factors that made those in the upper and middle income groups feel that there had been a vast social upheaval since before the war were (1) the very high level of taxation and (2) the drying up in the flow of domestic servants. But the former of these had only a slight connection and the latter no connection at all with the socializing measures of the government.

VI. SUMMARY

It is difficult to obtain a precise image of what the government would be like should the Labour Party again be returned to office, owing to the special circumstances during their former tenure of power which were due to the aftermath of war.

In the sphere of social security the Labour government took the country a step forward in a bold and imaginative way. But it must be stressed that this was in no way a new departure; rather it served to bring up to date a system which dated back to the Liberal government of 1906 to 1914, and had since been much amplified. The country had been prepared to expect a substantial new advance by the famous Beveridge Report. The most notable innovation was the extension of the general system of insurance, which had hitherto benefited "wage earners" only, to all classes of society.

Another innovation was the free health service, which, despite criticism of various particular points, has been highly popular.

The country was governed during this period by a very pervasive system of controls. These, however, were inherited from the war, and the very awkward and impoverished condition in which the United Kingdom found itself made it absolutely essential to have a further period of what may be called a "siege economy". It may be the case that many Labour Party members envisaged a system of tight controls as a permanent feature, but this is not certain; the Labour government did in fact remove many of the controls during its period of office. There is no likelihood that, should the Party be returned to office, it would reimpose a pervasive system of controls. These are largely discredited now. But it is possible that it would revert to a moderate amount of "controlling", especially if this seemed needful to implement an all-out policy of economic growth.

The Labour government nationalized a considerable sector of industry in rather quick time, and this was in some ways its most characteristic achievement. But here again there are qualifications. The coal-mining industry had become very much snarled up, and it is likely that even a Conservative government would have judged that there was no alternative to nationalization. The other nationalizations might also have been justified from the point of view of "middle-of-the-road" politics, since the industries were largely monopolies or public utilities, with which there had already been much interference by the government. The main defect in the programme was the lack of adequate forethought about the finance of these industries.

Nationalization has not been popular in the United Kingdom, and, whatever the inner thoughts of certain Labour Party members may be, no great emphasis has been placed upon it in successive General Elections.

It has been said in certain quarters, including left-wing quarters, that the Labour Movement will have to find a new philosophy. What shape this might take, it is impossible to predict; but it seems possible that its guiding idea may be that of greater economic growth. In the implementation of such a policy it might be expected to be willing to move further from traditional maxims and procedures than the Conservative Party.

CHAPTER 4

Industry

I. CHANGES IN PATTERN

While the somewhat restricted experiment in the nationalization of industry, described in the last chapter, has proceeded, all the multifarious activities required by a modern economy have continued under private enterprise. In the early post-war years work had to proceed subject to the trammels of the controls that were sustained in being after the war, of which the most important were material allocations and the requirement for licences for new construction and plant. The import controls had their advantages, as well as their disadvantages, from the point of view of producers, since they gave a temporary protection. The controls were progressively dismantled, and after 1951 there was little further encroachment by the state, except (1) by the stern application, from time to time, of monetary and fiscal restraints, and (2) by a number of measures to deal with monopolistic practices which, however, may be in sum rather more lenient than the anti-trust legislation of the United States. The main task of the country was to shift productive resources into industry, so as to fill the great gap on the external side, which was due to the financial losses of the war.

It may be interesting first to observe how employment shifted. We may start with 1948, as being the year in which the worst maladjustments following the war had been remedied. The year 1959 has been taken as the terminal date, because at the end of that year the statisticians made a rather large re-classification of employment by industries. This was doubtless a valuable and praiseworthy statistical readjustment, but makes things difficult for the patient student and expositor of time series.

Great Britain did not have in these eleven years much increase in its working population. This is shown in Table 15.

The increase of males available was only 400,000. It is to be noted that

TABLE 15

INCREASE PER CENT IN WORKING POPULATION, 1948–1959

	Great Britain	U.S.
Total . .	+ 5.2	+ 14.4
Male . .	+ 2.6	—
Female . .	+ 11.0	—

during this period there were large losses by emigration. The total loss on this account to the rest of the Commonwealth (males and females) was 1,321,000. At the same time immigration from the Commonwealth amounted to 640,000. Those lost were to a large extent people of high quality. In the year 1960, for instance, about half the males were respectively "professional and managerial" (20.7 per cent), "clerical, distributory and non-industrial" (16.2 per cent) and "students or of no occupation and retired" (12.7 per cent). The remaining half were fairly well distributed among industries. It is to be noted that those classified as "labourers" were only 4.6 per cent. This is a very great change of pattern from the typical emigration to such countries as Australia and New Zealand in the last century. On the side of immigration, while doubtless a number of immigrants were of good quality, a considerable proportion were from the West Indies and not on the whole available for higher grade work. None the less they have made a very valuable contribution to the total man-power situation.

If we look at this pattern as a whole, and take quality as well as quantity into account, it may seem doubtful whether there has been any substantial increase at all in the male population available for the tasks of the country. We may next note the way in which the population was absorbed or redistributed (Table 16).

Table 17 shows the percentage changes in the numbers employed by category. The disproportionate increase in distribution may be accounted for by the fact that this sector was very much squeezed during the war and immediately after it.

Table 18 shows more important changes in employment within the manufacturing industries.

TABLE 16

MAIN CATEGORIES OF AVAILABILITIES AND ABSORPTIONS OF LABOUR, 1948–1959 IN THOUSANDS

Gains		Absorptions	
Increase in working population	1,188	Manufacture	973
Released from:		Distribution	471
Defence	281	Professional, financial, and miscellaneous services	324
Agriculture	178	Local Government	81
National Government	162	Building and contracting	56
Mining	52		
	1,861		1,905

TABLE 17

CHANGES IN EMPLOYMENT, 1948–1959

Occupation	Percentage change
Manufacturing	+ 11.9
Distribution	+ 18.9
Professional, financial and miscellaneous services	+ 8.2
Agriculture	– 15.1

TABLE 18

CHANGES IN EMPLOYMENT WITHIN MANUFACTURING INDUSTRIES, 1948–1959

	Numbers (thousands)	Percentage change
Engineering, shipbuilding and electrical	+ 314	+ 17.7
Vehicles	+ 274	+ 29.3
Food, drink and tobacco	+ 182	+ 25.1
Paper and printing	+ 116	+ 25.0
Chemicals	+ 98	+ 22.3
Textiles	– 81	– 8.8

While the above tables show the shifting of man-power, they do not indicate the redistribution in the proportions of the output of the various categories, since productivity per person rose much more in some industries than in others. In Table 19 the various industries and occupations are ranked in a rough order of merit, as is seen by comparing the increase in the volume of output with the increase (or decrease) in the numbers employed. The coverage of the two columns is not the same, since Northern Ireland is excluded from the employment figures. But this should not make much difference to the general pattern.

TABLE 19

CHANGES IN OUTPUT AND EMPLOYMENT, 1948–1959

	Volume of output, U.K., per cent	Numbers employed in Great Britain, per cent
Chemicals	+ 92.7	+ 22.3
Gas, electricity and water	+ 78.2	+ 16.2
Agriculture	+ 29.4	− 15.1
Engineering and allied industries	+ 62.2	+ 21.7
Transport and communications	+ 24.5	− 6.4
Metal manufacture	+ 27.7	+ 3.6
Building and contracting	+ 27.6	+ 3.9
Distribution	+ 38.1	+ 18.9
Textiles, leather and clothing	+ 12.7	− 6.4
Mining and quarrying	+ 1.1	− 5.9
Food, drink and tobacco	+ 31.0	+ 25.1

The performance of the coal-mining industry has been somewhat better than indicated by the figures (in the tenth line) of the table, which relate mainly to coal mining. Between 1948 and 1955 the number of shifts worked per week fell from the average of 4.7 (1938 : 4.96) to 4.24. No doubt this change to a shorter working week, which was brought about by absenteeism, reflects an adjustment to the rise in wages, compared with before the war. It represents freedom of choice between more leisure and the arduous task of working underground.

As regards output per man shift, there has been a notable improvement since 1959. Output per man shift in 1938 was 1.14 tons, in 1948 1.11 tons, in 1959 1.33 tons, and in the first quarter of 1962 1.55 tons. At the coal face output per man shift was 3.0 tons before the war, 2.92

tons in 1948, 3.73 in 1959, and 4.47 in the first quarter of 1962. Thus productivity per man shift has risen rather notably.

The man-power engaged in this industry has dropped by 220,000 (on 782,000) since 1938. Recruiting has been difficult, but it must not be assumed that the movement away from coal mining has been uneconomic. The better seams have tended towards exhaustion, and it may well not be economic for man-power to remain engaged in an industry subject to diminishing returns. The occupation of coal mining cannot be regarded as a pleasant one, and it is rational that there should be a shift towards modern factory work, in which the value of output is higher. The net effect of this large curtailment of man-power combined with the smaller number of man shifts, although offset by a considerably higher productivity, has been a reduction of output by 690,000 tons a week (on 4,353,000). Meanwhile the domestic consumption of coal has been up by 280,000 tons a week. This has eliminated most of the margin available for export.

It may be well to consider the redistribution of emphasis as between different industries contributing to exports, as shown in Table 20.

Table 20

Composition of United Kingdom Exports

	1938	1961
Volume	100.0	214.6
	Percentage share in value of exports	
Food, drink and tobacco	7.3	5.6
Wool and other animal hair	1.7	1.9
Other basic materials	3.1	1.7
Coal, coke	8.5	0.8
Petroleum and products	1.0	2.6
Manufactures	75.6	84.7
Postal packages	2.5	2.5
	99.7	99.8

Manufacturers have had to fill the gap made by the large drop in coal. While manufactures have risen in price slightly compared with other exports the increase in the volume of manufactures is probably not far short of 130 per cent.

Some manufacturing industries in which there have been important increases or declines in their share of exports are given in Table 21.

TABLE 21

MORE IMPORTANT CHANGES IN COMPOSITION OF EXPORTS OF MANUFACTURES

	Percentage shares	
	1938	1961
Machinery	19.9	34.5
Road vehicles and aircraft	6.4	14.1
Chemicals	8.1	10.4
Scientific instruments, etc.	0.8	1.8
Woollen and worsted yarns and woven fabrics	5.7	1.3
Cotton yarns and woven fabrics	12.3	1.8
Clothing, footwear, travel goods	3.1	1.5

These shifts represent the response of the United Kingdom to the challenge to increase exports to nearly two-and-a-half times their previous level. There are varying views about the level of efficiency in British industry. They may be coloured by the particular sectors of which an individual may have knowledge and are very difficult to check by objective methods. There appears to have been a remarkable recovery after the war, followed by a less progressive phase during the nineteen fifties. Commentators are apt to lose sight of the all-important point, simply because the war is receding into a forgotten past, that the British have had the especially difficult task of raising exports by a large amount, without a countervailing increase in imports. This same balance-of-payments difficulty has also been inimical to total growth, because it has recurrently, especially since 1955, caused the adoption of measures by the governmental authorities deliberately devised to check growth. Producers, however highly efficient, will not expand their output of goods if a corresponding expansion of demand is prevented by governmental measures from coming into existence.

II. PRODUCTIVITY

It seems clear that the growth of productivity (i.e., output per person) is assisted by the growth of total production. This is because a higher rate of growth in total production may allow a larger spread of overheads, thus reducing unit costs, and also entails that a higher proportion of the equipment in use in industry at any one point of time is of more recent date and therefore presumably more efficient. Some countries, like Germany and Italy, have recently had very large increases in their industrial population, which partly accounts for their high growth of output per person. In the United Kingdom, on the contrary, the industrial population has, as shown above, increased little. This must mean that a higher proportion of the equipment used is of earlier design.

Much thought has been given to the need to increase efficiency. At one end of the scale is the supply of qualified personnel. It was generally agreed at the end of the war that there was a deficiency in the amount and quality of technological education. The causes of this have their roots in a rather far distant past. We may need to go back to the Industrial Revolution itself, when industry was, so to speak, self-created. Many of the inventions and innovations out of which modern industry has arisen were made on the workshop floor. The whole process was carried forward in this way, decade after decade. The technologists of British industry were self-educated amateurs, carrying their knowledge and traditions forward from one generation to another. It did not occur to them that the expertise of their own industries was something that ought to be, or could be, learnt at schools or institutes. Such traditions may have survived to times when they were already quite out of date.

A great effort has been made since the war towards enlarging and improving technological education. Rightly or wrongly, it was decided as a matter of deliberate policy not to set up brand new technological institutes, such as might aspire to vie with the MIT, but to enlarge and develop existing institutions, like the Imperial College of Science and Technology in London, or humbler technical colleges that already existed. Much progress has been made, but it is early yet to expect the full dividends.

It has always been the policy to seek to ensure that all universities should be of high quality. A number of universities—or rather colleges, which were only allowed to graduate to university status after a prolonged period of probation—were founded in the early part of the century. Thereafter there was a pause for a good many years. In the fifteen years after the last world war only one university came into existence, that of North Staffordshire, which is run on rather special lines. Currently, however, half a dozen new universities are in the process of formation. That of Sussex has already opened its doors. All universities are now dependent, as regards the greater part of their finance, on state aid. The only centres of education at the university level that are independent of state finance are the colleges of Oxford and Cambridge. (It is to be noted that these are of quite a different character from the halls of residence or colleges of any other university, in that they provide their own teaching, as regards the character of which they retain complete control and can use their own discretion. At Oxford also, although no longer to the same extent at Cambridge, it is the colleges, and not the university authorities, that appoint the great majority of persons destined to be responsible for the main work of teaching and research in the university.) Although all universities, subject to what has been said about Oxford and Cambridge colleges, are dependent upon state finance, a delicate system has been devised by which they continue to be effectively screened from any kind of state interference. Public money flows to them through the agency of the University Grants Committee, which is an independent body, although loosely connected with the Treasury, and of high academic standing.

A new university must acquire a charter. This is only granted after rather elaborate steps have been taken to ensure that the management of the new university is safely placed in hands that will ensure the maintenance of high academic standards. Subject to these safeguards, it is now planned to increase the output of university graduates at the greatest possible rate, to supplement the output of technological institutions. While the universities have in the past produced a substantial flow of scientists of the highest quality, it has to be recognized that there has not been a sufficiently large output of scientists of good quality. It is hoped that this will now be rectified.

There has been much discussion about whether universities should establish courses of training in management, or "business schools". Despite the high reputation of such places as the Harvard Business School, it seems that, on the whole, opinion in the United Kingdom is still sceptical of the utility of this kind of training. The academic fraternity is doubtful if the kind of material that could be used in courses is capable of giving training in exact thinking at the level which it is sought to maintain in university studies generally. Many of the shrewdest men of business are also doubtful if the kind of training capable of being provided in management courses would do anything to enhance the usefulness of recruits to business, and indeed fear that it might be the other way round. There is, however, a good deal of pressure from industrialists—perhaps from those less shrewd!—that more management courses should be instituted.

There may also continue to operate in some measure a deeper cause of the insufficiency of the supply of efficient personnel for the running of industry. Although the twentieth century has seen vast changes in British social attitudes and there is danger that foreigners may have a picture thereof, which is really a caricature, yet there still remain some effects of the age-old tradition that the occupations of production and distribution, those twin pillars of the economic system, lack prestige. It is not so easy to eradicate "feudal" roots. The ownership of property, public service of all kinds, the law, and professions connected with academic study or the arts, for many generations ranked, in prestige value, above production and distribution. Exchange, in the sense of high finance, was perhaps the first of the economic trinity to win acceptance.

In a certain sense all this is a thing of the remote past, but it may still have left effects, e.g., in the matter of recruitment. Many of the best brains in the country have no family connections with the business world whatever. All the universities have their Appointment Boards, which provide a channel for entrance into industry. It is probably the case that the largest firms have the biggest drawing power. But this may not be satisfactory. The linkages of business with the university are probably still not numerous enough to get recruitment on a wide enough scale.

Some time ago it was taken to be axiomatic in many circles that big business was also the most efficient. But I detect in the most recent period a certain shift of opinion in this matter. There are some who hold that the great firms, of famous name, are often centres of inefficiency, having become top heavy and bureaucratic through excessive growth, and that the most vital forces of progress are to be found rather in the firms of middling size.

If we may believe the supply of efficient personnel is improving, we also have to look to the other side and ask how the demand stands, in particular what the incentives are. In the forefront of the discussion has been the heavy burden of taxation. This may affect adversely the desire of the individual to enter industry. In the old days ambition might be fired by the prospect of turning a small business into a great one, or, from a more egoistic view, of building up a large fortune out of a small or negligible capital. If such ambitions are vain, then a greater drawing power may be exerted by the moderate incomes earnable in the Civil Service or professions, or even farming, where it seems possible for "expenses" to add more to the private "way of life" of the individual than is possible in other occupations. At the personal end of things, it has been impossible to save enough, after payment of income tax (and surtax) to grow rich, however much one might earn as one's income. And even at the business end it may be very difficult for an individual to enlarge a small business without reliance on outside sources, since he must draw out something to live upon himself. An individual, starting from small beginnings, may find that the only way to get rich by his own exertions is to engage in capital transactions, which make little or no contribution to the increase of the National Income.

The reduction of surtax undertaken by the Conservative government in 1961 has done something to ameliorate the bleak prospects described in the foregoing paragraph. Before this change surtax (tax chargeable in addition to the standard rate of income tax, now 37.5 per cent) began at an income level of not more than $5,600 a year and mounted steeply thereafter. By the aforementioned reform the bottom level has been raised to $14,000.

In a somewhat different field an attempt has been made to provide a growth incentive by "investment allowances". Shortly after the war it was decided to encourage investment by accelerated depreciation allowance. The "investment allowances" go further than this, by allowing an initial deduction from tax assessment in respect of capital outlay, which is not deducted from the value of the capital that can thereafter be claimed by way of depreciation allowance. Thus the investment allowance is in effect a subsidy to investment. These "investment allowances" have been taken on and off from time to time; they have been used in effect as one method of regulating the business cycle. They were in operation in 1962. The British are watching with interest the investment tax credit programme of the United States.

Despite these concessions, it is felt by many, although not by all, that the burden of direct taxation is still tending to diminish the incentives to enterprise, especially in the case where an individual owner runs his business and may not see advantage in taking on the additional work that would be entailed by efforts to expand it at home or in the export field.

III. THE PROBLEM OF MONOPOLY

The relation of efficiency to competition has also come into prominence in discussion. It was noted in the last chapter that before the war public policy was, contrary to ancient British traditions, inclined to be favourable to monopolistic (cartel) arrangements. These went under the blessed name of "rationalization". There has since been a considerable shift of opinion in this regard, and monopolistic arrangements have been frowned upon.

The British share with the Americans the Common Law by which all restraints of trade are in themselves illegal. But the operative effect of this overriding principle has been greatly whittled down over many years by court decisions, by which trading agreements of a basically monopolistic character were held to be "reasonable" expressions of the liberty of the individual to make such arrangements with trading partners or competitors as were most conducive to the success of his operations. Thus the Common Law had ceased to be a safeguard for the maintenance of competitive conditions.

In 1948 a "Monopolies and Restrictive Practices Commission" was established to make investigations and recommendations in regard to industries in which at least one-third of the output was controlled by a firm, or through arrangements between the firms. This body had a family resemblance to the Federal Trade Commission, and made numerous investigations (as revealed in private and public reports). These, however, did not lead to action, save in a few cases.

Its reports may have had an educative effect in relation to the complexities of the subject. The preconception of the man in the street is that there is a clear and simple issue. What we all want is competition, and any arrangements that restrict or hamper competition should be outlawed. But then arises a host of difficulties. The restrictive arrangements are of many varying degrees of formality or informality and of various kinds, and sometimes, although similar in outward form, are for differing objectives. They have grown up gradually by way of adjustment to particular problems and needs, which are often specific to particular industries owing to the organization of their marketing arrangements.

The general pleas that are apt to be made in favour of some price fixing or quoting arrangements are well known. It is held that irregularities and disturbances in selling outlets create uncertainties for producers, prevent the forward planning of long production lines and thus raise costs, so that the consumer is worse off in the end than he would have been under a régime of collective price fixing. Then there is the argument, much associated with the name of Schumpeter, that some monopolistic element is valuable as giving the security that is required by the producer if he is to make heavy investment in the production process, investment that will lower costs and benefit the consumer. How far are these pleas specious?

Troubled by the fact that the reports of the Monopolies Commission did not appear to be leading to much positive action, the government decided to adopt sterner measures, and in 1956 the Restrictive Trade Practices Act was introduced. By this the Monopolies Commission was left in being in a modified form with circumscribed duties. It was still required to report in cases where one firm controlled at least one-third of the output. Where the one-third control was due to arrangements between more than one firm, then this was a restrictive practice, which was to be dealt with in another way. The

Monopolies Commission was also left with the duty of investigating restrictive practices relating only to exports, so as to avoid the publicity entailed by the Court procedure about to be described. It is interesting to note that in the American case also the Webb-Pomerene amendment exempted agreements confined to the export trade from the severities of the Sherman and Clayton Acts.

This Act required that all restrictive practices should be "registered". The firms concerned could then either drop the practices, or request the Restrictive Practices Court, composed partly of judges and partly of laymen, to allow them to continue. In principle the Act condemned all restrictive practices; but the Court might allow them if it could be shown that the restriction in question conveyed specific and substantial benefits to the public, or was adopted in self-defence, e.g., against a powerful competitor outside the group, or in relation to monopolistic buyers or sellers of the product in question, or if the removal of restriction would cause serious unemployment in the area, or be likely to be damaging to the export business.

A great many restrictive practices were dropped by firms in consequence of this enactment. At first it seemed that the Court would be severe in upholding the general principle that restrictions were contrary to the public interest, and not allow itself to be impressed by the specious arguments for taking advantage of the exceptions allowed by the Act. There have, however, been a few decisions which have made it seem uncertain whether the Court will continue to take so firm a line. A plan for allocating tenders by the Water-Tube Boiler Makers' Association was allowed, as was a price-fixing agreement by the Black Bolt and Nut Association, and one by the Cement Makers' Federation. The Court was satisfied in these cases that there were safeguards against prices being fixed above the competitive level, and that the public would suffer from the irregular marketing that would ensue if the price-fixing arrangements were terminated. Thus it is not clear that the Court will in all cases condemn price-fixing arrangements as such.

The Act of 1956 laid down that the collective enforcement of re-sale price maintenance was illegal. On the other hand individual re-sale price maintenance was allowed, and indeed legal methods for enforcing it were strengthened. There is continuing discussion of the merits of re-sale price maintenance. It has to be admitted that there is a *prima facie* case for allowing retailers the right to compete freely, and for condemning restrictions on this along with all price-fixing arrangements. Is there not scope for increasing efficiency in distributive trades by healthy competition, just as much as in production itself? The case against re-sale price maintenance has sometimes been reinforced by arguments of a theoretical character derived from the theory of imperfect competition. Early expositors of that theory laid down that producers, trying to equate their marginal revenue with their marginal cost, would fix prices at levels giving them some surplus of profit, and that this would attract new entrants; this process would go on until the profits of producers were reduced to normal; but in this equilibrium, when established, there would be too many producers, each would be working below optimum capacity, each would have excessive overheads, and thus, while the producers made no abnormal profits, consumers would have to pay prices above the levels that would rule under perfect competition. These early doctrines of too rigid a kind have been largely discredited since, by the argument that producers would not take so short a view as to equate current marginal revenue with current marginal cost. If they looked ahead, they would see that the best way to maximize long-run profits was not to charge prices so high as to encourage new entrants, even if this meant that they were currently selling at an apparent loss (in terms of marginal cost and marginal revenue) at the margin. But, it is claimed that this doctrine, although inapplicable in the wider field of production, may come into its own in the area of re-sale price maintenance, and in consequence of it. If producers allow too large a margin, perhaps to maintain in being less efficient outlets, then the high profits earnable will cause too many shops to come into existence. Each shop will be having less than the optimum amount of turnover and will therefore have excessive overheads. In equilibrium the representative firm will not make an excess profit, but there will be an excessive number of firms. It is claimed that the abolition of re-sale price maintenance would cause greater concentration and rationalization of shopkeeping, from which the consumer would derive benefit.

As against all this it is held that arguments from the damage done by irregular marketing apply with special force in this field. It is claimed that firms will be inclined to quote cut prices by way of "loss leadership", as a ruse for attracting custom, and that consumers will not, nevertheless, benefit, because the losses on "loss leadership" will probably be recouped by higher prices for other goods, that the firms not desiring to compete in this way will tend to discard articles being sold at cut price, and that producers will be gravely damaged in their planning by the loss or diminution of sales to their regular outlets. Their planning of long-production lines may be disturbed and their costs of production increased, to the final detriment of consumers. It is also claimed that these practices may lead to a decline in quality.

It has not escaped attention in the United Kingdom that the Americans, who ever since the Sherman Act have taken a much stronger line against monopoly than the British, none the less thought it expedient to pass the Miller–Tydings amendment, followed by the McGuire amendment, by which States are allowed to have Fair Trading clauses if they wish, at their discretion, or subject to the verdict of their own Courts, including a "non-signer" clause. The idea naturally occurs that if the Americans, with their strong anti-trust tradition, have thought it expedient to make an exception in the case of re-sale price maintenance, they must have some rather strong reasons for doing so, derived from painful experience.

The matter has come into great prominence quite recently owing to the idea gaining ground that causes of inflation are to be found on the cost, as well as the demand, side. This has been exemplified in the recent "incomes policy" of the Chancellor of the Exchequer. It is felt that the campaign against inflation might be strengthened by allowing price competition among retailers. It is by no means clear at present on which side the balance of opinion will be.

IV. SUMMARY

It is difficult to classify the factors governing industrial growth, since these depend so much on the fund of human capacity for enterprise, adventure, efficiency and self-discipline; such human characteristics do not lend themselves easily to academic classification.

The United Kingdom is now a country of slow population growth.

And, since on average the quality of the man-power lost by emigration is higher than that of the man-power gained by immigration, if we take quantity and quality into account, we probably have to look upon the United Kingdom as a country with no increase in human resources, except to the extent that the existing resources are improved by better education.

The considerable shifts of employment as between the various sectors of the economy have been set out. These have been due not only to the normal incidence of economic progress, but also to the fact that the United Kingdom had to devote so much larger a proportion of its resources to exports owing to the financial losses of the war. The shift involved has been all the more difficult owing to the fact that the United Kingdom was already devoting a large proportion of its output to exports before the war.

As regards the human factor, great efforts are being made to expand the output of university graduates and also to expand and upgrade technological colleges. These efforts must take some time to bear fruit.

On the side of material equipment, it is usually supposed that the United Kingdom has still a long way to go to get up to date, despite the rise in the proportion of resources devoted to investment since before the war, which is now running above the American level as a fraction of National Income. An adverse factor is the stagnant working population. If the industrial population is growing, then at any one time a higher proportion of factory equipment is newly made and therefore presumably more up to date. In this respect some continental countries have had an advantage over the United Kingdom, since their industrial populations have been growing more rapidly. Note has been made of the attempts to encourage investment by accelerated depreciation allowances and investment allowances.

Modernization in the United Kingdom has not been helped by what has come to be called the "stop and go" policy, consisting of recurrent bouts of repressive measures in the monetary and fiscal fields, which will be described fully in later chapters. The principal reason for this policy has been continuing anxiety on the balance-of-payments side. The trouble is that industrial investment suffers not only during the periods in which the repressive policies are in force, but also owing to the fact that the prospect of the recurrence of such periods makes the future uncertain; it means that the outlay of funds on the enlargement and improvement of capacity is more risky and reduces the courage and adventuresomeness of industrial leaders.

On the side of industrial organization, official policy has been much more hostile to monopoly, including cartel arrangements, than it was before the war. In this respect the British have been moving nearer the American position. On the other side the high degree of specialization involved in modern science-based industry seems to require more mutual agreement between firms and the formation of consortia for great undertakings, e.g., in the field of nuclear energy. The whole question of the campaign against monopolistic tendencies bristles with difficulties, as the Americans have found from time to time, ever since the passage of the Sherman Act of 1890. Thus the future is not altogether clear; but on the whole it may be said that official policy has for some time been directed to encourage competition to the greatest possible extent.

CHAPTER 5

Monetary System

I. BACKGROUND

The Bank of England was founded in 1694 as a Bank of Issue, to hold the government account, and to advance money to the government from its subscribed capital. In the eighteenth century the ordinary deposit banks also issued notes. These banks were owned by individuals, singly or in partnership, and were not allowed to be incorporated into companies. The same motive actuated this prohibition as was at work in the United States law against branch banking. It was felt that the citizen should be in a position to judge the creditworthiness of his banker personally and not be beguiled by the high-sounding name of some emanation from a headquarters in London.

Thus the Bank of England had a monopoly of the note issue within the sphere of joint stock banking. But in 1826 this monopoly was restricted to a radius of 65 miles from London. The growth of joint stock banking in Britain was not, however, the effect of this change. The question was raised whether it was really necessary for a bank to issue notes at all; there was no law against joint stock banking, provided that no notes were issued; accordingly the Westminster Bank was started on a joint stock basis in London in 1833.

In 1844 the note issue business was drastically circumscribed by Peel's Bank Act. No new issues other than by the Bank of England were to be allowed and existing issue rights were to be terminated in the event of banks merging or wishing to turn themselves into companies. The Bank of England was restricted to a "fiduciary" issue of £14 million, and all notes, in addition to that, were to be backed a hundred per cent in gold. The private bank note issues lingered on in dwindling importance and absolute amount, as a vested interest. The importance of the Bank of England issue also declined as a result of the restriction placed upon it, and the great mass of the circulation consisted of gold coins until 1914.

During the nineteenth century the new joint stock banks grew apace with branches all over the country, although the private banks lingered on. There were many mergers. After the First World War the "Big Five" (Barclays, Lloyds, the National Provincial, the Midland and the Westminster) occupied an overwhelmingly predominant position.

It became the regular habit during the nineteenth century for the deposit banks themselves to deposit with the Bank of England. Thus the latter acquired what we now regard as the most important function of all of a "Central Bank", namely that of being a bankers' bank. To the extent that the various deposit banks formed the idea that they should hold a minimum fraction of their deposit liabilities in the form of notes or a deposit with the Bank of England, the Bank of England obtained the power to regulate the "money supply" by its lending policy.

A gold standard in its fullest sense was in operation. There had only been minimal changes in the gold valuation of the pound sterling since the reign of Queen Elizabeth the First. During the early part of this period, however, the bimetallic system was in operation, causing certain quite minor fluctuations in the gold price; the gold valuation of the pound was finally fixed by Isaac Newton, the astronomer, in 1717. The maintenance of the pound sterling at an almost exactly fixed value in terms of gold for a quarter of a millenium naturally gave it great prestige. There was, be it noted, an earlier period in which an absolutely fixed value had been maintained, without any depreciation or increase of alloy, namely for 200 years after 1066. During that period the silver penny continued to contain a one two-hundred-and-fortieth part of a pound of silver by Tower weight (the "Tower" pound differed slightly from the Troy pound). It was from this earlier period of stability and constancy of fineness, rather than the later one, that sterling derived its metaphorical sense, as when we say that a man has "sterling" qualities.

The working of the gold standard in the United Kingdom up to 1914 was fairly, although not completely, automatic. By Peel's Bank Act, the Issue Department of the Bank of England was separated from the Banking Department. When gold flowed into the Bank, the note issue was increased automatically, but did not necessarily go into active circulation. The extra notes were retained for the time being in the Banking Department, when those paying gold in did not wish to draw out notes. In this case the deposits of the deposit banks with the Banking Department would rise. This in turn altered (increased) the ratio of notes in the Banking Department to its deposit liabilities. This ratio was (and still is) known as "the proportion", and, in the days of the full gold standard, was regarded as the most significant quantity in the whole monetary system. A rise in the proportion might be taken to be a signal for an easier lending policy by the Bank of England. To the extent that this was adopted, the deposits held by the deposit banks at its Banking Department were further increased. This would place the deposit banks in a position in which, having regard to their ideas about a proper relation between their "cash" and their own deposit liabilities, they could be more generous in their lending policy. By "cash" was meant their deposits at the Bank of England plus vault cash. This increased willingness to lend would tend to increase the "money supply" (deposits at deposit banks plus notes in active circulation) for the community as a whole. This was one aspect of the automatic working of the gold standard. But it was not the most striking feature of its "automaticity".

At this point it is expedient to refer to two sets of specialist institutions in the London money market, which remain, to this day, of great importance. One was the group of Accepting Houses (merchant bankers), the expertise of which consisted in their knowledge of the creditworthiness of individual traders throughout the world. The most famous of these was Rothschilds, but there were others of hardly less importance. Their function was to "accept" bills (two-name paper) drawn by one trading firm upon another, usually for a period of three months, and thus turn them into assets of quite first-rate standing. The Accepting Houses were not primarily purveyors of money, but gave traders the benefit which their acknowledged excellence in judging creditworthiness conveyed to their signatures on bills.

The other specialist institutions were the Discount Houses (bill brokers). Their expertise was somewhat different. From early days they made it their duty to scrape together overnight money, or money that was available for very short term, and to use it for advancing to traders on their bills, and particularly of course on those bills which had been accepted by a good house. They were the conduit pipe by which very short money was made available to finance trade, and, through their services, London was often the cheapest place in the world in which to borrow for three months. The Discount Houses financed not only British exports and imports, but also much international trade which did not touch British shores. They took risks, since the money borrowed might be on shorter term than the money lent; and of course there was a possibility of default on some of the bills.

Stockbrokers played no significant part in the London short-term money market. The "call money" of the deposit banks went to bill-brokers, not to stockbrokers. The reason for this difference from the United States was partly the existence of the Discount Houses, which were always ready to take up any call money on offer, but probably also the fact that the London Stock Exchange did not require daily settlement. There was a fortnightly settlement, and also facilities for carrying over beyond that. Thus it was possible to speculate on a narrow margin, without requiring stockbrokers to make up the difference; this limited the use to which stockbrokers could put call money.

If gold flowed into the country the deposit banks acquired more cash, as described above. In the first instance they handed this over as additional call money to the Discount Houses. The call money position continues today to be adjusted each morning with the Discount Houses. An accession of extra cash for the Discount Houses caused the short-term rate of interest to drop. It dropped to the point at which supply and demand balanced again. The extra lending undertaken by the Discount Houses, in consequence of their having more money, went mainly to finance international trade. The drop of the rate in London attracted additional borrowers. Thus it is fair to say that, if gold flowed into Britain, most of it was re-lent abroad at once. This was the most central and distinguishing feature of the "automaticity" of the working of the British gold standard before 1914. A favourable balance of payments was very quickly offset by increased lending overseas; thus the favourable British balance did not affect the liquidity of the rest of the world to any great degree.

If the gold position was such that the market rate of discount remained low, this would have a gradual effect on the long-term rate of interest. If this also came down, British investors would fairly readily begin to look overseas for stocks on which the yield might be higher than at home. Thus an outflow of long-term capital might be generated to supplement the short-term outflow.

If there was an adverse balance of payments and an outflow of gold, all the above-mentioned processes would operate in reverse. The interest rates in London would go up and international borrowing from London would be discouraged. It has sometimes been stated that this system was not satisfactory for the outside world, on the ground that the United Kingdom, by reducing its lending, was exporting its difficulties. This is not a tenable position. If the United Kingdom had an unfavourable overall balance of payments with the outside world, the outside world must be having a favourable overall balance of payments with it. In these circumstances a curtailment of short-term lending by Britain could do no harm to the outside world. Since it had a surplus on its account with the United Kingdom, it could afford not to borrow so much. Of course, if a critical phase of the business cycle occurred in the United Kingdom, this could infect other countries. This is always liable to happen when a particular country has important external relations, and it is not specifically connected with the working of the gold standard. It must not be assumed that British crises always had their origin inside the United Kingdom.

The system described was worked on the basis of a very narrow gold reserve—some £20 to £30 million. By however much one multiplies that sum, to allow for the increase in the sterling value of world trade, it would still appear to be derisory by modern standards of what countries require as liquid reserve. It is true that there was also some gold locked up behind the notes in circulation, in accordance with Peel's Bank Act; but that gold never had to be released between 1857 and 1914. Furthermore, there was a vast mass of gold coins in circulation, which might be regarded as an ultimate war chest; it was used as such after 1914.

While its external automaticity was the most outstanding feature of the British gold standard, incoming gold being so readily re-lent abroad, the gold flow did have some effect on the internal economy. When money was easy, the deposit banks, although operating in the first instance by increasing call money, in due course got around to other forms of lending, so that there would be an expansionist tendency in the whole economy. And conversely in the opposite situation.

The Bank of England was not a purely passive spectator of this automatic process. Two principles may be mentioned which were accepted by the Bank largely in consequence of the tireless advocacy of Walter Bagehot, for many years editor and leader writer of *The Economist*; his writing did much to win renown for that paper in its early days.

First, he held that if internal conditions were proceeding towards boom, the Bank of England should be more restrained in its lending, whatever the condition of the "proportion". This was contrary to the advice given by Peel when his Bank Act was passed. He had held that the only specific feature of the Bank of England was its right to issue notes, and, since that had been rigidly defined and controlled by the Act, the Bank might conduct its banking and lending operations just like any other banks, competing with them for business as much as it wished. In fact he ignored the special position of the Bank of England as being the bank which held the deposits of the others banks, on the basis of which they could make a manifold increase of their credit. This wrong precept was corrected by Bagehot, and in due course the Bank came to pay more attention to business-cycle conditions inside the country. After a time the method of lending by way of discounts and advances by the Bank of England declined, except for old customers and except on the occasion of a crisis. Thus it came to rely more, for the regulation of credit conditions, on what we now call open-market operations. It had a technique of selling consols (undated government bonds) for cash, while buying them forward. This created a temporary "credit squeeze".

Secondly, of very great importance were Bagehot's recommendations for how the Bank should behave in a time of crisis. He held that it should put the Bank Rate up to any level that it thought expedient, however high, and then express willingness to lend on good paper to all comers without limit of quantity. This principle is crystallized in the phrase "lender of last resort". In the early part of the nineteenth century the United Kingdom was subject to periodic crises of considerable severity. What happened was that, when the boom came to its turning point, there would be a sudden collapse of values; assets became unrealizable except at a heavy loss; this made everyone unwilling to enter new commitments, to lend money, or even to pay cash due out, if they did not fear immediate legal enforcement; thus everyone was placed in a position in which assets were unrealizable, no new money could be borrowed, and dues in might not arrive; this in turn made them unwilling to lend or to part with liquidity, save under necessity; thus the whole financial system became frozen up. Many, including, of course, banks, who could not escape a legal obligation to pay cash at once, found themselves bankrupted, even although their fundamental positions were perfectly sound. It was Bagehot's view that, in order to unfreeze the economy, the Bank of England should express complete willingness to lend to all and sundry, however low its own reserve might be, but at a Bank Rate of its own choosing. People would not mind paying a high Bank Rate, to save themselves from bankruptcy, for a short loan. This did serve to unfreeze the system. Those unwilling to pay dues out, because they feared that they would not get dues in, had their minds relieved; they could always go and get temporary accommodation at the Bank of England.

It was largely due to this doctrine that the United Kingdom did not have any severe internal crises after 1866. They continued to take place in the United States periodically, one of the most severe being in 1907; and one may perhaps reckon as a crisis of this type the events of 1932–1933. The last mentioned, however, was different, because it came, not at the turning point of the boom, but after three years of harrowing slump.

The automatic working of the gold standard on the external side was based on a very strong creditor position. The vast mass of funds locked up in bills due for payment by foreign firms within three months or less was very great indeed compared with sight or short-term liabilities. Between the two world wars the situation changed somewhat. Before the First World War some countries held reserves in the form of "sterling balances", but these were of modest amount only. In the decade after that war these sterling balances grew somewhat, especially after the return to the gold standard by Britain in 1925. This was not due to a change in British policy. It has sometimes been said that the United Kingdom adopted the imprudent policy of borrowing short and lending long during this period. That is to put the matter in a false light. The build-up of sterling balances was due to a different cause, epitomized in the resolutions of the international Genoa Conference of 1922. Owing to the fact that the currency value of gold was not re-adjusted for thirteen years after the First World War, all currencies including sterling and the dollar having become inflated in terms of goods, the goods value of gold stocks in the world was much depressed; there was, in fact, an acute gold shortage, accentuated by the fact that much gold had gone into American reserves during and after the war. In order to economize in the use of gold, the Genoa Conference recommended that, when the countries returned to the gold standard, they should not put gold coins into circulation again; and it also recommended that Central Banks should hold part of their reserves in the form of foreign currency. The foreign currency then most readily acceptable for compliance with this recommendation was sterling. This was probably the most important cause of the build-up of sterling balances held abroad, which was not particularly desired by the British.

The build-up of sterling balances was vastly reinforced by the events of the Second World War. The United Kingdom, being very hard pressed, and having to take as much man-power as possible away from the export trade, simply told the various countries that sterling acquired by sales to the United Kingdom would have to be kept in "special accounts" and would only be encashable, in one way or another not specified, when the war was over.

This led to a great problem at the end of the Second World War, to be discussed in the next chapter. What it is important to note, in relation to the working of the domestic monetary system, is the effect on its management of the fact that Britain was now a heavy debtor on short-term international capital account. The use of the Bank Rate to influence the flow of short-term capital movement is much more effective when it is a question of attracting or repelling foreign short-term borrowing from time to time, than it is when it is a question of repelling or attracting short-term lending. The latter is obviously a much weaker position to be in. In particular a high Bank Rate will not serve to attract much lending if there is lack of confidence in the future of the country, particularly as regards any possible devaluation of its currency. The same obstacle does not occur when it is merely a question of reducing the amount of foreign borrowing by a high Bank Rate. It is true that the Bank Rate appears to have worked very successfully in attracting lending during 1960 and the winter of 1961–1962. But the operation of the Bank Rate in this matter has not been uniformly effective in recent years.

II. CREDIT CONTROL

In what remains of this chapter it is proposed to concentrate on the internal working of the monetary system. It is relevant in this connection to note that there has been a considerable decline, proceeding over several decades, in the use of bills to finance international trade. This may be partly due to traders operating with more working capital than was their habit in the nineteenth century; in the United Kingdom itself there is also a much more extensive use of banking facilities for overdrafts. It has also no doubt been due to currency disorders—exchange controls, fears of devaluation, etc. At the same time there has been a great growth in the volume of Treasury Bills in the British Discount Market; this happened in both the world wars. For a number of years only about one-tenth of the bills discounted in the London market were commercial, although there has been some rise quite recently. The remainder have been Treasury Bills. This change in the character of the paper handled has made a great difference to the Discount Market.

The Bank of England policy has continued to be strongly influenced, in line with its tradition, by the external situation. But it has always paid some regard to the internal situation, and now has much more sense of responsibility for it than it had before 1914, and one might even add before 1932. This is due, not primarily to the nationalization of the Bank of England, but to a change of point of view among economists and the general public, no less than among Central Bankers. It was about 1922 that the Federal Reserve System began to direct its policy specifically to the state of the business cycle, as manifested in the internal

United States economy. Between 1932 and 1951 the United Kingdom endeavoured to implement a policy of ultra-cheap money, so that problems of domestic credit restriction did not arise. In the following decade certain difficulties have arisen in the operation of traditional methods of credit regulation, which in earlier times had worked very smoothly.

The traditional method consisted in the use of open-market operations in conjunction, if necessary, with changes in the Bank Rate. On certain occasions, if only a small change was required, it might suffice to tighten credit by open-market operations, without the need for any change of Bank Rate. Sometimes the Bank Rate would be changed without any open-market operations, simply to comply with trends manifesting themselves in the Discount Market, when these were held not to be undesirable by the Bank of England. Or a change in Bank Rate might produce its effect on money market interest rates without there being any need for open-market operations. Or the change in Bank Rate might have to be reinforced by open-market operations also.

Since the Second World War the deposit banks have adhered rigidly to a ratio of 8 per cent between their cash (as defined above) and their deposit liabilities. Before the war it is thought that they had a somewhat higher ratio. In their monthly statements they usually showed between 10 per cent and 11 per cent; but this was affected by "window dressing" each month, which by general agreement has been abandoned since the war, so that the true ratio to which they were then working for most of the time may have been below 10 per cent; but it was probably above 8 per cent. In this regard the British system is different from the American. The British banks do not, like the members of the Federal Reserve System, hold excess reserves. They push out any excess reserve above 8 per cent very promptly into the Discount Market as call money; or, if the Bank of England judges that this will lead to an unwanted fall in interest rates, it will cut off the excess reserves by open-market operations. Nor, on the other hand, do the banks borrow from the Bank of England, as member banks do from time to time from their Federal Reserve Bank. Such borrowing as is done from the Bank of England is undertaken by the Discount Houses, and even then only at very short term. The reason for its being at very short term only is that the official

Bank Rate is penal for the Discount Houses. Thus, so long as they are in debt to the Bank of England, they are losing money day by day. (For borrowing from the Bank of England below Bank Rate, see page 101.) While the Federal Reserve Discount Rate may at times be above the rate earned by certain member bank assets, which, however, they may not wish to dispose of, it is not, on the whole, a penal rate for them. And, although they have their tradition against borrowing from the Federal Reserve, they may take some time to repay, according to their convenience; they are not on hot bricks, as the Discount Houses are when they borrow from the Bank of England at its official rate.

Now this rigid adherence by the British deposit banks to the 8 per cent ratio, without indulging in borrowing from the Bank of England on one side or allowing excess "reserves" to pile up on the other, would seem to put the Bank of England into a much stronger position to regulate the "money supply" than the Federal Reserve is in. In a general way this is true, apart from the difficulties that I am shortly about to explain.

If the Bank of England conducts open-market sales with a view to the tightening of credit and thus reduces the "cash" of the deposit banks, their first line of response is to call in call money from the Discount Houses. An adjustment of the amount of call money outstanding is effected every morning. This calling in of call money must tend to send up the discount rate in the open market. The Discount Houses have to keep their books in continual balance, and, if they are deprived of cash, then, although they can temporarily recoup themselves from the Bank of England, they must quickly put rates up to reduce borrowing. If the Bank of England wishes to see a really substantial rise of discount rates in the market, it will put the Bank Rate up as well as imposing an open-market squeeze. The Bank Rate is always kept somewhat above the open-market discount rate, so that it can remain penal. In the old days a rise in the rate of interest in the Discount Market would promptly cause a reduction in the offering of commercial bills for discount. Why should those concerned go to London if they found they could borrow more cheaply in Switzerland or Holland? As the medium of this market was mainly commercial, the supply of it to the market was elastic. Thus the chain of events was simple: the Bank of England reduced the supply of "cash" to the deposit banks, they reduced the amount of call money they put into the Discount Market, the Discount Market rate went up and less paper (mainly international) was offered to it. The consequence of all this was that the "money supply" in the economy as a whole was reduced. The cut in lending to the Discount Market meant a cut in total lending, and, by the principle that "loans create deposits", the quantity of bank deposits in the hands of the general public went down.

This was not the end of the story. The deposit banks have always had some regard to what is called "second line" liquidity. It is now customary to refer to the ratio of the sum of "cash", as defined above, call money lent to the Discount Market (or elsewhere) and bills discounted by the deposit banks themselves, along with their holdings of Tax Reserve Certificates and foreign currencies, to total deposit liabilities as the "liquidity ratio".

In recent years the deposit banks have not allowed their liquidity ratio to fall below 30 per cent. In certain seasons of the year, it is usually kept above 30 per cent with the view that in other seasons the liquid assets available are liable to drop. There is a difference between the 8 per cent ratio and the 30 per cent ratio in that the former is adhered to, subject to fine margins, without plus or minus, while the latter may be taken to be a minimum.

In consequence of this desire to maintain their liquid assets, the banks will, after the immediate day-to-day adjustment of their call money, seek, if the credit squeeze continues, to reduce their other assets. They may sell out bonds, especially those of reasonably short date, on which they can restrict their loss. But then, in the long run, if the squeeze is continued, they will seek to reduce customer loans. In this matter they like to use their own discretion and proceed at their own pace. Some have the idea that, in the last analysis, the most important duty of these banks is to provide their customers with accommodation to the extent that this is justified by sound banking principles. The banks do not like to be rushed into curtailing customer loans. But this they will nonetheless do if that is dictated by a shortage of resources, as expressed in the 8 per cent ratio or in the 30 per cent ratio.

III. RECENT DIFFICULTIES

An essential link in this chain of causation was the elasticity of supply to the Discount Market. But we have seen above that, in recent years, by far the biggest medium of investment by that market is the Treasury Bill. And the supply of Treasury Bills is by no means elastic to changes in the rate of interest charged on their discount. The British government must get the money it needs week by week. It would be rather undignified to tell creditors due for payment for goods and services rendered, or otherwise, that it was short of money for the moment because borrowing in the Discount Market had become rather expensive. Nor does it peddle its Treasury Bills in foreign Discount Markets. Perhaps it ought to. And so this great mass of paper which the Discount Market is expected to take up week by week is rather inelastic in supply.

Part of the "floating" debt of the government itself is held in capital funds belonging to agencies of the government. The floating debt consists mainly of Treasury Bills but includes short-term borrowings from these agencies, known as "ways and means advances". A section of the Treasury Bills is issued directly by the Exchequer to these agencies, which may be called the Public Departments, from time to time, and these are known as "tap" bills. The remainder are "tender" bills. These are issued, as required, each Friday, to keep the government in cash. The Discount Houses agree on the price which they are prepared to pay for these bills. It has sometimes been suggested that this represents monopoly action by the Discount Houses, but this is not really so. The price named by the group is truly a competitive price, since it is directed, not to profit maximization, but solely to balancing supply and demand; they have a certain amount of cash in hand and aim at naming the right price to get that supply taken up in the purchase of the bills. There are also outside bidders for the bills, on whose behalf the deposit banks may act. Many of the outside bidders are foreign banks. All those outside bidders who offer a higher price than that named by the Discount Houses get their bids met in full. The Discount Houses bid for the whole tender, in accordance with an unsolicited and, of course, revocable undertaking of long standing. They will get a certain proportion of their bid, namely the whole tender minus that part of it which is assigned to the outside bidders. Outside bidders who name a lower price than that offered by the Discount Houses get nothing. Accordingly it is up to the Discount Houses to name a price that will, in their judgement, get them the precise proportion of the total tender that will match the cash at their disposal.

If, owing to a squeeze implemented by the Bank of England, their cash has been reduced, they will not be able to hold so many bills. Accordingly they will drop their price, i.e., raise the rate of interest that they charge to the government. If they get more bills than they desire, which they have to take up in equal quantities on each of the days in the week following, they will have to raise sufficient cash somehow. There is a ready method for them, namely resort to the Bank of England. Normally they will have to pay Bank Rate for funds obtained in this way. And this is higher than the rate that they would be earning on their bills in hand. Accordingly in the following week they will have to consider dropping their price (i.e., raising the rate of interest charged) still further.

Thus all depends on the responsiveness of outside bidders to the higher rate of interest which they can earn on the bills. If the rise in the rate of interest attracts outside bidders strongly, all may go forward smoothly, and of course the market for Treasury Bills is interlocked with that for commercial bills and other temporary short-term accommodation. The Discount Houses may be put in cash through less commercial bills being offered for discount, or by less requests for other short-term money, or by more short-term money coming into the Discount Market. By any of these methods the shortage of cash may be relieved. But in certain cases supply and demand may not be elastic.

And this constitutes the big difference between the condition of the Discount Market in recent years and that before 1914. The government demand for accommodation by way of Treasury Bills—and that is the big factor in the market as a whole—is inelastic. When the main medium of the market was commercial paper, conditions were elastic, and it was relatively easy, by a rise in the interest rates, for the Discount Market to balance its books at the end of each day.

If conditions in the Discount Market are notably inelastic, then the Discount Houses can be in a fourfold quandary. It may be that the cash available to them is cut down, that raising the rate of interest has no marked effect on outside borrowing or lending in the market, that the Discount Houses, feeling obliged to bid for the whole tender, have to pay out more money on this account than they have in hand, and that they can only raise the extra money by borrowing from the Bank of England at a rate that involves them in loss.

During the long easy-money period, when there was seldom any desire to impose a credit squeeze, a technique was developed by which the Discount Houses got accommodation from the Bank of England, not at Bank Rate but at the running market rate. If the Bank of England had misjudged the requirements for cash in its open-market operations, and if there was no desire to impose a credit squeeze, then it was sensible to let the Discount Market have the cash required below the Bank Rate, i.e., at less than the penal rate, by what is sometimes known as the back-door. When it was decided to re-introduce a more active monetary policy in November 1951, it seemed desirable to get away as much as possible from the back-door technique. At the same time, in the case of the fourfold quandary described above, it may still be thought sensible to use it, and it is so used very frequently.

But when it is used, the effect of the open-market operations, constituting the initial credit squeeze, is frustrated. The "back-door" lending increases the cash basis of the deposit banks. If this increase is maintained week by week, then the effect of the open-market operations is offset and there is, in fact, no credit squeeze at all. So what is to happen? One recipe would be a still higher Bank Rate, introduced in the hope that the consequential higher market rate would produce that elasticity of supply and demand that is desired. But it may be considered undesirable to have a still higher Bank Rate, and in certain circumstances that too may be ineffective in making the market more elastic. Thus we seem to have a block in the system.

The only way out of this difficulty is for the government to reduce its offer of Treasury Bills. If the reduction of cash available to the Discount Market is matched by a reduction of the value of the Treasury Bills that it has to take up, then all can go forward smoothly, and the money supply available to the whole community will have been reduced. And, in due course, the deposit banks, having regard to their

30 per cent liquidity ratio, may proceed to shift part of the onus of the squeeze off the Discount Market, by selling investments and reducing customer loans. And so the question has to be considered as to whether the government can normally be in a position to reduce the amount of tender Treasury Bills in order to enable a credit squeeze to be carried out smoothly.

The need of the government to borrow in any week, or run of weeks, is determined by the annual Budget and the seasonal pattern of the government's expenditure and revenue. Its need to borrow in the market is also influenced by the flow of funds by non-market borrowing (small savings, etc.), by the requirements of the Exchange Equalization Account, by receipts from extra-budgetary funds, and the growth of the fiduciary note issue. Subject to these, the amount that the government has to borrow in all in any week can usually only be altered once a year, on Budget Day, by changing the balance between revenue and expenditure on the whole. On two occasions in recent years there have been intercalary budgets, namely in November 1955 and July 1961. This is not a satisfactory procedure nor one which is likely to become a normal practice. Both were occasions when the government thought it desirable to give a striking demonstration that it was dealing manfully with an allegedly critical state of affairs; actually its measures on the former occasion were not very manful, and on the second occasion the crisis was, in a deeper sense, bogus. This will be discussed in a later chapter. The budgetary method of altering the supply of tender Treasury Bills is somewhat slow-working, even if resort is had to an extra budget.

This brings us to the other method by which the government should be able to alter the amount of its weekly offer of tender Treasury Bills, namely by funding them. This does not alter the total size of the National Debt at any one time, but alters its composition as between three-month bills and securities of longer term. It might be thought that this could readily be done by a new issue of bonds. But a distinction has to be drawn between nominal funding and true funding. When the government makes an issue, it is not underwritten in the style of corporate issues. If the public does not take up the whole issue, the residue is taken up by the Public Departments. Of these the major one is the

Issue Department of the Bank of England itself, but there are also Insurance Funds, etc. But as the capital of these funds cannot, for the moment, be increased, and is indeed governed as to its amount by long-run trends, the Departments can only take up the residue of a new issue by disgorging other securities that they have on hand, notably Treasury Bills. To take an extreme example, if the government decides to fund £500 million of Treasury Bills by a new issue, and none of the new issue is taken up by the public, then the Public Departments have to release Treasury Bills worth £500 million in order to enable them to take up the new unwanted bonds, and, the amount of tap bills having been reduced by £500 million, the amount of tender bills will, despite the nominal "funding", be unchanged. There will have been a nominal funding of £500 million Treasury Bills, but there will have been no true funding at all.

Contrariwise, there can be true funding without any nominal funding. If the Public Departments can, in any month, sell £50 million of bonds to the general public, then they can take £50 million extra of Treasury Bills through the tap and relieve the Discount Market of the need to tender for that amount. And so we come to this point. If in any given period it is desired to reduce the flow of Treasury Bills into the Discount Market, this can be done to the extent that the authorities can persuade the public to buy government bonds. Putting the matter in still wider terms, it can be said that the money supply can be reduced by the authorities (taking the pattern of government revenues and expenditures as fixed and given) precisely to the extent that it can persuade the non-bank world to invest more in government paper, bills and bonds together.

In the old days there would have been no difficulty about this. In one respect the system ought to work more smoothly now, namely owing to the large size of the capital funds in the hands of the Public Departments, the composition of which can be varied at the will of the authorities as between bills and bonds. But there is another, and much more important, respect in which the situation has deteriorated seriously. It is no longer as easy as it used to be to push out into the hands of the non-bank public a given quantity of government bonds in a given period. The gilt-edged market has become much less resilient.

There are two reasons for this. One affects the supply of, and the other the demand for, government bonds ("gilt-edged stock").

As to supply, before 1939 the British government was normally a net repayer of National Debt in peace-time. Certain Sinking Funds existed for its redemption. There were not always honoured in effect, being sometimes "raided" by Chancellors of the Exchequer, who wished to present a favourable Budget. But some part of the National Debt, even if only a small one, was paid off every year. This was naturally a strengthening factor in the market for gilt-edged stock.

Since the Second World War this has not been the case. The government has taken on new commitments of vast magnitude. We may mention the two most important of these. It was explained in Chapter 3 why it seemed necessary to expedite the provision of new houses by authorizing the local authorities to build on a large scale. The Conservatives have placed more emphasis on private building, but a substantial part (more than a third) of new house building is still done by the local authorities. Finance has to be found for this. (Note. This is quite a separate point from the provision of housing subsidies.)

Before the war the local authorities were largely left to their own devices in raising fresh capital. During the war it was thought expedient, in the interest of combating inflation by the most streamlined system of public finance, to centralize its provision, and the local authorities were authorized to apply to the Public Works Loans Board (itself supplied directly by the Exchequer) for what capital they required. This system was retained after the war, still in the interest of streamlining. Those were the days of easy money, in which the raising of loans by the central government was no problem. But after 1951, when it was decided to initiate a more active monetary policy, the fact that the government had to raise additional funds by the issue of gilt-edged stock for this purpose began to be an encumbrance, in the way already described, in relation to monetary policy. The system was altered in 1955, a year in which it was most desirable to have a credit squeeze, and in which great difficulties had been encountered. The local authorities were requested to try to raise their own capital, by the issue of bonds and by mortgages, before coming to the Public Works Loans Board. This change of system has on the whole worked well. More recently the local authorities have taken to raising considerable sums by short-term "Deposit Receipts"; these have played a significant part, but have not crucially interfered with monetary policy, because the Discount Market is under no obligation to invest in them, if it lacks spare cash for that purpose.

A still larger burden on government finance has been constituted by the nationalized industries. These are heavy capital users, and the government has to find the capital for them. It was stated in Chapter 3 that the provision of finance was much the largest unsolved problem bequeathed by the nationalizing of industry. From the beginning the funds required by the coal-mining industry were provided directly from the Exchequer, while electricity, gas and transport were allowed to make their own issues of bonds. But these issues carried a Treasury guarantee, and, when they were not taken up by the general public, they were taken into the portfolios of the Public Departments, just in the same way as if they had been ordinary government issues. In fact the issues of these nationalized industries operated on the balance of supply and demand in the gilt-edged market in the same way as ordinary government issues.

In respect of these also a change was made in 1955, owing to the aforementioned difficulties which arose in that year. But in this case there was no relief of the burden weighing down upon the government. Those nationalized industries that had previously made their own issues were instructed to desist from doing so and, instead, to get the capital they required direct from the Treasury. The change was made in this case in order to give the government more control over raising the capital for which, in the last analysis, it was responsible. "One effect expected from this change was that it would facilitate debt management. Issues of government stock could be better suited to the condition of the market, both in respect of timing and in respect of terms of issue that had proved manageable with issues of Guaranteed Stock."[1] The system continues. Thus every year the government has to borrow large sums. Instead of decreasing the National Debt by a small amount

[1] *Report of the Committee on the Working of the Monetary System. Principal Memoranda of Evidence.* Vol. I. Memorandum submitted by the Bank of England, page 30.

each year, it has to increase it by a large amount, and this gravely weakens the market for government bonds.

Expenditures for the local authorities and the nationalized industries are shown in the British Budget "below-the-line", and constitute the main part of the items there shown. (But local authority borrowing has been much reduced since 1955; see above.) The below-the-line items constitute what may be regarded as a "Capital Budget". The division between above-the-line and below-the-line does not correspond precisely to current and capital, but does so subject to minor trimmings. From time to time Chancellors of the Exchequer have sought to cover a large proportion of the below-the-line items out of taxation. There are probably some who hold that in an ideal Budget all those items would be so covered; that is pointed to by the frequent use of the expression, below-the-line "deficit" or overall "deficit". If these items were so covered, this would greatly ease the problem of funding, since the National Debt would no longer be growing. But the idea that these items ought, taking one year with another, to be covered by taxation, is utterly wrong. In the years immediately after the war, and in certain particular years during the nineteen fifties, when the United Kingdom was subject to great inflationary pressure, it was quite a good thing to cover as many of these items out of taxation as possible; a Budget surplus is a correct fiscal remedy for inflationary pressure. But to cover them out of taxation normally would cause severe deflation and depression. More than 40 per cent of all the fixed industrial capital formation in the U.K. is within the public sector. An attempt to get all this covered by taxation would produce a most violent distortion in the economy. Before the war all these items, capital for electricity, transport, mining, etc., and for new house building, was found out of the savings of companies and individuals. In certain periods saving may have been running somewhat short, although by no means so recently. It is fantastic to suppose that the voluntary savings of all individuals and companies in the United Kingdom are only sufficient to cover 60 per cent of investment requirements and that the rest have to be covered by compulsory savings in the form of a Budget surplus.

Thus we have a conflict of interest which has already been doing serious damage to the British economy. From the technical money market point of view, heavy government borrowing, viz., on behalf of the nationalized industries, etc., is a dreadful nuisance and makes it difficult to implement a correct monetary policy. Therefore the technicians of the Treasury and the Bank of England will always tend to be anxious to press upon the Chancellor of the Exchequer the desirability of covering as many of these below-the-line items as possible by taxation. But from the wider point of view of a balanced economy, with investment and voluntary saving matching one another, any such idea would be perfectly disastrous.

So much for the point that, on the side of supply, conditions in the United Kingdom government bond market have entirely altered. On the demand side too there has been a great change. Preference among the great mass of investors has swung over from gilt-edged stock (government bonds) to "equities" (common stock). There were beginnings before the war. The great insurance companies were already carrying large amounts of equities in their portfolios. During the war they invested most of their additional funds in gilt-edged stock for patriotic reasons. Since the war they have been readjusting their portfolios back towards a higher proportion of equities. This movement has now become widely extended, not only among institutional investors, including pension funds, but also among private people. In the old days a person of modest means would normally hold most of his capital, on the advice of his banker or broker, in gilt-edged stock, and only venture a minor fraction in something more interesting. Now the position is altogether changed. Institutional investors and private persons alike have become primarily interested in equities and regard investment in gilt-edged stock as a "mug's game". The Trustee Acts have been altered to allow trustees to put funds into equities.

It is often said that the main reason for this change is the fear of inflation. There are probably deeper reasons also, since the movement had started before the war, when there was a nineteen-year period of deflation. It may be connected with the fact that the risk element in many great industrial companies, whose shares are sought for this type of investment, has been much reduced since the nineteenth century or the early years of the twentieth. Previously investors had been willing to forego the prospect of dividend increases in the interest of safety. But if the risk of investment in a great corporation is much reduced, why forego the prospect of dividend increases?

The result is that we are confronted with a violent paradox. On one side the issue of gilt-edged stock has to be increased year after year in large quantities; and, on the other side, investors are showing a growing repugnance to the purchase of gilt-edged stock. It is no wonder that the government broker finds it difficult to get the public to buy substantial extra quantities of gilt-edged stock at times when the authorities wish to impose a credit squeeze. It cannot be too strongly stressed that the nationalizing of industry has led to a financial impasse of the utmost gravity. If any other countries seek to experiment in the nationalizing of industry, they should make sure in advance that this financial problem has been solved. The idea of covering 40 per cent of the country's industrial investment out of taxation is not acceptable.

A further point may be noted. It is probably the case that the authorities, having in mind the great awkwardnesses arising, when they have found the gilt-edged market unwilling to absorb extra supplies on a large scale, have sought to sell as much gilt-edged stock as they conveniently could, whenever the market seemed favourable. But this is not in itself at all a good thing. It may be that the gilt-edged market is favourable for government selling at a time when the economy is really in need, not of a restrictive, but of an expansionist, policy on the side of the authorities. The sale of gilt-edged stock in substantial quantity inevitably has some deflationary effect. It is easy to understand the point of view of the authorities; conscious of previous embarrassments, they argue, "Let us take this favourable opportunity of unloading on to the public redundant holdings of gilt-edged stock in the Public Departments. That will give us greater freedom of action." But there is faulty reasoning here. What is required, if inflationary pressures begin to develop, is that the authorities should be able to unload government paper into the hands of the non-bank public *at that time*. It is not the absolute amount of government paper held by the authorities that matters, but potential flexibility in unloading or reabsorbing that paper, from time to time, according to whether the current phase of the business cycle requires a restrictionist or an expansionist monetary policy.

The year in which the aforementioned difficulties became most acute was 1955. We have already seen that certain changes were made at that time, both in regard to the local authorities and the nationalized industries. A sort of impasse had been reached before these changes were made. Fairly early in the year the authorities began to move, quite rightly, towards a more restrictive policy. The Bank Rate was raised by one half per cent in January and by another 1 per cent in February. The money supply was somewhat curtailed. The deposit banks reacted primarily by selling short-dated investments. But when they had got to the end of that part of their portfolio which they could sell without much loss, it did not seem that the credit squeeze was sufficiently strong. If the Bank of England had acted according to the old traditional rules of reducing the "cash" of the deposit banks still further, the latter would have been driven to reducing their accommodation to the short-term market. And thus they would have encountered the difficulties that have already been explained. The Discount Houses would have had to re-borrow from the Bank of England, thus frustrating the effect of the open-market operations. Had they been allowed to continue to do so through the back-door, this frustration might have been perpetuated. Should they then be charged the penal rate in the ordinary way? But then they would have been driven to desperation. They might have come to the point when they protested, "We just cannot go on tendering for the whole Treasury Bill issue every week any more." Unhappily, after June 1955 (for reasons that will be explained in the next chapter) there was some loss of confidence in sterling abroad, so that the high Bank Rate did not have much effect in attracting foreign holders of Treasury Bills. It was in these circumstances that a novel expedient was adopted, which made people at home and abroad rightly think that the British monetary machinery was beginning to creak. Doubtless there was some conversation between the Governor of the Bank of England and the Chairmen of the deposit banks; the Chairman of the Committee of London Clearing Banks wrote to *The Times* (June 30, 1955) to explain that, in the national interest, Her Majesty's Government wished to restrict the total volume of credit and that the banks hoped that their customers would understand and keep their requirements for credit as small as possible. This essay in moral suasion was not very well taken. Finally, on July 25 the Chancellor of the Exchequer explained publicly that he had written to the Governor of the Bank of England, asking him to urge upon the banks the desirability of reducing customer loans. This time the banks made a greater effort to state uniform principles for the guidance of their branch managers, so that these would be in a position to deny their customers accommodation that would in normal times have been given, without the fear that a competing bank would take advantage of the situation to capture their customers' business.

All this seemed very strange. The essential point is as follows. By the ancient traditional mode of procedure, the Bank of England would just have reduced the cash of the deposit banks and left it to them to reduce their own extensions of credit at their own discretion and in the way that best suited them, first by curtailing loans to the Discount Market, and then, under the influence of the idea of a 30 per cent liquidity ratio, by selling investments or refusing accommodation to customers. What made this normal procedure impossible was the condition of the Discount Market—its obligation to bid for the whole tender of Treasury Bills and the inability of the government to reduce its offer of Treasury Bills, because it was unable to conduct "true funding" owing to the state of the gilt-edged market. So, instead, the authorities had to proceed in reverse order, by which the Discount Market was by-passed. First, by moral suasion it prevailed on the deposit banks to reduce their customer loans, and then, as and when that was done, it trimmed down the cash basis of the deposit banks to match, in accordance with the 8 per cent ratio. It is to be noted that, although everything was done by mutual agreement between the Governor of the Bank of England and the deposit banks, there was a latent power on the side of the Bank of England, ever since its nationalization in 1946, to issue directives, legally binding, had a gentleman's agreement been impossible to obtain.

It may possibly be an over simplification, but is a statement of the essential truth, to say that the difficulties of imposing an outright credit squeeze in 1955 and the somewhat embarrassing essays in moral suasion that had to be undertaken, were directly due to the nationalizing of industries, or, at least, to their having been nationalized without any suitable provision having been made for their finance. It is to be noted that they were requiring heavy capital during 1955. They made issues of stock of £315 million between mid-July and early October; most of this was not taken up by the public and had to be held by the Public Departments, and an equivalent amount of Treasury Bills had to be transferred from tap to tender. In fact, the nationalized industries were being financed in that phase by Treasury Bills, which really means, having regard to the complex relations already described, that they were being financed by the printing press.

The matter is stated very clearly by the Bank of England in its memorandum to the Radcliffe Committee on the Working of the Monetary System.[2] "If banks' balances at the Bank are increased by open-market operations, the banks have a strong inducement to increase their earning assets and thus their deposits, but if they are reduced, the banks can adjust their position by calling upon their most liquid assets other than cash. The bank can control the price at which this can be done, by making effective or altering the rate at which they will lend or re-discount, action that first affects the Discount Market, but also, through the Market, the general structure of interest rates. But their power is limited by the need to be lender of last resort, which in practice today means ensuring that the current requirements of government are met. In the last resort these requirements must be met by direct advances from the Bank, which have the effect, as the disbursements take place, of restoring the cash reserves of the banking system."

IV. A NEW GADGET

After the submission of this memorandum, but before the "Radcliffe Report" was published, the Bank of England proposed a new technique. This was said to be provisional only, pending recommendations by the Radcliffe Report, but, since the latter proposed nothing to the point, this technique has been kept in being and used.

In effect the new technique consists of varying the "reserve requirements" of the deposit banks. This is in line with the power now enjoyed by the Federal Reserve System and by some other Central Banks. It is not, however, thus designated. What is stated is that the deposit banks can be required to hold "Special Deposits" with the Bank of England,

[2] *Op. cit.*, page 105.

these deposits not counting as part of the 8 per cent cash basis (or 30 per cent liquidity). The reason why this special nomenclature is adopted is not a desire of the British to be different from other people, but because there are in fact no "legal" reserve requirements at all in the British system. The 8 per cent ratio and 30 per cent ratio are based only on custom and agreement. Thus one could not call the new procedure one of "varying the legal reserve requirements", when there are no legal reserve requirements! However, the Bank has an underlying right to impose legal reserve requirements if it wishes, and, if the deposit banks countered the requirements to have Special Deposits of amount equal to 3 per cent of their own deposit liabilities by reducing the conventional cash basis to which they worked to 5 per cent, thus leaving their effective cash basis the same as before, namely 8 per cent, there would be trouble! Naturally the deposit banks would not dream of doing any such thing; but, if they did, the Bank of England could bring its latent power into play and legally "require" them to have a cash basis of 11 per cent.

There has been much discussion in the United States about the alternatives, when it is desired to ease or tighten credit, of conducting open-market purchases or sales on the one hand, or lowering or raising reserve requirements on the other. Some of this discussion may apply to the British case also. But, whatever the broader considerations, the advantage in the British set-up comes out very clearly.

We may consider the case where it is desired to tighten credit. It has been explained that this can only be done smoothly if the government can reduce its weekly offer of tender Treasury Bills, and that it can do this only if, at the same time, some of the gilt-edged stock in the hands of the Public Departments can be unloaded into the hands of non-bank holders. A block arises if the condition of the gilt-edged market makes it impossible to conduct this process of unloading with sufficient celerity. By the new technique, the Banking Department of the Bank of England can absorb (buy) a given quantity of Treasury Bills, which are thus withdrawn from the tender, and thereby enlarge the cash basis of the deposit banks, without producing a general credit expansion. If the amount of Special Deposits which the Bank of England newly requires the deposit banks to hold, is £X, then £X worth of Treasury Bills can be withdrawn from the tender and bought by the Bank of England, without giving the deposit banks any new money to play with. The requirement for this new technique arises essentially from the inelasticity within a short period of the amount of government paper that the banking system as a whole has to hold, in order to enable the government to meet its day to day requirements.

The new technique was brought into use in 1960; an initial requirement for Special Deposits, amounting to 1 per cent of the deposit banks' deposit liabilities, was quickly followed by a requirement for 2 per cent. In 1961 a further requirement of 1 per cent, thus making 3 per cent in all, was imposed. The working of this arrangement can be seen very clearly in the published figures. In June 1960, Special Deposits came into existence in accordance with the formula to the amount of £70 million, and in August this was raised to £143 million (the deposit liabilities of the deposit banks having gone up slightly in the interval). At the same time in June the government securities held by the Banking Department of the Bank of England rose from £218 million in May to £330 million (the May figure was abnormally depressed the average for the first four months of 1960, being £264 million), and to £429 million in September. In September 1961 the Special Deposits went up to £221 million, while the government securities held by the Banking Department of the Bank of England went up from £405 million to £477 million. It is to be noted that the government securities held by the Banking Department had been running fairly level in the preceding years at about £250 million. Thus the increased holding of government securities by the Banking Department matched the requirement for Special Deposits very closely.

What was the effect of these operations? The Banking Department was enabled to enlarge its holdings of government securities by some £220 million, without increasing the cash basis or the availability of credit in the country at all. If it had made these purchases without requiring Special Deposits, then the cash basis of the deposit banks would have increased by £220 million and the deposit banks would then have been able, in accordance with the 8 per cent ratio, to increase their lending by about £2,500 million. This would, of course, never have happened. But given the state of government requirements and the condition of the gilt-edged market in the two years, this extra £220 million would have had to be found somehow for the government. The simplest way would have been for the Bank of England to give the deposit banks enough extra cash, by open-market purchases, to enable them to lend the Discount Market, or themselves take up, some £200 million more Treasury Bills. This would have had the double effect (1) of raising the total amount of deposits in the country by £200 million and (2) of raising the "liquidity ratio" of the deposit banks, thus inclining them to be more liberal in their customer loans, etc. If we assume that such an increase of credit would have been undesirable on the three occasions (taken together) in question, then it follows that the new arrangement was a very helpful one.

It is to be noted that in neither year was there any downward pressure, except for brief intervals, on the cash available for the deposit banks (i.e., on their cash less their Special Deposits) or in their deposit liabilities outstanding. Thus the operation of the requirement for Special Deposits on these occasions was not designed to produce a monetary deflation, but rather to prevent the exigencies of government finance causing a monetary inflation. But in other circumstances it might be held desirable to produce a positive deflation, and then the new technique could be used effectively for this purpose.

While the technique has thus enabled the authorities to get a better grip upon the situation, it has probably not solved completely the problem arising from the nationalizing of industries. Difficulties arise if an attempt is made to push any one technique to an extreme limit. Two unsatisfactory features remain. First, as already noted, the exigencies of government finance probably make the authorities anxious to take advantage of any favourable opportunity for getting as much gilt-edged stock as possible into the hands of the non-bank public. But such favourable opportunities may not coincide in time with the need, from the national business cycle point of view, of credit restraint. The unloading of gilt-edged stock into the hands of the non-bank public is bound to have some net deflationary influence, and this may be undesirable at favourable opportunities for unloading. Secondly, the authorities are naturally inclined to wish the Chancellor of the Exchequer to cover as much of his below-the-line expenditures as possible out of taxation.

Since the problem of unloading gilt-edged stock is a perennial headache, this wish is likely to be present fairly continuously. But from the point of view of the balance of the national economy and the objective of growth, it may often be undesirable that the Chancellor should finance any of the below-the-line items out of taxation.

It is my conviction that during the last seven years the authorities have been much too much inclined towards a restrictive monetary policy from the point of view of growth. This view depends on other matters which have still to be discussed. But, whatever the growth policy, it is most desirable that the monetary authorities should at all times be in firm control over the situation, so as to be able to exert a restraining influence when that is genuinely required. It is accordingly most unfortunate that the structure of the monetary system, as it is at present, gives them a bias in favour of deflationary measures. Their aim of keeping control over the situation is an eminently laudable one; that makes it all the more regrettable that doing what they, perhaps rightly, feel they must do in order to retain that control, inevitably involves more deflationary pressure than is good for the economy.

CHAPTER 6

Sterling

I. BACKGROUND

Sterling has gained some notoriety in the world recently, as being one of the two major key reserve currencies. While this is sometimes vaguely thought to be an arrangement that dates back into a long past, in fact it really represents the reversal of an earlier position, which has been accidental. What does date back is the importance of sterling in world trade. This importance did not consist mainly in its being a reserve currency.

There are two aspects of the present position of sterling. One consists in its being, in a certain sense, the currency for the whole of the sterling area, and the other in its being widely used as a medium of reserve and settlement outside the sterling area.

We need have no doubt that the principal reason for the world-wide importance of sterling was the growth of British overseas trade and investment. This was important for the United Kingdom from early times and accelerated in the nineteenth century. While the enterprise and energies of the American people were absorbed in pushing out their frontier and developing the great land mass that constitutes the United States, the British, with a rapidly increasing population and, in consequence of the Industrial Revolution, rapidly increasing output per head, but with only small island territories of their own, had to turn their energies outwards and undertake increasing trade and investment overseas. Since the British were the active party in these developments, it was natural for their currency to follow trade and investment.

Another aspect, connected yet separate, was the growth of the Commonwealth. The consequent extension of the use of sterling proceeded in different ways in different parts of it. It was natural for settlers, e.g., in Australia and New Zealand, to take their home currency with them. Where it was a question not of settling, but of taking over the administration of already populated regions, what happened depended on the circumstances. Where the monetary system was very primitive sterling was introduced. In other cases, the already existing currency was allowed to continue for the time being. The Indian rupee, a silver coin, may be given as an example of this. For many years after the establishment of British rule, the Indian rupee continued as an independent silver currency. Owing to the world-wide operation of the bimetallic system, there was a fixed par of exchange between any silver currency, such as the rupee, and any gold currency, such as sterling. When the bimetallic par was ruptured in 1873, never to be restored, the Indian rupee was allowed to continue on its own way for twenty years as a silver standard currency. This meant that it depreciated. This was a happy thing for the population of India, because, during those twenty years, gold standard countries experienced deflation, gold prices falling rather severely. The Indians, with their silver standard currency, had the benefit of more stable prices. However, certain inconveniences began to be felt in consequence of the fluctuating exchange between the rupee and the various gold currencies, and the depreciation of silver was proceeding so fast—by the early eighteen nineties it was already at a discount of nearly 50 per cent against gold—that there were dangers that India might become involved in inflation. Accordingly the silver standard was suspended in India in 1893, and the rupee was allowed to appreciate against the value of its silver content, although not of course to its old gold parity; a discount of a third on that was perpetuated. Towards the end of the century, it was stabilized in terms of gold. Since it would have been an unwarrantable extravagance for a poor country to buy gold, in order to introduce gold coins and gold reserves, what has come to be known as a "gold exchange standard" was introduced; the silver rupee was made convertible into gold at a fixed rate by British administrative arrangements. In practice this meant that it was convertible into sterling, itself a currency convertible into gold, and one might prefer to call this a "sterling exchange standard".

It does not make much difference which designation one uses, since sterling was in the fullest sense a gold standard currency. And this illustrates a wider point. The distinction between sterling and gold itself was less marked than it became in certain periods that followed. Sterling was simply a part of a world-wide gold standard system. To distinguish sterling, as such, from other gold standard currencies, e.g., the dollar, would have seemed meaningless at the time. Sterling was simply a denomination, meaning basically a certain weight of gold, which happened to be used by the United Kingdom and associated territories. All gold standard currencies were intimately linked together as being in fact certain weights of gold.

The development of world-wide trade and investment, including, for example, investment in Latin America, is the origin of the world-wide use of sterling, as noted above, while the growth of the Commonwealth is to be associated, although not too strictly, with the sterling area.

The world-wide acceptability of sterling must primarily be related to the very strict adherence by the Bank of England to the principle of unimpeded convertibility, as reinforced by Peel's Bank Act (1844), by which all notes over £14 million had to be backed a hundred per cent by gold. But almost equally important in this connection was the existence of the Accepting Houses and the Discount Market in London, which have already been referred to. It was the knowledge and expertise represented by these institutions that, more than anything else, created what may be called the sterling system. Together they gave traders throughout the world the opportunity to finance their trade in London at the lowest possible cost.

The most important feature of the sterling system was the practice of *invoicing* trade and *settling* the liability in respect of it in terms of sterling. If one intended to finance the trade in London, then it was expedient to express its value in terms of the currency which would have to be used for that purpose. Settling in sterling was, and remains, the most central feature of the sterling system.

Much less important in early days, but a contributory factor, was the habit in certain quarters of holding central reserves in the form of sterling. This had already begun in a minor way before 1914.[1] There was a considerable growth in this practice after the First World War for reasons that have already been given.

The next crucial point came when the United Kingdom was driven off the gold standard in 1931. It was then evident that sterling was likely

[1] J. M. Keynes, *Indian Currency and Finance*, Chapter 2, Macmillan, 1913.

to fluctuate against the dollar for some time. The question arose in the minds of certain central bank authorities outside the Commonwealth, whether it would not be better to hold their respective currencies at a fixed parity in relation to sterling, rather than at a fixed parity in relation to gold. It may be noted that there was an earlier precedent for an outside country doing this; when Hungary restored the convertibility of the pengo after the First World War in 1924, it decided to fix its value in terms of sterling, Britain not yet having returned to the gold standard then, rather than in terms of gold. Thus after 1931 there came into being something like what has since been called the sterling area. It consisted of the Commonwealth, less Canada, and the Scandinavian countries. And for periods between 1931 and 1939, other countries also attached themselves to sterling, such as the Argentine, Portugal, Turkey, Japan.

Thus, by this time the sterling system had three features. There was the widespread practice of settling in sterling, by no means confined to the Commonwealth. There was a less widespread practice of holding reserves in sterling, which was regular in the Commonwealth but not confined to it. There was the practice of making the currency convertible at a fixed rate of exchange into sterling, rather than into gold; this was the rule in the Commonwealth, but also adopted, from time to time, by other countries. Even within the Commonwealth there was a certain flexibility; for instance, in 1930 Australia depreciated its pound against sterling generally.

Then came the Second World War. The loose, undefined and irregular sterling system had to be considered in relation to the exchange controls that had to be imposed. These controls involved legal enforcement, and the consequence was that the British, contrary to their instincts and traditions, had to make precise definitions. For legal purposes certain countries were grouped together and came to be known as the "Scheduled Territories". They included not only the whole Commonwealth, except Canada, but also Egypt, Palestine, Iraq, Jordan, Iceland and Libya. Between 1931 and 1939 the pound had floated freely against gold and the dollar. But in 1939 a fixed parity with the dollar was re-established ($4.03 to the pound). The United Kingdom adopted, and imposed on certain territories, an exchange control, and actuated the other territories of the sterling area to initiate exchange controls of like pattern. The essence of the exchange control was that all earnings of currencies other than sterling had to be surrendered to the authorities and that means of payment other than sterling had to be obtained from them.

Within the Scheduled Territories sterling was always fully convertible into outside currencies, including the dollar, according to need; but it was understood that the countries concerned would restrict their needs to the greatest possible extent, and enforce the restrictions by control. In return for the advantage of convertibility, the countries agreed to continue to surrender their dollar earnings to the United Kingdom, in accordance with a procedure of long standing, and the United Kingdom held on their behalf what came to be known as the "dollar pool". Sterling held by the United States residents remained fully convertible into dollars throughout. Meanwhile arrangements were made with other countries in due course for the establishment of "Special Accounts". Sterling accruing to their residents by sales to the sterling area (i.e., Scheduled Territories) or otherwise, would be surrendered to their Central Banks and paid into these Special Accounts. The British secured agreement that payment should be made out of these Special Accounts, only to discharge obligations to the sterling area. The sterling in the Special Accounts was not convertible into other currencies.

As the war proceeded, some of these accounts began to build up. In effect the United Kingdom was living on credit. One may ask why these various countries consented to extend it this credit. The main answer is that outlets for trade were very restricted during the war, and these countries felt it to be in their interest to export to the United Kingdom or other parts of the sterling area for credit, rather than not have opportunities for export at all. Exports to the United Kingdom enjoyed the advantage of British convoys. By the end of the war a huge debt had been built up in this way.

Before the war there were £540 million of outstanding sterling balances, of which £330 million were in the Commonwealth. After the war there were £3,700 million worth of such balances, of which £3,000 million were in the sterling area. The sterling area at that point included certain countries no longer in it: Egypt, Sudan, Palestine, Iraq.

If we regroup the countries according to the present extent of the sterling area, there were £2,500 million of balances in the sterling area and £1,200 million outside.

It was this great accumulation of indebtedness, built up to meet the exigencies of war, that has provided the outside world with such a large volume of sterling, which has continued to be held by it, although with a varying distribution of ownership, ever since. Thus the function of sterling as an important medium of reserve in the world outside the sterling area—within the sterling area it was always an important medium—has been the accidental result of the way in which the United Kingdom managed to get credit, in order more effectively to wage war. Had it had to pay for all its imports by exports, its warlike endeavours would have been considerably circumscribed.

While the holding of reserves in the form of sterling was one feature of the sterling system before 1939, as already described, it was by no means the most important feature—anyhow apart from the sterling area itself. And it was quite a minor feature of the sterling system before 1914, although sterling was more important as a world currency then than it has ever been since.

II. POST-WAR PROBLEMS

The war bequeathed to the United Kingdom two major problems in regard to sterling. First, there were the very grave losses on non-merchandise account in the current balance of payments that have been described in Chapter 2. Secondly, there was the problem created by the great mass of indebtedness, amounting to £3,700 million. As things have worked out, it has been the former problem that has imposed the major strain and burden on the United Kingdom. The indebtedness has not proved to be a burden, since in fact, although its ownership has changed, it has never been paid off! But it has been a constant source of anxiety and has played its part in influencing British economic policy, sometimes causing it to take directions out of line with business-cycle requirements.

It has been seen that sterling held in "Special Accounts" was at that time usable only to discharge liabilities to the sterling area. When the war was over, the Americans were very anxious that sterling should be made "convertible" again at the earliest possible date, with a view to expediting progress towards the re-establishment of a world-wide system of multilateral non-discriminatory trade, which had been sadly damaged, not only by the war itself, but also by the various restrictive and bilateral arrangements made by countries in consequence of the pressures of the world slump of 1929–1932. It has now become clear, however, that the Americans were somewhat impeded in their friendly efforts at that time by a very imperfect understanding of the workings of the sterling system.

They did, however, clearly see that this great mass of sight indebtedness would hamper the British in re-establishing the convertibility of sterling and in re-introducing a non-discriminatory commercial policy. It was accordingly proposed in the agreement, by which an American loan to the United Kingdom was granted on very generous terms, that the sterling balances should be drastically dealt with. It was hoped that some countries might agree to a reduction, as a post-war contribution to the defeat of Hitler. It was proposed that some proportion of the balances should immediately be made convertible—I believe that the Americans did not fully understand that the greater part of the balances, viz., those inside the sterling area, always were convertible—out of the proceeds of the American loan. The rest of the balances were to be funded, i.e., taken right out of the monetary system. Thereupon the British entered into negotiations with their various creditors, but did not succeed in getting either a scaling down, except in the cases of Australia and New Zealand, or an agreement to funding. Rightly or wrongly, the British felt that they could not impose funding against the will of creditors, despite what had been agreed to with the Americans; they took the view that unilateral action would be dishonourable. Convertibility was re-established in the summer of 1947, in accordance with the United States Loan Agreement, and this proved to be a fiasco. Creditors outside the sterling area ran down their balances at an unmanageable rate.

After the breakdown, the management of sterling proceeded on similar lines. There were four main kinds of sterling, apart from that held by residents in the United Kingdom. Sterling area sterling continued to be fully convertible for the Central Banks or currency authorities which held it; for ordinary citizens in this area, it was convertible subject to the exchange controls as enforced in the various countries. Sterling held in American accounts was fully convertible. Sterling held in Special Accounts was of two main categories. In one class of cases its use was subject to a bilateral agreement by which it could be used only for discharging liabilities in the sterling area. In another class of cases, countries were grouped together in a "transferable sterling" area; sterling in these countries could be used to discharge either their liabilities in the sterling area or liabilities in the transferable account area. Inclusion of a country in the latter implied that it was agreeable to receiving sterling from another transferable account country in discharge of a debt due. The composition of the transferable account sterling varied from time to time. There was also what was known as "administrative transferability", by which, with permission readily granted in many cases, sterling could be used for making payments between countries not officially in the transferable account area. It was the aim of the British authorities to extend the transferable system as much as possible, and in 1954 it was extended to include all countries outside the sterling area and outside the area of the American account countries. The latter included those countries in the Western Hemisphere whose own currencies were fully convertible into American dollars. There was also an important class of sterling, known as "security sterling", which arose out of the sale of British securities by foreigners and could be used only for the purchase of other British securities.

During this period there was a vast mass of different quotations for sterling (in black markets) amounting at times to over fifty, depending on the precise status of the sterling in question, e.g., as covered by one or other of the bilateral agreements. The most important quotation was for transferable account sterling. This complex system served to see the United Kingdom through a difficult period. Immediately after the war the position looked very grave. At the worst point of the war, exports had fallen to a third of their pre-war level; but they pulled up very rapidly when the war was over. The United Kingdom was helped out of its immediate difficulties by large loans on generous terms from the United States and Canada. The out-turn for the years 1946 to 1947 is given in Table 22.

TABLE 22

UNITED KINGDOM BALANCE OF PAYMENTS, 1946–1947

£ million			
Merchandise deficit	— 576	Australian and New Zealand gifts	+ 30
Deficit on current invisibles	— 161	U.S. line of credit (out of total of £1,339)	+ 856
Current account deficit	— 737	Canadian line of credit (out of total of £494)	+ 239
Repayment to U.S. and Canada	— 56		
Other net governmental repayments and loans	— 131		
Outflow of capital including Unrecorded Transactions	— 202		
	— 1126		+ 1125

In order to judge the importance of quantities shown by such figures as these, i.e., how they would feel if applicable to the American economy, the American reader would do well to multiply them by 20 (or by just a little more). The components of this multiplier are, very roughly, 4 to convert sterling into dollars, 3 to allow for the larger size of the American population in civil employment and 1.8 to allow for the higher output per head in the United States. By this reckoning the deficit on current account for these two years would amount to no less than $15 billion. This was despite the fact that in the two years together the volume of British exports had almost regained its pre-war level, while the volume of imports was less than three-quarters of its pre-war level. This is yet another way of illustrating the weight of the burden that the United Kingdom had to carry, owing to war-time financial losses.

Nevertheless, by a vigorous push of exports, the United Kingdom managed to achieve a balance on current account in 1948 (a surplus of £7 million). The accounts showed a substantial surplus in every year for the next ten years, except for a slight lapse in 1955 and a more serious one in 1951, the latter being caused by circumstances arising out of the Korean War.

This favourable result was achieved neither by the automatic working of the economic system nor by good luck. It was the consequence of artificial measures deliberately introduced to meet a difficult situation. Even the most extreme advocates of the automatic working of market mechanisms could hardly contend that exports, which already before the war absorbed a large fraction of United Kingdom production, would, under the ordinary working of market forces, rise up by 65 per cent in *excess* of imports in a couple of years. The necessity to have such a rise was due to the war, an event of large magnitude, which cannot be regarded as a normal incidental aberration in the smooth course of economic growth.

Exports had to be boosted. Apart from the usual moral suasion represented by such an expression as "Export or die", definite measures were taken. The most powerful of these was provided by the control system still in force for the allocation of materials. The automobile industry, for instance, was told that it would be allocated steel only if it showed that a given high proportion of its output (at one point as high as 75 per cent) was exported. The pottery industry was directed to export its output, except for a bare minimum of utility articles and spoilt ware. It was under such influences that exports rose to more than five times their war-time low in the space of five years.

At the same time imports were rigidly controlled. This is clearly shown in the volume of imports running for so long below their pre-war level.

While these events were proceeding, the question of the restoration of sterling convertibility continued to be canvassed. It is to be stressed that sterling throughout remained convertible for sterling area holders. (There was continuing confusion in American minds, in relation to sterling convertibility, between those facts which result from sterling being the currency of the sterling area and those which result from its use *outside* the sterling area.) The convertibility within the sterling area was modified for its residents by the existence of exchange controls analogous to those operating in the United Kingdom. It was further modified by the periodic meetings of Commonwealth Finance Ministers.

At times, when the position of the sterling area, taken as a whole, showed signs of deteriorating, its Finance Ministers would agree to tighten up restrictions. Apart from territories directly administered from London, this was all on a purely voluntary basis. The British were able to point out that, if sterling collapsed, the whole sterling area would suffer grave detriment. Its own reserves were largely in sterling. If the British were able to make a good case from facts and figures, the other Ministers felt that it was a sensible thing for them to proceed more cautiously in admitting imports from outside the sterling area, particularly dollar imports. It is to be remembered that in that period there was a world-wide "dollar shortage", so that other foreign currencies were relatively "soft". These restrictions on imports from outside the sterling area naturally helped British *exports* to the outer sterling area. It may be noted that the decline of the British share in sterling area imports, which has occurred more recently, is a natural consequence of the adventitious aid that they had previously received, and need not be taken as implying any decline in British competitiveness. In the period 1955–1959 the British share of world manufactured exports to the *non*-sterling area hardly declined, which means that it must have risen per head employed in British industry.

Meanwhile sterling held outside the sterling and dollar areas was inconvertible. This gave British exports an advantage; it was a kind of "protection" for them in foreign markets. This must be a rare, perhaps unique, case of a country's industries enjoying protection in foreign markets. Countries holding sterling balances, but short of dollars, would deflect their purchases on to British goods even when they were more expensive.

While the United Kingdom thus enjoyed a measure of protection for a time, the sterling held outside, both in the Commonwealth and beyond, continued to impose anxieties, and indeed burdens. If the outside sterling area ran a deficit with the rest of the world, the United Kingdom had to pay. And its bilateral arrangements did not wholly exempt it from having to finance some of the external deficits of non-sterling area countries also.

All the time the British authorities had to keep two separate accounts simultaneously in mind. An illustration may be given from the two post-war years already referred to. The overall United Kingdom balance, as shown in Table 22 (page 125), had its importance. But of more immediate moment was the gold and dollar balance. An adverse balance with a non-dollar country could be financed in certain cases, *pro tem.*, by an increase of the sterling balance held in its Special Account. There was no such means of financing a deficit with American account countries. Furthermore an overall deficit of the outer sterling area regions with the dollar account countries had to be financed by the United Kingdom in gold or dollars. Table 23 shows that the gold and dollar balance was worse in those two years than the overall balance.

Table 23

United Kingdom Balance Payable in Gold or Dollars, 1946–1947

£ million

Merchandise deficit with dollar area	— 727	U.S. and Canadian Loans *net*	+ 1040
Deficit on invisibles with dollar area	— 78	Long-term capital including balancing item	+ 79
Current account deficit with dollar area	— 805	Purchases of gold from sterling area	+ 159
Other inter-government loans	— 17		
Dollar payments on account of rest of sterling area	— 372		
Gold or dollar payments to, or on behalf of, non-sterling non-dollar area	— 226		
	— 1,420		+ 1,278

	£ million
Decline in gold and dollar reserve	+ 98
Drawing on the I. M. F.	+ 60
	158
Less decrease in dollar area sterling balances	— 16
	+ 142

It so happened that the outer sterling area ran a very heavy deficit with the dollar area in 1947. It is fair to add that in the following years the United Kingdom made a net gain from its association with the sterling area. Part of the last adverse item shown in the main table was due to the brief abortive experiment in sterling convertibility. Some of the outside countries took the opportunity to encash part of their sterling holdings for dollars.

It was in consequence of these various events that so large a proportion of the American and Canadian lines of credit (see Table 22, page 125), were used up in the first eighteen months. This alarmed the British authorities. Things improved rather quickly in the following year. The current account of the United Kingdom came into balance in 1948; the overall account of the outer sterling area showed a surplus; something still remained of the American and Canadian lines of credit.

III. CONVERTIBILITY

There was thereafter much argument about how soon the United Kingdom should again attempt to re-establish convertibility. The failure of the attempt in 1947 caused much discouragement. One influential school of thought held that the whole idea of convertibility was a mistake. They took the line that, since the United Kingdom needed a great volume of imports, it should use this as a bargaining counter to make other countries accept an equivalent quantity of its exports on a bilateral basis. I was never able to have any sympathy with this point of view. First, it struck me as being of paramount importance, not only in the interest of the free world as a whole, but in the long run interest of the United Kingdom also, that world trade should develop on a multilateral non-discriminatory basis. Secondly, I was convinced that the protection given by sterling inconvertibility was not viable as a permanent system. Indeed, it probably lasted as long as it did, only because the British authorities recurrently held out hopes that convertibility would be coming along in the not too far distant future. Had it ever become plain that the British never intended to return to convertibility, the various countries would have refused to accept payment for their exports to the United Kingdom in sterling; thus, any protection given by the inconvertibility of sterling would have withered away, and the United Kingdom would have been faced with the appalling problem of having either to encash, for gold or dollars, the vast outstanding mass of sterling liabilities, as their holders would strongly demand, or alternatively of having simply to default on them.

In 1949 came the unfortunate incident of the devaluation of sterling from $4.03 to the pound to $2.8. It has already been suggested (Chapter 2) that the development of prices in the United Kingdom and the United States did not point to the need for any such devaluation. In retrospect it may be judged that some much smaller devaluation would have been in place, e.g., one of 10 per cent, and that this should have been executed, not in 1949, but somewhat later, probably in 1952. In the latter year the British economy was underemployed and world prices were falling, so that the demand-inflationary and cost-inflationary effect of a devaluation would not have been so damaging.

The trade figures do not suggest that the devaluation had any lasting effect on the United Kingdom balance of payments. In the particular circumstances of the case devaluation did not, and could not, have its normal effect of reducing imports, since all imports, except those absolutely necessary, were already being excluded by stringent controls and price was not a consideration in regard to imports allowed to come in. Even the immediate effect of devaluation in increasing the volume of exports was almost entirely offset by the deterioration in the terms of trade, which was its consequence. That it had very severe adverse effects, both on demand and on cost inflation, cannot be doubted. In the United States the demand inflation, caused by post-war readjustments, appears to have terminated in 1948; in the United Kingdom there was an appreciable easement in 1949, and there would probably have been room for a substantial increase of exports without a great increase in demand inflation being caused. But the further upsurge in the volume of exports by 15 per cent in one year did impose a severe strain for the time being. And the subsequent easing off in the volume of exports was also ill-timed, since in 1952 the British economy went into a recession. The cost-inflationary effect of the devaluation was even more unfortunate. In 1948 the Labour Chancellor of the Exchequer had managed to secure a "wages pause", and in the two following years wages certainly rose less than productivity. The large and cumulative rise in the cost of living, which followed the devaluation, made it absolutely impossible to maintain this wages pause. In the following years there occurred a spiralling between wages and prices, which was quite inevitable. Incidentally this took away much of the price advantage given to British producers by the devaluation. It might be objected that by stern discipline wages could have been held down; but this is quite unrealistic; by no reckoning could it be supposed that, after ten years of severe austerity, British wage-earners could be expected to have their real standard of living reduced by 10 per cent or more. Discipline might have availed to keep the wages pause in being in relation to a moderate devaluation, but not in relation to one which was so grossly excessive. The breakdown of wages restraint had further unfortunate effects. It is quite possible that the habit of expecting a substantial wage increase each year, which grew up immediately after the war, would have lapsed, the previous increases being regarded as part of a post-war readjustment. But when, for half a dozen years or more, renewed wage increases were fully justified by the steep rise in the cost of living, which was the consequence of devaluation, the habit became more deep seated, so that the expectation of annual increases continued even after its justification, which resulted from the devaluation, ceased.

On external account 1950 proved to be a bumper year. This was partly due to a substantial destocking, later naturally reversed, and partly to a better external balance on the side of the outer sterling area. It has been claimed that the latter effect was due to the devaluation, but this is not clear. In 1949, prior to the devaluation, the Labour government had been determined not to have one, and summoned a meeting of Commonwealth Finance Ministers in July, which agreed to tighten up import restrictions, not only in the United Kingdom but also throughout the Commonwealth. This was put into effect despite the fact that the subsequent devaluation might have been judged to make it unnecessary. It accounted for the destocking in the United Kingdom in 1950, and was probably the main cause of the improvement in the external balance of the outer sterling area. So good did the position appear to be in 1950 that the Labour government renounced the United Kingdom's share in Marshall Aid, which was due to come in for another eighteen months. While this would have been an admirable gesture had the situation been fundamentally sound, the United Kingdom had not, in fact, made the full structural adjustments necessary—import restrictions were still very strict—and it could be argued that the United Kingdom's war effort entitled it to its full share of the Marshall Aid so generously provided by the Americans.

It may be asked why, despite all that has been said, the devaluation occurred. The Labour government was quite sincere in announcing that they had no intention of executing one. It has to be admitted that the fault in this case was partly on the American side, and this has not been the only case, since the war, where foreign diagnosis of the British condition has been incorrect and led to unfortunate consequences. In fact British exports had been rising very well, and much better than had been expected at the end of the war, right up to 1949, as shown in Table 12 (page 31). There was a slight relapse in the middle of that year, but this was entirely due to the world-wide rumours at that time that devaluation was impending. Purchasers began to wait for the devaluation before placing orders. And heavy "leads and lags" in trade payments began to take place during the summer.

American opinion took the line that a devaluation of sterling should be tried, so as to make possible an earlier return to convertibility and the removal of import restrictions. This may have been reinforced by a reluctance of Labour spokesmen to state that in the last resort, e.g., when Marshall Aid came to an end, they would be willing to administer the disagreeable medicine of deflation, should that prove necessary when the time came.

There were those who thought, and I must confess myself one, that deflationary measures should have been adopted at once. But in retrospect this does not look very sensible. The only effective form of deflation would have been a curbing of investment, since consumption was anyhow being held down to a pitiably low level. Despite the evidence available to travellers in the United Kingdom, there were widespread misconceptions about this abroad, increased by misunderstandings, already referred to in an earlier chapter, about lavish expenditures in the new "Welfare State". In retrospect it seems that it would have been neither sensible, nor an appropriate gesture in relation to American generosity, to have cut down investment in the United Kingdom in 1949. For what purpose was Marshall Aid being provided, other than to enable the United Kingdom to have rather more investment, with a view to increasing its economic strength, than it could for the time being afford out of its own savings? The right thing for the Labour government to have done, to satisfy American public opinion, would have been to promise faithfully that, as soon as Marshall Aid came to an end, it would take all necessary measures to tailor down investment, as required to make the country solvent without external aid. But to expect such a promise from politicians, who are mainly preoccupied with day-to-day problems, would be expecting rather much. In the event, no such measures would have been required, as the year in which Marshall Aid would have terminated, had it run its full course (1952), was one of internal recession in the United Kingdom and a favourable external balance.

When the Americans, labouring under the aforesaid misconceptions, disseminated the view that the United Kingdom would be wise to try devaluation, this set up a world-wide pressure on sterling, which made some devaluation, although not necessarily so large a one, unavoidable.

After the bumper year of 1950, the United Kingdom had what was ostensibly a very bad year, the worst that has occurred between 1947 and 1962. This was deemed to be a severe "crisis", which was partly responsible for the return to power of the Conservative government. Imports soared. Their value was higher than in any subsequent year until 1957 and their volume as high as it was in any year until 1955. The soaring was partly due to the removal of the extra restrictions that had been imposed in 1949, prior to the devaluation.

TABLE 24

UNITED KINGDOM IMPORTS AND BALANCE OF PAYMENTS ON MERCHANDISE AND CURRENT ACCOUNT, 1950–1952

£ million

Year	Imports	Balance of payments on merchandise account	Balance of payments on total current account
1950	2,390	− 136	+ 297
1951	3,501	− 749	− 419
1952	2,959	− 128	+ 227

The two main causes of the great rise in imports, however, were the worsening of the terms of trade and heavy stock-piling, both the consequence of the Korean War. This worsening of the terms of trade was superimposed on that due to the devaluation of 1949. A comparison of Table 25 with Table 24 shows what part of the adverse balance was due to the terms of trade being worse in that year than in the preceding and following years.

TABLE 25

UNITED KINGDOM BALANCE OF PAYMENTS ON MERCHANDISE AND CURRENT ACCOUNT, 1950–1952, IF TERMS OF TRADE IN 1951 HAD BEEN EQUAL TO AVERAGE OF 1950 AND 1952

£ million

Year	On merchandise account	On total current account
1950	− 136	+ 297
1951	− 467	− 137
1952	− 128	+ 227

World prices soared up after the Korean outbreak, largely in consequence of world-wide (especially American) stock-piling. Thereafter they turned down somewhat. It was generally believed, not only in the United Kingdom but in the United States also, that this down-turn constituted a "lull", on the ground that the vast prospective American defence programme was bound, in due course, to make world prices move further upwards. This was, perhaps, a reasonable expectation, although it was not fulfilled. It was the cause of the heavy stock-piling in the United Kingdom in that year. This is shown in Table 26.

It could not, perhaps, have been foreseen in 1951 that there would be some improvement in the terms of trade thereafter. But it could have been foreseen, at least had prompt and adequate statistics been available, that there would be an improvement owing to the cessation of stock-piling. Thus there were exaggerated views about the gravity of the "crisis". They led to an unfortunate increase in import restrictions, which the French felt bound to match by increased restrictions of their

TABLE 26

VALUE OF PHYSICAL INCREASE OF STOCKS AND WORK IN PROGRESS IN THE UNITED KINGDOM

Year	£ million
1950	− 210*
1951	+ 575
1952	+ 50
Average 1949–1960	+ 193

* Fall due to import restrictions.

own, and these were a setback to the movement for the liberalization of intra-European trade. Internal measures of restraint were adopted which led to a recession in the following year.

Thereafter the United Kingdom had four years of good progress. In the autumn of 1952 there was an important meeting of Commonwealth Finance Ministers, at which it was agreed to work for the re-establishment of the convertibility of sterling at a fairly early date. It is believed that there was an unpublished addendum, which had its influence later, that it would be desirable to have wider margins within which sterling could fluctuate.

In the following years organized commodity markets were re-established in the United Kingdom, which involved at least a partial relaxation of control over the imports of the commodities in question. (Markets had been opened for the commodities, tin and rubber, of which the sterling area was the principal supplier, at an earlier date.) This was interpreted, no doubt correctly, as a kind of partial restoration of the convertibility of sterling, since it enabled sterling holders to use sterling for the purchase of commodities at world prices in the United Kingdom, even although these were not produced in the sterling area. Previously the sterling prices of some of these commodities had been above their dollar prices at the ruling rate of exchange.

Ever since the war there had been around the world what the British regarded as "black" markets in the various forms of inconvertible sterling. From the British point of view these forms of sterling could be used only to meet liabilities in the sterling area, or, in the case of transferable account sterling, in the transferable account area. But actually, through the existence of the black markets, devious means were found for using this sterling for other purposes, and particularly for the purchase of dollar goods. At times, during the post-war years (very notably before the devaluation of 1949), these sterling quotations fell to a low level.

The "devious" means were many and various, as any American banker, who was operating in foreign exchange in 1949, may recall. It will suffice to give a much over-simplified example, merely to illustrate the principle. A holder of sterling in the non-sterling non-dollar area is willing to sell it for dollars at a discount. With the dollar proceeds thus acquired on the side, he may be able to buy dollar goods which can be sold at a high profit, precisely because of the restrictions on the import of such goods. An American, making a purchase from the sterling area, is glad to buy sterling at a discount, in order to discharge his debt, rather than at the official rate. He cannot buy inconvertible sterling outright, as the Bank of England would stop the cheque. But through an intermediary it can be arranged that the sterling area product *appears* to be sold to a non-dollar country when, in fact, it has been sold to an American. When the resident of the non-dollar country makes payment against an invoice showing the export of a commodity from the sterling area to his country, the Bank of England thinks that all is in order; but, in fact, the American reimburses the resident in the non-dollar country by giving him dollars, but at a rate of exchange for sterling lower than the official one. It is obvious enough why such a transaction is advantageous to the American; he gets his sterling cheap. It is advantageous to the resident of the non-dollar country, only if he believes that there is no early prospect of sterling convertibility by which he could obtain the dollars at the official rate, which is of course higher. Any belief that sterling would become convertible soon thus raised the quotations for sterling in the black markets.

So far as the British authorities were concerned, the devious operations were detrimental. In the example given, instead of the British authorities receiving dollars in payment for the sale of the sterling area product into the dollar market, they merely received payment in the form of inconvertible sterling previously owned by the third-party country. In fact, by this arrangement, the third-party owner was "converting" his sterling into dollars, although not allowed to do so, and the British authorities were losing that quantity of dollars. And the truth of the matter is that, if the British had not held out hopes of early convertibility, the use of the black markets would have become more and more important, whatever the British authorities might do to stop it, and the use of the official markets less and less important. Thus, a back-door kind of convertibility would have been thrust upon the British against their will; they would have found themselves paying off large quantities of the outstanding balances in dollars or gold, which they could ill afford to do; and there would have been a complete *dégringolade* of the sterling system.

With the United Kingdom making good progress, and the belief that convertibility would come in the fairly near future, the rate for transferable sterling, the most important of the black market rates, was within 1 per cent of the official rate for most of 1953 and was above the lowest point for the official rate for some months in early 1954. At such levels there was not sufficient margin for the profitable use of transferable sterling to buy dollars, since the devious methods of so using it, which may be compendiously called "commodity shunting", inevitably involved some payments to intermediaries. In April 1954 the British authorites unified the whole non-sterling non-dollar area, subject to minor exceptions, into a single transferable account area. At the same time it took the important step of re-establishing the gold bullion market in London. This looked promising as it seemed to portend an early return to convertibility.

Unfortunately at this time a recession occurred in the United States, which discouraged the British authorities. They were always subject to some pressure by those opposed to convertibility on principle. This caused the British Chancellor of the Exchequer to make a cautious statement at the annual meeting of the International Monetary Fund in 1954, in which he contended that the return to sterling convertibility must be conditional on the Americans adopting a more liberal commercial policy. The reference to this condition, namely a more liberal American commercial policy, suggested to many minds—which was perhaps quite unfair to the Americans—that the British intended to postpone convertibility until the Greek Kalends. Accordingly black market quotations for sterling dropped and commodity shunting started up. It may be convenient to call a quotation that allows a margin of profit on commodity shunting, after payment of expenses, the "commodity shunting point", by analogy with the "gold export point" which refers to the quotation at which, on a full gold standard, gold export becomes profitable, after all expenses are paid.

In February 1955, the Bank of England took the bold step of intervening in the black markets. History does not record how full a Cabinet discussion there was on this topic; it may well have been represented that this was a purely technical question, about which the Bank of England would know best. But in fact it was not a technical question at all. It constituted in truth the *de facto* return by the United Kingdom to sterling convertibility, a little less than ten years after the war. This was despite the fact that the basic balance was not yet wholly satisfactory, import restrictions being stiff, and that the great liabilities, in the form of sterling balances outstanding, were undiminished.

The British intervened in these markets, which could hardly be called "black" any more, now that official cognizance was thus taken of them, so as to prevent sterling falling in them below the commodity shunting point. This meant that the quotations were held within about 1 per cent of the official rate. Thus the convertibility was not quite complete, since there was still a discount of up to 1 per cent on the transferable sterling. But it was good enough. Commodity shunting was at an end. Holders of sterling had not much to complain of if they could sell it at any time at a discount of 1 per cent, since this variation from parity was less than might quite easily have been adopted for variations in the official rate itself.

This courageous action by the Bank of England may have come in the nick of time to rescue the sterling system from destruction, and great credit is due to them. The event more commonly referred to as constituting the restoration of sterling convertibility, but inherently much less important, was the action taken in December 1958 to eliminate the discount on transferable sterling and thus to amalgamate official and transferable sterling. A still more formal step was taken in the spring of 1961 when the British accepted the obligations of Article 8 of the International Monetary Fund. The earlier steps had been unilateral in the sense that they could have been reversed by the British authorities, although it was widely recognized that they were most unlikely to be. The final step could not be reversed without application to the International Monetary Fund.

It may be well to review events up to the crucial point of the return to *de facto* convertibility in February 1955. An aggregated balance of payments for the United Kingdom is presented in Table 27 for the seven years from 1948 to 1954.

It appears that over these years the United Kingdom had only a narrow balance on current account. Its proper discharge of its duty in making long-term capital available to other countries was offset by its receipt of Marshall Aid, defence aid, etc. The Unrecorded Transactions in this period should probably be added to the proper resources of the United Kingdom itself. It may be held that it was quite right for the United Kingdom to proceed with its capital investment overseas, although at the same time depending on assistance. Marshall Aid, etc., by helping the United Kingdom in its tasks of recovery, enabled it to carry out its overseas duties, which were of value to the free world, during this awkward period of post-war reconstruction.

It will be recalled that, for the years 1946–1947, two tables were presented, one showing the overall balance of the United Kingdom, and the other its gold and dollar balance. In the following seven years this distinction remained. The United Kingdom had a strongly favourable balance outside the dollar area and an unfavourable one with the dollar area. When we look at things from this point of view, we see that the United Kingdom met all its overseas investments with the aid of its surplus on current account with the non-dollar world, while Marshall Aid, etc., enabled it to cover its deficit with the dollar world. Even if it had made no overseas investments, it would have still needed the Marshall Aid, etc., to cover its dollar deficit. This is shown in Table 28.

It may be observed in the table that about the same amount of gold and dollars was gained from the surplus of the outer sterling area as the United Kingdom had to pay to non-sterling non-dollar countries. This caused a reduction in the sterling balances held by the latter and an increase in the sterling balances within the sterling area. From the bankers' point of view this was satisfactory. Whereas it was understood

TABLE 27

AGGREGATED UNITED KINGDOM BALANCE OF PAYMENTS, 1948–1954

£ million

Merchandise Balance	− 1,748		Long-term Capital Outflow	− 1,331
Balance on Account of current services	+ 1,978		Subscription to I.R.B.D.	− 173
		+ 230		− 1,504
Australian and New Zealand gifts		+ 16		
Repayments to U.K. govt. of loans previously made by it		+ 56		
Net loans to U.K. govt.		+ 116		
Marshall Aid	+ 681			
Less net contributions to European monetary arrangements	− 113			
		+ 568		
Defence Aid		+ 276		
Appreciation of gold reserve	+ 149			
Less devaluation payments	− 75			
		+ 74		
Unrecorded transactions		+ 105		
		+ 1,441		

Change in Reserve Position

£ million

Assets (increase: +)		Liabilities (increase: −)	
Gold Reserve	+ 474	Increase in sterling balances	− 293
Reduction in holding of foreign currencies	− 24	Debt to European Payments Union	− 120
		Short-term capital liabilities	− 100
	+ 450		− 513

TABLE 28

UNITED KINGDOM GOLD AND DOLLAR BALANCE, 1948–1954 INCLUSIVE

£ million

Marshall Aid . . .	+ 681	Merchandise deficit	– 1,334	
Net capital inflow into U.K.	+ 252	*Less* surplus on services	+ 78	
				– 1,256
Net receipts from surpluses of outer sterling area . .	+ 439	U.S. and Canadian loans to U.K. .	+ 157	
Purchases of newly-mined gold from sterling area . .	+ 585	*Less* repayments of loans . . .	– 159	
				– 2
		Gold or dollar payments to or on behalf of non-sterling non-dollar countries (including devaluation payments: £75)		– 428
	+ 1,957			– 1,686

Change in Reserve Position

£ million

Assets (increase: +)			Liabilities (increase: –)	
Increase in gold reserve . . .	+ 474		Increase of American account countries' sterling balances	– 79
Less accretion in its value owing to devaluation . .	– 149		Repayment (net) to I.M.F.	+ 25
				– 54
Increase in gold reserve . . .		+ 325		
To which must be added £149 increase in sterling value owing to devaluation				

that balances held by other sterling area countries would be used only to meet a deficit, there was the danger that the non-dollar non-sterling countries might at some stage wish to use their holdings, not to finance their own deficits, but because they might at some time decide that they would prefer to hold a greater proportion of their reserves, if not all of them, in gold or dollars rather than in sterling.

Such was the broad picture in the seven years prior to *de facto* convertibility. It would be desirable to look at what was happening in that year itself, but it happened to be quite an abnormal one. Each year at that time had its own peculiarities, so that the best that can be done may be to look at the aggregated balances for the three years, 1954 to 1956. Table 29 shows the aggregated overall balances for 1954 to 1956, and also the aggregated gold and dollar balances for those years.

The gold and dollar balance was still giving rather more difficulty

TABLE 29

(a) UNITED KINGDOM OVERALL AGGREGATED BALANCE OF PAYMENTS, 1954–1956 INCLUSIVE

£ million

Net merchandise balance	− 602		Net loans to and repayment of loans by U.K. Govt.	− 124
Net balance on account of current services	+ 998		Long-term capital outflow	− 540
Current account balance		+ 396		
Unrecorded transactions		+ 159		
		+ 555		− 664

Change in Reserve Position

£ million

Assets (increase: +)		Liabilities (increase: −)	
Decrease in gold reserve	− 100	Increase in foreign-held sterling balances	− 86
Increase in foreign currencies held	+ 4	Reduction of debt to European Payments Union	+ 73
	− 96		− 13

(b) UNITED KINGDOM AGGREGATED GOLD AND DOLLAR BALANCE, 1954–1956 INCLUSIVE

£ million

Long-term capital inflow .	+ 108	Net merchandise balance . . .	– 522	
Earned by outer sterling area	+ 84	Net balance on account of services . .	+ 276	
Purchase of newly-mined gold from the sterling area . .	+ 534	Current account balance . . .		– 246
		Repayment of loans .		– 134
		Paid to or on behalf of non-sterling non-dollar countries . .		– 582
	+ 726			– 962

Change in Reserve Position

£ million

Assets (increase: +)		Liabilities (increase: –)	
Decrease in gold reserves .	– 100	Decrease in holding of sterling by American account countries	+ 25
		Drawing on International Monetary Fund† . .	– 161
	– 100		– 136

† Occasioned by the Suez crisis.

than the overall balance. In the latter we find an overall deficit of £109 million, taking the three years together. This was not very serious.

We may consider the deficits as percentages of turnover. In the longer period from 1948 to 1954 the aggregated deficit constituted 5.4 per cent of total merchandise imports. But part of the expenditures that had to be made were those on invisible imports. The aggregated deficit constituted 4.3 per cent of the aggregated imports, visible and invisible. In the period 1954 to 1956, the deficit constituted 1.1 per cent of aggregated merchandise imports and 0.9 per cent of aggregated imports, visible plus invisible.

IV. SUBSEQUENT FLURRIES

Although the situation was still precarious, and the great outstanding sterling balances still gave ground for anxiety, the return to convertibility cannot be regarded as an act of great imprudence. Unluckily, soon afterwards fresh troubles began to arise. The United Kingdom's investment boom culminated in 1955, and inflationary pressures were operating. Rather heavy stock-piling occurred in that year. British prices were rising, although, it should be added, not more markedly so than elsewhere. Anxieties were caused abroad by two rather serious strikes in May. But the serious exchange troubles that arose later in the year were caused by an unco-ordinated action on the part of British representatives, which has never been explained and probably never will be. There was an OEEC meeting in Paris to discuss what should be done with the European Payments Union in the event of all, or some, of its members making their currencies convertible. One proposal was that the monthly settlements of the EPU should be continued, but with 100 per cent of the balances arising being paid in gold. The British did not much like this, feeling that these gold settlements might prejudice the operation of the exchange markets, and, indirectly, the use of sterling as a reserve currency, which, whether one liked it or not, was still to be desired, since the alternative would be to pay off those colossal sterling balances. Accordingly the British took the line that in the event of such settlements, they would like to see a 3 per cent margin of fluctuation on either side of par. It was a curious suggestion at a time when for four months they had successfully been holding transferable sterling within 1 per cent of par. The world took it to mean that the United Kingdom would like to have a 3 per cent devaluation of sterling, and adverse speculation continued for the remainder of the year, although the Chancellor of the Exchequer tried to correct the impression that had been made in Paris at the annual meeting of the International

Monetary Fund at Istanbul. Thereafter things went more smoothly and the Suez crisis did surprisingly little damage to the British position.

In 1957 a crisis arose, which of all those that have occurred since the war must be pronounced the most totally bogus. Nonetheless, it caused the Chancellor to raise the British Bank Rate to 7 per cent. The background was some unfavourable talk, especially in the Western Hemisphere, about inflationary tendencies in the United Kingdom. Actually these had not been recently any more marked than in competing countries, while the British economy was running rather slack, as was clearly demonstrated by the great recovery which started a year later.

The cause of the crisis was the consideration then being given to the realignment of European currencies in the event of the Common Market, or a wider Free Trade Area, coming into being. It was thought that these matters should be discussed at the September meeting of the International Monetary Fund in Washington, prior to a subsequent meeting of the Ministers of the European countries in Paris. For years already the French franc had been considered overvalued. During August it came under irresistible pressure and had to be devalued. This made everyone on the alert for other possible changes. Much well-informed opinion in the United Kingdom, incredibly and without sufficient thought, took the line that the German mark should be valued upwards. But at that time the Germans had a cast-iron case against valuing the D. Mark upwards against the dollar, since they were in substantial deficit with the dollar area. It was therefore assumed that the British would be prepared to have sterling devalued against the dollar and the D. Mark. There was accordingly heavy speculation against sterling in favour of the D. Mark; this included "leads and lags" in trade payments.

At the September meeting of the International Monetary Fund in Washington, the German and British representatives both said that they contemplated no revaluation and Dr. Jacobsson, head of the International Monetary Fund, said that he saw no reason for any further change in currency values. The prospective meeting in Paris to consider this was accordingly cancelled. In the following three months the speculative positions were reversed.

The underlying position of the United Kingdom had been quite sound throughout as is shown in Table 30.

TABLE 30

UNITED KINGDOM BALANCE OF PAYMENTS ON CURRENT ACCOUNT, 1956–1957

£ million

Year	Merchandise balance	Balance on services	Total balance
1956	− 51	+ 309	+ 258
1957	− 56	+ 328	+ 272
1957 First half (annual rate)	− 50	+ 286*	+ 236

* Slight fall here (and in total) compared with 1956, principally due to reduced interest and profits from overseas.

The United Kingdom has gained the reputation of being subject to recurrent crises since the war. In fact most of them have been due to rather minor oscillations, and have been blown up into what at the time seemed more serious events by pessimistic talk based on misunderstandings of the true situation both at home and abroad. Doubtless this would not have happened, however, had the British position not remained precarious, both because the gap on current account, caused by financial losses during the war, had not yet been quite filled, and because of the external sterling balances. The most serious of the crises was naturally that nearest the war, when in 1947 the United Kingdom was still running a heavy deficit on current account, and had not yet had sufficient breathing space to make the preliminary readjustments in its post-war position. But even that crisis was in part artificial, being associated with a premature attempt at convertibility in accordance with the terms of the United States Loan Agreement. The 1949 crisis, leading to the lamentable event of sterling devaluation, was largely bogus and due to unfounded talk abroad, as has already been shown; steady progress was being made during that year. The crisis of 1951 may be attributed exclusively to the Korean War; the adverse turn in the terms of trade was a genuine factor, but the visible deficit was in part due to stockpiling, which would inevitably have a counterpart of de-stocking in due course. The events of 1955 were no more serious than one might expect to happen on the occasion of the peak of an investment boom; but foreign opinion was unfavourably impressed by the creaking of the internal monetary mechanism in that year, which was described in full in the last chapter. The 1957 crisis was due to the expectation of an upward valuation of the D. Mark at that time and was entirely bogus, *both* so far as the British internal economy and the external balance were concerned.

It is fair to add that the various so-called "crises" were accompanied by declines in foreign confidence, which presented the British authorities with severe problems; these enabled them to find good arguments to justify actions that were untimely and unfortunate in relation to the requirements both of business-cycle policy and of growth policy.

It is only when we draw nearer the present time that things have moved in a way that gives ground for more serious anxieties.

It has been noted that, while the United Kingdom was almost in balance around the time of the return to *de facto* convertibility (1955), its position was still buttressed by strict import restrictions. I have always favoured, since the end of the war, the quickest possible dismantling of import restrictions, even when the reserve looked rather narrow in relation to that purpose. But I also continued to urge in the early nineteen fifties[2] that the British should proceed cautiously in dismantling restrictions round about the time of the return to convertibility. Import restriction is one form of protection, and, as has already been explained, inconvertibility is another form. In my opinion, the restoration of sterling convertibility would be a more important contribution towards the development of non-discriminatory multilateral trade than the dismantling of a particular set of import restrictions, and that, accordingly, sterling convertibility should have priority in the programme of a return to normalcy. The Americans and Canadians, looking at the matter from a somewhat different point of view and, not unnaturally, from that of their own interests, were inclined to argue that the removal of import restrictions was just as important as, if not more important

[2] Cf. R. Harrod, Report in International Monetary Fund Staff Papers, April 1953, and *The Dollar,* Macmillan, (London), and Harcourt, Brace, (New York), 1954.

than, the restoration of convertibility; the Britsh authorities appear, in my judgement, to have been too much influenced by this point of view. Be that as it may, there were rather sweeping moves towards import de-restriction in the period between the *de facto* return to convertibility in 1955 and the more formal return at the end of 1958.

The very low level of imports in 1954 and 1955 might well give rise to anxieties about what would happen when the remaining restrictions were removed. No one could foresee in advance. That would surely be a reason for going cautiously. The British seem to have lost their caution in this phase, perhaps owing to influence of some particular Minister.

In 1954 the volume of imports still stood only at 97.2 (1935–1938 = 100), while the volume of exports stood at 162.2 and the National Income (at constant prices) at 124.5. This did really point to the likelihood of a substantial rise of imports when these were freed.

Table 31 shows the composition of imports in 1954. A substantial saving had been made on the side of food, owing to the encouragement given to agriculture during the war and subsequently. The amount of manufactured goods coming in was still not above the level of 1938.

TABLE 31

UNITED KINGDOM IMPORTS (VALUE) IN 1938 AND 1954
VOLUME OF IMPORTS IN 1954 WAS 96.4 (1938 = 100)

Percentage of Total Imports			
Year	Food	Raw materials	Manufactured goods
1938	47.1	27.2	25.7
1954*	39.3	37.1	23.6
1954†	42.7	30.6	26.7

* Allocating fuel between raw materials and manufactures.
† Assuming prices had risen by same ratio in all three categories.

The year 1955 was one of general increase in imports (Table 32). All except food were up on the pre-war level but only slightly.

TABLE 32

UNITED KINGDOM IMPORTS (VOLUME) IN 1955 (1954 = 100)

Food	Raw materials	Fuels	Manufactured goods
106.8	105.3	120.7	124.9

Volume of imports in 1954 was 97.23 (1935–1938 = 100)
Volume of imports in 1955 was 108.7 (1935–1938 = 100)

Since 1955 the situation has changed rather drastically (Table 33).

TABLE 33

COURSE OF UNITED KINGDOM IMPORTS BY VALUE SINCE 1955 (1955 = 100)

Year	Food	Basic materials	Fuel	Manufactures for further processing	Finished manufactures
1956	100.6	98.0	101.5	96.8	113.9
1957	103.6	103.8	114.1	94.6	131.4
1958	104.4	80.3	107.6	86.6	147.2
1959	106.4	84.1	114.4	95.8	181.7
1960	107.6	95.9	117.5	131.4	251.1
1961	104.0	88.9	118.5	122.2	271.6

It must be remembered, however, that even in 1961 imports were still only 32 per cent above the pre-war level, while exports were 105 per cent above. It was in the sphere of finished manufactures that the de-restriction of imports came last. It is obvious from the table that the upsurge of imports, which was largely concentrated on finished manufactures, was due to the de-restrictions.

Spokesmen have recurrently put forward the view that this was not so. The authorities appear to have been confused by the events of 1960. A further table is given showing the volume increase (Table 34). The figures here are subject to a margin of error, being based on the assumption that the prices of manufactures for further processing and finished manufactures varied together, since volume indices and price indices are not supplied separately for these two categories. The error, however, should be only a small one.

TABLE 34

COURSE OF UNITED KINGDOM IMPORTS BY VOLUME SINCE 1955
(1955 = 100)

Year	(Manufacturing production)	Food	Basic materials	Fuel	Manufactures for further processing	Finished manufactures
1956	(100)	102	97	96	95.7	112.5
1957	(102)	106	101	94	95.0	132.2
1958	(101)	111	89	102	90.2	153.3
1959	(110)	110	96	119	98.9	187.5
1960	(114)	113	104	130	132.7	253.0
1961	(114)	113	96	136	121.1	269.3

It appears from Table 34 that the imports of basic materials, and, still more, the imports of manufactures for further processing, did not respond sensitively to the upsurge in manufacturing production that occurred in 1959. It seems likely that in the case of manufactures for further processing there was some running down of stocks in the preceding four years. The figure for 1960 clearly involved some stockpiling, as evidenced by the relapse in the following year. By contrast, finished manufactures rose progressively without intermission from 1955 onwards, and continued to rise even in 1961 when imports in total fell.

The deterioration in the basic position of the United Kingdom has been the most serious that has occurred since the end of the war. It is only in these last years that the economy has been exposed to the full brunt of competition in the field of finished manufactures, and the sudden increase of importation of these has been the sole cause of the British troubles in the last few years. The disclaimers of the authorities on this point may be unhesitatingly set aside. As I observed in the second chapter, the United Kingdom had a unique task in having to raise exports by 65 per cent above imports owing to financial losses on current account, directly or indirectly due to the war; even taking the adverse figures of 1961, five-sixths of the required structural readjustment had been achieved. It is doubtless disappointing that the whole readjustment has not been achieved; but such are the facts.

The authorities are naturally unwilling to take a backward step in the matter of import restrictions, having regard to the British objective, which is no different from that of the United States in this regard, of getting the quickest possible approach to non-discriminatory multilateral trade. But the facts remain what the tables show them to be. It is most unlikely that the remaining part of the structural imbalance, as it is correct to call it, could be rectified within a year or two years.

CHAPTER 7

Labour

I. INTRODUCTORY

The time has not yet come to survey the trends and requirements of economic policy. We have already seen what the difficulties are that at present confront the smooth working of a domestic monetary policy. On the one side there has been the difficulty of enforcing a monetary policy of restraint promptly. On the other side this very difficulty has led to a tendency to adopt a deflationary policy in circumstances when it is inappropriate in relation to the current phase of the business cycle. This takes the form both of a tendency to unload gilt-edged stock into the hands of non-bank holders and to have an above-the-line budget surplus, when neither of these are required by the current phase.

Then we have seen that there have been constant balance-of-payments anxieties, consequent upon the difficult situation bequeathed by the war. These anxieties have in turn given rise to recurrent crises. The events directly responsible for these crises have sometimes been of quite minor importance, and the crises would never have arisen but for the fact that against a background of admitted difficulty minor events cause disproportionate anxiety. This anxiety and a certain propensity in foreign circles to underrate British achievement have had a mutually inflammatory effect, whereby a mole-hill is magnified to the scale of a mountain.

The United Kingdom has, like other countries, had a recurrent problem of inflation since the war. This has not been nearly so severe as that in some other countries, such as France, and hardly more severe than in the United States. But it has been more acute than in Germany, at least since the currency reform there of 1948.

II. DEMAND INFLATION AND COST INFLATION

In this connection I judge it to be of vital importance to distinguish between demand inflation and cost inflation. That this distinction is fundamental is not yet recognized by all economists; this, in turn, has caused, in my judgement, both confusions and deviations from correct policy. This distinction has a bearing on United States economic policy, no less than on the British.

There are, admittedly, difficulties in defining the distinction correctly. In my submission, demand inflation should be defined as a condition when the aggregate demand for goods and services, as it stands at the level of prices currently obtaining, is greater than the economy can meet. This state of excess demand gives rise to what may be entitled "inflationary pressure". This inflationary pressure does not necessarily eventuate in a proportionate increase of prices. Part of the excess demand may just not be met; this involves a lengthening of delivery dates. If delivery dates are lengthening to a degree beyond the normal on average through the whole economy, then we should say that inflationary pressure is present, even although there is no increase of prices. To the extent that excess demand is not confronted with delivery denied, it must lead to a rise of prices, which is what we mean by inflation. It is important to note that it is an essential feature of such a rise in prices that it is a rise in excess of paid-out costs of production (or paid-out incomes). If a given rise of prices, which was due to a demand in excess of what the economy could meet, was at once matched by a rise in paid-out incomes, then the aggregate of money demand would rise correspondingly further. Thus what a situation of excess demand requires, and will cause, except to the extent that it is met by a lengthening of delivery rates, is a rise of prices *over the rise in paid-out incomes.* And it is precisely this excess in the rise of prices over the rise in paid-out incomes that marks the presence of demand inflation, to the extent that that is not met by a lengthening of delivery dates.

I define a cost inflation as a condition in which paid-out incomes rise in greater proportion than the increase in the volume of goods and services produced. This will raise money costs and the flow of money incomes available to be used in the demand for goods *simultaneously.*

Thus, whereas a demand inflation consists essentially of a rise of prices over costs, a cost inflation consists of a rise in prices and costs together. This is a clear-cut conceptual distinction, and one that it is possible to utilize in the interpretation of statistics.

It has been suggested that the two definitions should contain a reference to causation. I do not believe that this is workable. It must be admitted that a demand inflation may cause a cost inflation. It is suggested that a cost inflation, in as much as it is caused by a demand inflation, should itself be considered as part of a demand inflation. There are real difficulties in this method of approach to the problem of definition. It might be, for instance, that, with unemployment at 10 per cent, no increases of pay would be demanded; but it might be that, if unemployment fell below that level, say to 5 per cent, owing to an increase of demand, increases of pay would be demanded even beyond any increases in productivity. Such an increase of demand might not be for any excess of goods and services over and above what the community could easily produce; is a rise of prices due to the fact that an increase of demand of such sort causes an increase of wages such as would not otherwise occur, to be called a demand inflation? I suggest that this would be absurd. I suggest that there should not be said to be a demand inflation unless the demand at current prices for goods and services is greater than the economy can produce.

I am not convinced that post-war experience suggests that in fact an increase of demand, less than one setting up demand inflation as defined, causes a greater cost increase than would otherwise occur. And there have been cases outside that experience, as on the occasion of the first accession to power of the socialists in France (1936), when cost inflations have occurred in times of very slack demand.

We have even to recognize that there may be opposite cases in which a decline in demand actually causes a cost inflation. There have been fairly clear examples of this in the United Kingdom, and I believe that examples may also be found in the United States. It is to be recalled that the concept of cost inflation involves a *ratio* between money rewards and output per person. Thus, there would be a cost inflation if output per person fell, money rewards remaining the same. A demand *deflation* may cause output per person to fall. This is because, at a given point of time, many industries are subject to "increasing returns", so that a drop in output means a higher cost in labour per unit of output. All these points have, unfortunately, to be carried in the mind simultaneously.

With a view to sorting out these problems in the British case, I have constructed certain tables. For these I laid down a programme in advance and did not deviate from it when, in the case of particular years, the results differed from what seemed to me to be *a priori* likely. Rather I endeavoured to modify my theory in the light of the out-turn of the programme. By and large, however, the results confirmed what I have been arguing over a number of years.

This matter is highly relevant to the United States, where correct policy depends, no less than it does in the United Kingdom, on an understanding of the difference, and even contrast, between the phenomena of demand inflation and cost inflation. Accordingly I ask the reader to bear with me while I take him through certain tables.

The leading element in cost inflation is naturally the movement of wages. This gives rise to a problem in policy which will be discussed in the ensuing chapter.

During the war the relative position of wage-earners in the United Kingdom appears to have improved; but this improvement cannot be defined with precision owing to some doubt about the movement in the cost of living. The official index of wage *rates* increased by 65 per cent, while wage *earnings* doubled. During the war there was an unofficial concordat between the government and labour leaders that there would be an amnesty in regard to demands for wage increases, if the cost of living were held down. This has already been discussed in relation to food subsidies (compare Chapter 3). The cost-of-living index that was officially published when the war broke out was still based on sample enquiries into typical working-class expenditure made in the first decade of the present century. The objects of expenditure had clearly much altered since then. Even the expenditures forty years earlier were not faithfully represented, since beer and tobacco were deemed to be noxious luxuries which were no part of the "cost of living". This index, based as it was on obsolete data, had risen by only 31 per cent in 1947 over 1938. It had been artificially held down by food subsidies, etc., on the supply side and by restrictions in consumption (rationing, etc.) on the demand side. But the index of the cost of the articles contained in "consumer expenditure", as used in subsequent statistics relating to the National Income, had risen by 82 per cent. Thus it may be a matter for legitimate doubt whether wage *rates*, in "real" terms, had risen more or less than the cost of living. It may be that the true cost of living for those concerned had risen somewhere between the rise in the old obsolete index and that in the general index covering consumer expenditure; the latter was probably closer to the true cost of living for wage-earners whose habits of life had changed much since the dawn of the century. Wage *earnings* had risen somewhat more than either index. That there was a real increase in the share that wage-earners took out of total National Income is evidenced by the fact that in the National Income White Paper (1947) wages are represented as getting 40 per cent of private income, as against 36 per cent in 1936, while the cost of living of wage-earners had probably gone up somewhat less.

We may thus base results on the view that wage-earners had improved their relative position somewhat during the war. Nonetheless this was not a great advance, since the National Income itself had barely grown, as shown above, and the consumer was oppressed by lack of freedom of choice, including rationing, etc.

Before we proceed to the tables which set out recent trends, it may be well to consider the difference between the increase in the index of wage *rates* and the increase in wage *earnings*. The excess of the latter over the former has come to be known by the expression the "wages drift". This wages drift has constituted a positive quantity for most years since the war, although it fell below zero in certain years of stagnation during the nineteen fifties. It is important to observe that of its four main components, two may be expected to operate in boom years only, one being actually reversed in years of pause or recession, while the other two may be expected, to the extent that the economy is at all progressive, to operate in good and bad years alike.

The four components are as follows: (1) In boom years wage earnings may rise above wage rates because more overtime is worked; and conversely. (2) In boom years average earnings may rise over the rates embodied in the official index, which represents those reached in Trade Union bargains or by official tribunals, because some especially prosperous firms, in order to attract or firmly secure their labour supply, may bid up their offers of wages above the rates as fixed by bargaining or officially. (3) There is all the time a process going forward, perhaps more strongly in boom years, but in pause and recession years also, by which workers are up-graded, so that a greater proportion come to earn skilled or semi-skilled rates. Thus average earnings in a given factory may go up, even although no change has been made in the rates for skilled, semi-skilled or unskilled. (4) The operation of a piece-rate (or bonus) system may cause a rise of earnings, even although there is no change in the scale of piece rates or bonuses. New plant may be introduced or a redeployment of labour effected, by which operatives are enabled to produce more pieces during the day. Even if they do not get the full benefit of this, they may get part of it, although there is no change in the official rates. This is a process that clearly may go forward, so long as there are some progressive firms, during a pause or recession. Consequently a wages drift is not to be regarded as a symptom of inflation; but if there is no wages drift at all, that may be taken to be a sign that the economy is rather decidedly depressed.

It may be expedient first to take the period of immediate post-war reconstruction, in which there was an excessive demand likely to lead to demand-inflationary pressure. This is shown in Table 35.

TABLE 35

PRICE AND COST INCREASES, 1947–1949

Percentage increases in year over preceding year						
Year	Import prices	Consumer prices	Wage rates	Wage earnings	Industrial Production per person in industrial employment	Gross Domestic Product* per person in civil employment
1948	+ 13.5	+ 7.6	+ 5.6	+ 9.4	+ 9.8	+ 0.9
1949	+ 2.0	+ 2.0	+ 2.8	+ 4.2	+ 5.3	+ 2.5

* At constant prices.

The strong rise of import prices in 1948 is to be noted. This alone would have caused a substantial rise of consumer prices. Imports may be taken to constitute roughly 20 per cent of the goods and services available for consumption. The rise of consumer prices in 1948 was clearly somewhat greater than could be accounted for by the rise in import prices alone. But it may have been indirectly due to the latter. At this point wage-earners would not be content to see their standard of living cut by 3 per cent; I take this figure as about the amount of rise of prices that a 13.5 increase in import prices *alone* would cause; such a rise in the cost of living would undoubtedly provoke wage demands. These in turn, to the extent that they exceeded any rise in productivity, would further raise consumer prices. In these years, and in the following years also, it is a perplexing problem as to how far one should regard wage increases as the effect of prior increases in the cost of living—but those wage increases would undoubtedly further increase the cost of living—or how far the rise in the cost of living was the effect of wage increases due to some other cause. This is an insoluble problem.

The increase of wage earnings (as distinct from that of wage rates) somewhat exceeded the increase in consumer prices, so that the wage-earning class as a whole made a small gain in 1948.

In that year there was a very strong difference between the increase of industrial production per person and the increase of the Gross Domestic Product per person. If we take the former index, even the increase in wage earnings was fully justified, i.e., covered by the increase in productivity. But the latter index is very relevant to the whole problem of inflation. This brings us to the heart of the difficulty of finding a correct solution in terms of a wages policy based on "productivity". Those engaged in industrial production, conscious of what is proceeding to raise industrial productivity, may feel that they ought to have a commensurate increase in earnings, since otherwise their employers might luxuriate in excessive profit—especially if it is known to wage-earners that "administered" prices are not currently being reduced. But outside the field of industrial production, increases in productivity may be much less. By competition, increases of wages in industry will affect the wages of those engaged in the provision of services. Thus if industrial wages go up in line with industrial productivity, and all wages do not lag too far behind, there is bound to be a rise in the price level of consumer goods and services, in fact there is bound to be inflation.

In 1949 all was quieted down. The further increases that occurred may well be attributed to the gradual working through into the whole economy of the preceding rise in import prices.

I now propose to present another table (Table 36), which ventures to isolate the factors showing respectively cost inflation and demand inflation. I have called column (ii) the "index" of cost inflation, since this gives a precise numerical measure of how much cost inflation there was. It is not, of course, intended to deny that part of this cost inflation may have been *caused* by the demand inflation proceeding. On the other hand I have called column (iv) an "indicator" of demand inflation. This means that the figures in this column, and in those so designated in subsequent tables, do not profess to give a numerical measure of the precise extent of demand inflation, but only a general indicator of its strength and direction.

The second column simply measures the extent to which the increase in money rewards exceeded the increase in the quantum of goods and services produced by those receiving the money rewards. The latter quantum is subject to what errors those who compile our National Income statistics may make. While minor deviations may be due to error, the general trend of the figures in this table and those that follow may be accepted as valid.

The tables do not claim to provide an exhaustive analysis, but, rather, a challenge to research in the United States no less than in the United Kingdom. The facts, when thoroughly analysed in terms of the concepts of demand inflation and cost inflation, may give the lie to many prevailing beliefs.

The amount of demand inflation, as implicitly defined in the tables, may not give correct readings for the strength of demand-inflationary pressure. This is owing to the fact that this pressure can cause delivery delays as well as an upward movement of prices. For what it is worth, the evidence of the tables slightly suggests that the price increases consequent on excess demand tend to be prior to the increasing backlog of unfilled orders.

The two years that will give special problems to the research workers are 1951 and 1955, when the amount of "demand inflation" fell—in 1955 it had a negative figure—while other indicators suggest that these were years of maximum inflationary pressure. This is not altogether clear for 1951, however, the interpretation of which has been somewhat blurred owing to its political significance, as the occasion when the Conservatives ousted Labour from power. The course of events in 1955 merits very careful research.

TABLE 36

INDICATORS OF INFLATION, 1947–1949

Year	(i) Personal incomes (money)	(ii) Excess of increase of personal incomes (money) over increase in Gross Domestic Product (constant prices). Index of cost inflation	(iii) Undistributed incomes of companies and public corporations (money)	(iv) Excess of increase of undistributed corporate income over increase of total domestic expenditure (money). Indicator of demand inflation
	Percentage increases in year over preceding year			
1948	+ 6.1	+ 2.9	+ 20.9	+ 14.2
1949	+ 5.9	+ 2.2	+ 0.9	− 4.1

Column (iv) represents the best indicator of demand inflation that I can think of. If it is the essence of demand inflation that aggregate receipts rise more than paid-out incomes, then undistributed corporate incomes may be a fair guide to this excess. For it is undistributed corporate incomes in the aggregate that reflect the excess of receipts from sales over paid-out incomes.

What strikes the eye in this table is that, if column (iv) provides a good indicator, and in the subsequent years it fits in fairly well with what we know on other grounds, demand inflation had ceased in 1949.

This was the year of the devaluation of sterling. It has already been shown that, on the basis of consumer prices and export prices, as compared with those in the United States, there was no ground for more than quite a small devaluation in 1949. Exports were continuing to rise rapidly, at a rate that would have exceeded all expectations in 1945.

Marshall Aid was being generously provided by the Americans to enable the United Kingdom to have rather more investment than it could afford out of its own savings, and to balance its deficit on *dollar* account, as distinguished from that on overall account. And now we have Table 36 which suggests that demand inflation itself had died down. It had terminated in the United States in 1948. No doubt its dying down in the United Kingdom was itself due in part to the existence of Marshall Aid. Meanwhile cost inflation was still proceeding in 1949, but at a moderate pace only, and certainly not by enough to give a pointer to the need for a devaluation of 30 per cent.

In the ensuing period the whole pattern of costs and prices was dominated by the devaluation. I have chosen 1952 for the concluding year of this phase, as being one in which the worst impact of devaluation was over. But the figures given in Table 37 indicate that its full effect had not even then worked through the whole economy.

TABLE 37

PRICE AND COST INCREASE, 1949–1952
PERCENTAGE INCREASES IN YEAR OVER PRECEDING YEAR*

Year	Import prices	Consumer prices	Wage rates	Wage earnings	Industrial production per person employed in industry	Gross Domestic Product† per person in civil employment
1950	+ 17.0	+ 3.9	+ 1.8	+ 4.6	+ 5.7	+ 1.6
1951	+ 33.3	+ 8.5	+ 8.1	+ 10.0	+ 0.4	+ 2.8
1952	− 1.8	+ 5.2	+ 8.4	+ 7.9	− 1.7	+ 0.7
1949 to 1952	+ 53.1	+ 18.6	+ 19.3	+ 24.1	+ 4.3	+ 5.1

* Except for last line.

† At constant prices.

It is to be noted that in 1950 the increase of wage rates was very moderate. This was due to the wages pause secured by Stafford Cripps when he was Chancellor of the Exchequer, which was also responsible for the increase in wage rates being quite small in 1949 (see Table 35, page 158). At the end of the period shown above (1952) consumer prices had clearly not yet caught up with the direct and indirect effects of devaluation.

Wages rates were doing little more than keep pace with consumer prices; nothing was gained by those receiving them from the increase of output which occurred in this period. It is to be noted that whereas in the years 1947 to 1949 industrial production increased far more than the Gross Domestic Product, this was no longer so in the later period. The vastly greater increase in the earlier period was no doubt due to the dire shortages of material goods; in the later period people could look around to satisfy other conveniences.

Wage earnings, on the other hand, more than kept pace with the rise in consumer prices. In fact the "real" income of wage-earners rose more or less in line with the increase in the Gross Domestic Product.

One point that it is very important to bear in mind in relation to this matter is that Trade Union leaders, who are responsible for looking after the interests of their members, have to address their minds to wage rates rather than to wage earnings. For many of their members may not be in a position in which to acquire the high earnings, which are an overall average, because they are simply doing their duty in their own positions or grades, and have no access to supplementary payments. This is indeed at the centre of the wages problem. Trade Union leaders are bound to consider how much wage rates have risen in relation to the cost of living, and they might well be discontented in 1952 to see that over three years they had risen barely more, while the increase of output per person had risen considerably.

Table 38 shows the indicators of inflation.

The year 1950 appears to have been one of strong demand inflation. This may have been due mainly to the large temporary boost in the volume of exports consequent upon devaluation. In 1951 there was no further increase in the volume of exports, indeed a slight decline, while import controls were relaxed. Thus the demand inflationary pressure eased off. It is interesting that 1951, not 1950, was the year of "crisis". There was little cost inflation in 1950, but this came on strongly in

TABLE 38

INDICATORS OF INFLATION, 1949–1952

Percentage increases in year over preceding year				
Year	Personal incomes (money)	Excess of increase of personal income (money) over increase of Gross Domestic Product (at constant prices). Index of cost inflation	Undistributed incomes of companies and public corporations (money)	Excess increase of undistributed corporate income over increase in total domestic expenditure (money). Indicator of demand inflation
1950	+ 4.6	+ 1.6	+ 27.2	+ 18.0
1951	+ 9.0	+ 5.1	+ 13.2	+ 1.6
1952	+ 7.0	+ 6.8	− 13.6	− 16.6

1951, and also in 1952, a year of recession in economic activity. We may hold that the cost inflation was the effect of the great upward push coming from the side of import prices, as shown in Table 37.

We do not know enough to say for certain whether a demand inflation may be expected regularly to cause a cost inflation. Those who insist that there is such a regular causal relation, argue that we may expect a time lag; accordingly the cost inflation of 1951 and 1952 would be deemed due to the demand inflation of 1950. When, however, we have surveyed a wider period, it will not appear that there is any regular connection between a demand inflation and a cost inflation, even when the latter is lagged. I believe this to be true of the United States also. The cost inflation in 1951 is sufficiently explained by the rise in import prices; that in 1952 may also have been in part the delayed effect of this, but it is arguable that it was partly caused by the demand *deflation* in that year. The decline in turnover raised unit costs of production.

We next pass to a period when import prices were not rising. It is to be recalled, however, that it is hardly likely that internal prices had risen into equilibrium with import prices by the end of 1952. The devaluation of sterling was continuing to have a cost-inflationary effect in the subsequent years (Table 39).

TABLE 39

PRICE AND COST INCREASES, 1952–1955

Percentage increases in year over preceding year*						
Year	Import prices	Consumer prices	Wage rates	Wage earnings	Industrial production per person employed in industry	Gross Domestic Product† per person in civil employment
1953	− 9.1	+ 1.0	+ 4.7	+ 9.0	+ 5.2	+ 4.6
1954	− 1.0	+ 2.0	+ 4.3	+ 6.4	+ 5.2	+ 2.6
1955	+ 3.0	+ 3.0	+ 6.7	+ 9.6	+ 2.3	+ 1.5
1952 to 1955	− 7.3	+ 6.2	+ 16.5	+ 23.5	+ 15.5	+ 8.1
1949 to 1955	+ 42.0	+ 26.0	+ 39.0	+ 53.2	+ 23.7	+ 13.5

* Except for last two lines.

† At constant prices.

It will be seen that consumer prices were rising more moderately than before. Wage rates did not rise in the three-year period much more than consumer prices plus the real increase in the Gross Domestic Product per person. Wage earnings, however, rose substantially more.

In the last line of Table 39 aggregated increases are given for the longer period from 1949 to 1955. The increase in import prices consequent upon devaluation was still substantially greater than the increase in consumer prices. The question has to be asked whether the new relation established in 1955 between consumer prices and import prices was an equilibrium one. Although 1949 showed an equal balance on the current external account, this was still buttressed by severe import restrictions. Thus, somehow it would be needful further to boost exports. For this to happen it may have been necessary that internal prices should continue to be held at a substantially lower level than world prices, in order to give a special motive for cultivating export markets, and as a shield against an excess of imports at such time as the restrictions should be completely removed. Whether this is right or not, the disparity between domestic wages and prices on the one side, and, on the other, the much higher level of world prices, was bound to give rise to domestic pressures on the cost side.

In Table 40 the indicators of inflation for this period are shown.

TABLE 40

INDICATORS OF INFLATION, 1952–1955

Percentage increases in year over preceding year				
Year	Personal incomes (money)	Excess increase of personal income (money) over increase in Gross Domestic Product (at constant prices). Index of cost inflation	Undistributed incomes of companies and public corporations (money)	Excess increase of undistributed corporate income over increase in total domestic expenditure (money). Indicator of demand inflation
1953	+ 5.6	+ 1.3	+ 8.2	+ 1.1
1954	+ 6.0	+ 4.3	+ 9.4	+ 3.6
1955	+ 7.8	+ 4.7	+ 6.5	– 1.6

In 1953 there was recovery from the recession of 1952; a strong investment boom, as evidenced by orders placed and factory building started, developed in 1954. Some demand inflation developed during 1954, although this was only slight compared with such years as 1948 and 1950. The reason for the lower level of demand inflation in 1954 was doubtless that the economy had become substantially underemployed in 1952, so that there was slack to be taken up. Pressure of demand only begins to exert a marked effect on prices (and thereby on undistributed profits) as the economy approaches a state of full employment.

I was surprised to find that in 1955, the peak year of the investment boom, my indicator ceased to show demand inflation, but a slight move in the opposite direction. It is to be remembered, however, that the authorities had begun to adopt restrictive measures early in 1955, and these may have exerted their appropriate influence during the course of the year in checking demand inflation. The more closely one examines the post-war history of the United Kingdom, the more it appears that economic policy measures exert their influence upon the economy very promptly. Production continued to rise during 1955, but there was a substantial increase in the labour force.

It is interesting to notice that in both crisis years, 1951 and 1955, demand inflation had already abated. Cost inflation proceeded.

We now proceed to the final period. It may be thought that the influence of the devaluation of sterling was now over. This it not altogether safe. There were considerable time lags before "administered" prices were raised, as a final concession to the pressure of cost increases. For instance, it was only in this last period that the price of postage stamps was raised for the first time since before the devaluation.

TABLE 41

PRICE AND COST INCREASES, 1955–1961

	Percentage increase in year over preceding year					
Year	Import prices	Consumer prices	Wage rates	Wage earnings	Industrial production per person employed in industry	Gross Domestic Product* per person in civil employment
1956	+ 2.0	+ 5.2	+ 8.1	+ 7.9	0	+ 1.8
1957	+ 2.0	+ 3.7	+ 4.8	+ 4.6	+ 1.0	+ 1.2
1958	− 7.5	+ 3.0	+ 3.6	+ 3.5	+ 0.5	+ 0.7
1959	− 1.0	+ 0.5	+ 2.6	+ 4.6	+ 5.2	+ 4.1
1960	+ 1.0	+ 1.0	+ 2.6	+ 6.6	+ 3.9	+ 4.0
1961	− 2.0	+ 3.4	+ 7.7	+ 6.2	− 0.1	+ 0.6

* At constant prices.

There was a marked abatement in the increase of wage rates during the years 1958 to 1960, although 1959 and 1960 showed a strong increase in the level of activity. It may be argued that this moderation was partly due to strong efforts at moral suasion made in 1957. It may have been more due to the drop in import prices in 1958, which was the first of any importance since 1953. (But in 1953 the economy was still in the toils of readjustment to the devaluation of sterling.) This drop in import prices in 1958 may have enabled producers to absorb their increases in cost and thus to call a halt to the upward movement of ex-factory prices and consumer prices. Consumer prices and wage rates doubtless reacted on each other in a favourable sense. It is to be noted that the increase in wage rates was less in the two years of strong expansion, which may be another example of rising demand having a cost-*deflationary* effect. The moderation in the rise in consumer prices may confidently be attributed to rising demand and turnover in those two years. Of course, this cost-deflationary effect may exhaust itself after two or three years of revival.

It is to be noted that the method by which the figures are presented shows one year as a whole by comparison with the preceding year, and not what was happening during the course of each year. The reader's patience might be exhausted if he were given too many different kinds of figures! Table 41 shows 1959 and 1960 as years of high production increase. In fact this increase came to an end very early in 1960, the average level in 1960 being higher than in 1959, mainly owing to the fact that production was rising strongly throughout 1959.

It is to be noted that in the three slack years, 1956 to 1958 inclusive, wage earnings rose fractionally less than wage rates, and more markedly so in the recession year, 1961. It has been already noted that in the normal course of progress one must expect wage earnings to rise somewhat more than wage rates in average years. When they do not, this can probably be taken as a sign of decidedly subnormal activity.

I next present in Table 42 the indicators of inflation for the concluding six-year period.

It is to be noted that this period was predominantly one of demand deflation. This accounts for the lower growth rate during this later period compared with the earlier period, as already recorded in Chapter 2. Even the period of reviving production, 1959 and the first few months of 1960, shows only a slight release from the pressure of demand deflation. The very strong demand deflation of 1961 is to be noted. This was the combined effect of a strong increase in personal savings with an

TABLE 42

INDICATORS OF INFLATION, 1955–1961

Percentage increases in year over the preceding year

Year	Personal incomes (money)	Excess of increase of personal income (money) over increase in Gross National Product (at constant prices). Index of cost inflation	Undistributed incomes of companies and public corporations (money)	Excess of increase of undistributed corporate incomes over increase in total domestic expenditure (money). Indicator of demand inflation
1956	+ 7.8	+ 5.2	+ 2.7	− 3.9
1957	+ 5.3	+ 4.0	+ 3.1	− 2.2
1958	+ 4.9	+ 4.9	− 2.2	− 5.6
1959	+ 5.4	+ 2.2	+ 1.8	− 0.6
1960	+ 7.6	+ 3.0	+ 9.2	+ 1.7
1961	+ 7.4	+ 5.1	− 4.2	− 14.5

increase in the Budget surplus provided by the Chancellor of the Exchequer.

Cost inflation meanwhile proceeded merrily. Once again the cost inflation appears to have been greatest when the economy was in pause or recession and demand *deflation* was greatest. If we take all the periods together, there does not appear to be any correlation between demand inflation and cost inflation, even if we allow for time lags. Rather the correlation seems to be the other way round.

If we compare the whole period from 1948 to 1955 with the period from 1955 to 1961, we find that the average rate of cost inflation in the former was 5 per cent and in the latter 4.1 per cent. This is an astonishing result, in view of the fact that the effect of the devaluation of sterling in 1949 had mostly to be absorbed in the former period. If we allow for that, it would seem that the purely internal forces making for cost inflation were stronger in the second period than they were in the first. The second period was characterized by lower growth and by demand deflation. These figures present a challenge to economists to do further research on the hypothesis, which I, provisionally, believe to be correct, that demand inflation and cost inflation are normally *inversely* related to one another (unless the former is very strong). It may anyhow be said that the attempt to bring a halt to cost inflation by demand deflation during the period 1955–1962 was a total failure. But it has had the undesirable result of reducing the British growth rate, undesirable both from the point of view of the welfare of the British people and also from the point of view of what the United Kingdom might have contributed towards assisting the developing countries of the world.

III. COMPLEXITY OF THE WAGES PROBLEM

From time to time there has come to the surface the view that, after all, wage trends should be tackled directly, and not merely left to find their own level through the indirect method of pressures on demand. It has already been seen that Stafford Cripps, when Chancellor of the Exchequer, succeeded in getting an informal understanding with labour that wage increases should be moderated, and this understanding had an effect for about two years, although the cost of living had already begun to rise strongly under the influence of the devaluation of sterling in the second year. Mr. Harold Macmillan, when Chancellor of the Exchequer, also made an attempt, not wholly unsuccessful, at moral suasion, combining this with securing a pause in the increases of administered prices by the nationalized industries. In connection with the bogus crisis of 1957, there were further attempts by Mr. Thorneycroft (then Chancellor) at moral suasion, which also may have had some effect for a limited period. All these attempts imply that correct monetary and fiscal policy, as regulators of aggregate demand, will not automatically ensure that wages do not rise excessively, especially if there is a political commitment not to allow unemployment to become too severe.

More recently Mr. Selwyn Lloyd took vigorous action in relation to the limitation of wage increases, involving both a long-range plan and a short-range plan. In regard to the latter, he combined a general proposal for a "wages pause", supposed to be applied throughout the range of private enterprise, with action to check, or postpone, wage increases in cases in which the Treasury had some say, e.g., government employees. After a period of a little more than six months, the idea of a total pause was replaced by the "guiding" thought that, for the time being, wages should not increase at more than the rate of $2\frac{1}{2}$ per cent a year.

Unfortunately the manner in which this wages policy was proposed and executed gave great offence in labour circles. It involved interference with the awards of tribunals, some of which, e.g., the Burnham Committee on Teachers' Salaries, had long-established reputations for fair dealing. It has been thought that any interference with the awards of such bodies will be bad for smooth working over a longer period, since their high reputations had made those concerned willing to accept their awards without question. It has also been argued that the Chancellor should have taken responsible labour representatives into his confidence before announcing this new departure. The counter plea was that a "crisis" was on hand (July 1961), and that time did not admit such advance consultations. This "crisis" occurred at the time of a heavy drawing by the United Kingdom on the International Monetary Fund; the need for this had been long foreseen, and, accordingly, it could be argued that there had been plenty of time for the Chancellor to consult representatives on the labour side in advance of taking the various measures simultaneously adopted in July 1961 to cope with the balance-of-payments situation.

The longer range plan was connected with the setting up of the National Economic Development Council. The functions that this body has to perform are not yet clear. The idea is that it should make investigations into the cause of the low growth rate of the United Kingdom, and chart out possibilities for the future growth of the main sectors of the economy: investment, consumption, exports, government spending, etc. Then, on the basis of these projections, it might assess what increases of consumption, and of personal incomes, could be allowed without causing a cost inflation. From the point of view of getting such projections widely accepted, it was rightly considered desirable that the Trades Union Congress should be represented on this body. It took some months to persuade the Trades Union Congress to accept the idea of representation, partly because of the ill-will caused by the methods of implementing the short-run pay pause, and partly because it seemed doubtful to them if the government was sufficiently convinced of the need for a policy of stronger growth or willing to proceed far enough in the direction of economic planning to get a growth policy implemented. If the projections and plans contemplated lower growth than was really obtainable, then there was danger that there might be some kind of indirect moral involvement by the Trades Union Congress, which would seem to lead to its having to acquiesce in lower increases in rates of pay for wage-earners than the economy could really afford to allow.

To the extent that the National Economic Development Council is intended to have influence in securing the implementation of a non-inflationary wages policy, it may, presumably, be compared with the American National Advisory Committee on Management and Labor.

And thus there is at present a live question as to whether a body of this sort, and plans of this sort, can have a real effect in cutting out the causes of cost inflation at the roots, namely where wage increases are bargained for and granted. The Trades Union Congress has protested, correctly, that it has not the right to interfere with the attitudes or the bargaining of individual Trade Unions.

The position is not made easier by the fact that the British Trade Union structure is a very complex one. It had its beginnings already in the early part of the nineteenth century, although the first attempts at forming Unions failed by being too ambitious. But by the middle of the century some notable successes had been scored; there had been effective resistance to the "Document" by which some employers sought to make employees undertake not to join a Trade Union. Many responsible employers were beginning to hold that Trade Unions could play a useful part in making industrial relations smoother; there was a Royal Commission on the subject in 1867, which was followed by an Act of Parliament, giving Trade Unions part at least of what they required by way of special status; the Trades Union Congress was formed in 1868.

Unions that became strong during the nineteenth century were mainly organized on the basis of craft. Many of these craft unions, or their successors or amalgamations, still exist. They cover and serve to protect the interests of what might be thought of as the aristocracy of labour. In due course other types of Unions came into existence, some organized by industry, like the National Union of Railwaymen, and others based on a particular industry, but gathering together under their aegis a wide variety of members who had no Unions of their own, like the Transport and General Workers' Union and the General and Municipal Workers' Union, both having very large memberships. Gradually a great many Unions of many varying types came into existence. It has been stated that there were no less than 666 Unions in 1955.[1] It has not been the British practice to form a Union comprising all workers for a particular firm. That may be a good thing. It means that a given advance has to be along the whole front and that workers in weaker firms are protected. On the other hand, advances are restrained, since wages that might be obtainable from a very strong firm might, in certain cases, be obviously in excess of what many other employers of Union members could afford to pay.

The consequence of the complex structure is that a single firm often has a great many Unions represented among its employees, and it has to negotiate separately with them. This, in turn, has brought into prominence the shop stewards, who are responsible for labour relations generally in each particular factory. As conditions are bound to be different in detail from factory to factory, the shop stewards have a significant part to play through their intimate knowledge of conditions on the spot. They are not always well looked upon by employers, or, indeed, by Trade Union officials themselves, and they have some reputation with the general public for being trouble makers. Nonetheless, by and large, they probably do good work, and constitute a part of the machinery for industrial relations that could not well be dispensed with. It is thought that they tend to provoke "unofficial" strikes, i.e., those not approved by the Unions of which the strikers are members. It is to be noted, however, that unofficial strikes may occur through the sheer boiling-up of feelings among the rank and file.

On the whole it may be said that industrial relations in the United Kingdom have been good since the war—much better than they were in the decade following the First World War or in the years immediately preceding it. A very small number of days has been lost by strikes.

However, this problem of getting a non-inflationary wages policy is

[1] Allan Flanders, *Trade Unions*, page 54. Hutchinson University Library, 1960 (first published 1952).

something that transcends the traditional problems of industrial relations and the traditional methods of bargaining and securing agreement.

Anyone making a manful attempt to get a non-inflationary wages policy widely accepted has to face the following problems:

1. The cardinal principle of free collective bargaining has to be maintained. It is unthinkable that the rank and file would accept anything in the nature of dictated wages, or waive its right to withhold labour by strike action, if the terms of employment were not acceptable. There is an element of compulsion in the awards of "Wages Councils". These are descended from "Trade Boards" but have somewhat enlarged powers since the Second World War. The first Trade Boards were set up in 1909, to deal with a limited number of "sweated" trades, and much multiplied after the First World War to cover trades where the men had not been able to form effective Unions. On the whole their job has been to protect the less fortunate classes of wage-earners by establishing minimum rates and conditions, which are statutorily binding. As the main function of their work is to protect workers unable to protect themselves, they are not thought to violate the principle of free collective bargaining. Similar bodies deal with agricultural wages.

2. If an important Union gets an increase of a given amount, this may lead to intensive pressure in other Unions, even if profitability in their trades is not so great. It is felt that the disparities between one trade and another should not be excessive.

3. The structure of wages rates, in relation both to differentials between grades and to piece work, is often extremely complex, so that only a great expert can understand its true working. It may be difficult to relate such a complex structure to the terms of a given national wages policy.

4. There is the problem of differentials between industries. The question arises whether an industry showing a high profit margin and making rapid progress, ought to attract labour to itself by establishing higher rates than those prevailing in other industries. How otherwise is the mobility of labour towards industries (or localities) where it is most needed, from the national point of view, to be secured? This problem is made more difficult by the prevalence of full employment. In the old days the progressive sectors might be able to attract labour simply by

being able to offer jobs. Is it desirable that the more progressive or rapidly extending sectors should pay higher wages? And how is that to be related to any given national policy that, on the overall average, wages should not increase by more than so much a year?

5. There is the whole question of the "wages drift", the four elements in which have already been stated.[2] If it is a fact that in a progressive economy one must expect there to be a positive wages drift on average, taking good years and bad years together, then standard wages must rise less than average Gross Domestic Product per person employed, if price inflation is to be avoided. How is this fact to be related to some agreed overall principle for moderating wage increases? For instance, if the National Economic Development Council decided that the consumption of wage-earners could not go up by more than 4 per cent a year,[3] and if it seemed likely that the wages drift would amount to 2 per cent a year, then the average standard wage rates could not go up by more than 2 per cent a year without causing price inflation. Would it not be difficult to get acceptance for the principle of a 2 per cent increase only? The workers might ask—what happens if the wages drift is not so great as is expected? It varies from year to year and even its long-run trend cannot be predicted.

If there is to be any success in getting agreement on both sides of industry for a non-inflationary wages policy, there will have to be an initiative extending over a much wider front than anything that appears yet to be contemplated.[4] It is not only a question of getting agreement in principle with the Trades Union Congress, an agreement which, at best, can be in principle only; consultations are needed with the Trade Unions themselves. There might be separate consultations with each of the larger Unions, while some of the others might be grouped. All this would require a large expert staff, which would have to be coached in the underlying principles guiding the discussions. It would have to be made plain at the outset that no unilateral actions were intended, and

[2] See pages 157–8.

[3] Since the time of writing it has given its endorsement to the figure of 4 per cent for the whole gross Domestic Product, which implies a somewhat lower increase of consumption.

[4] The establishment, since the time of writing, of a National Incomes Commission, may be written off as of little value, owing to insufficient forethought and faulty terms of reference.

that everything must go forward in accordance with agreed principles. One fault in previous excursions into this field has been that Trade Union action tends to come up for criticism only when a particular demand is put forward. This is quite wrong. The wider discussions should not be expected to assess the justification for particular requests, which would be invidious and might run the risk of seeming one-sided. Rather the discussions should be expected to have influence upon the pattern of requests over a number of future years. The discussions should be based on the following objectives of policy.

1. The main basis should be an affirmed intention of the authorities to raise the real standard of living of wage-earners as a whole over a term of years. It may be difficult to assign a particular figure in advance. The authorities could pledge themselves not to embark upon a deflationary policy if growth was proceeding at a lower rate than that projected. If the proposed growth really proved impracticable, then matters agreed upon in the discussions would have to be subject to review. I suggest, for instance, that the intention should be stated that the real standard of living of wage-earners should be raised by 50 per cent over a period of twelve years. This would be a notable departure from the policy of the last twelve years, which was content with a lower rate of growth, and introduced measures for damping down the activity of the economy for extraneous reasons, such as the external balance of payments.

2. It should be affirmed that the best effort would be made to achieve this target in any case, but that success would be gravely jeopardized by undue wage demands. Although it would be wrong to make pursuance of the policy conditional on the rise of exports at any particular rate, it should be made clear that if exports did not rise harmoniously, that would make the achievement of any given growth rate more difficult. Indeed that is one of the main reasons why a non-inflationary wage policy is to be regarded as essential to the achievement of the best possible growth rate. If exports did not rise sufficiently, imports might have to be restricted, and that would deprive the country of the benefit of expanding foreign trade, which is itself an important ingredient in the achievement of the maximum growth in the real standard of living of the people. On the other hand, it would be wrong

to postulate that growth of domestic activity should be deliberately held down if foreign trade did not expand commensurately. This seems to have been the philosophy implicit in the statements by Mr. Selwyn Lloyd (Chancellor of the Exchequer 1960–1962). His adoption of this attitude is a very grave matter, which could have a seriously adverse effect on the prosperity of the country. It does not appear that the Chancellor had any democratic mandate for adopting such an attitude. Indeed a survey of economic policy may make one doubt whether a democratic constitution enables the democracy to have an operative influence on those parts of policy that matter most. Although a convinced life-long Free Trader, I cannot blind myself to the facts of arithmetic so far as not to recognize that reducing economic growth does far more damage to economic welfare than marginal interference with the freedom of foreign trade.

3. In order to get goodwill on the side of the wage-earners, it is clearly necessary to have some specific policy in relation to other kinds of income. Why should one class only have to bear the main burden in checking inflation? It can, of course, be fairly argued that during the war and until quite recent times, the wage-earners have had the lion's share of increases in consumption and that it is their turn to do a little "pausing". No doubt this is a point that could come up as an integral part of the discussions. But it does not justify a total absence of a specific policy for keeping other incomes under restraint. A partial recognition of this point is made in the recent fashion of referring to the need for a national "Incomes Policy", as distinct from a mere "Wages Policy".[5] A British Chancellor of the Exchequer recently took the line that no immediate measure in regard to profit restraint was needed, since profits had recently been below par. This is true enough, as shown in Table 42, and the reason is not far to seek—the Chancellor's own policy in damping the economy. If he reverted to a growth policy, as pre-supposed in the discussions in question, profits would soon rise up again. The wage-earners would feel entitled to know what the authorities intended to *do* in such an eventuality. It is not good enough to leave the matter entirely vague.

The difficulty here is that the principles underlying profit making and

[5] Cf. White Paper on *Incomes Policy*, Cmd. 1626. 1962.

dividend distribution are altogether different from those underlying wage payments. A wage-earner is worthy of his hire and expects to be paid at the standard rate, agreed upon in advance. Profits by contrast arise in quantities not predetermined, and depend upon efficiency and good luck. Efficiency is to be particularly noted. It is to be expected, therefore, that different firms will make different rates of profit on their capitals employed. It would be the death of private enterprise to impose an overall restraint on profit making or dividend distribution. The efficient are entitled to their higher rate of reward; many may make losses.

Accordingly, the restraint of incomes paid out by dividend distributions must take a different form. Now that good National Income statistics are available, it should be possible to implement a policy of taxing dividends by means of a special levy in years in which these constituted a larger share of the national cake than in some standard years. Such a levy would leave the favourable position of the more efficient relatively to the less efficient unimpaired. Allowance would presumably have to be made for the rise in the quantum of capital employed, representing the investment of fresh savings. Nowadays these fresh savings are largely derived, via financial institutions, from the hard-won earnings of middle and lower income groups. Wage-earners might argue that dividends should receive, not a constant, but a falling share of national cake. This would be a point to be argued about. A general policy for the more equal distribution of incomes in society is already implemented by progressive rates of taxation. Furthermore it is no longer clear that the majority of dividends go to the most favoured income groups.

4. Some hold that, in relation to cost inflation, restrictive labour practices have a worse effect than money wage increases. There are differences of opinion about how damaging these restrictive practices are. Whatever the true view, they ought to be included within the range of discussions covered by the kind of initiative here proposed. This is a further reason for holding that it is not nearly good enough to contemplate only a top level Round Table with Trades Union Congress representatives. Restrictive practices (including apprenticeship rules) vary much from one trade to another; furthermore they are often connected with "demarcation" problems, which affect inter-Union rules. Thus

there should not only be general discussions at a high level, but also involved and detailed discussions, Union by Union.

The underlying presupposition must be that restrictive practices that hold down productivity are bad. There should also be an underlying presupposition that restrictive practices in most cases reflect some genuine human need. There are, of course, some practices which are merely obsolete relics of past conditions, or reflect demarcation problems that ought to be resolutely overcome. Among the various human feelings underlying restrictive practices a leading one is a fear of redundancy. In an all-out attempt to solve the wage inflationary problem, the question of redundancy must be squarely faced. We have already passed beyond those *laissez faire* modes of thought, by which the ruthless dismissal of workers is regarded as part of the normal functioning of a free economy. Measures must be explored for giving wage-earners in most cases a greater security of tenure, such as is enjoyed by those engaged in more highly paid occupations. It would be impossible to cover the whole field of employment, but it would be helpful to make a beginning.

It is to be noted that the policy of the last seven years of stunting growth has made the redundancy problem more acute than it was in the decade after the war. Since the war, employers have themselves been much more reluctant to stand off hands than they were in pre-war days. That may be partly due to a more tender social conscience; it may be due also to the conditions of greater labour shortage that have prevailed; and it may be partly due to the more powerful position of Trade Unions or shop stewards. Whatever the cause, it is a fact. The result is that, when the Chancellor of the Exchequer takes measures to damp down the economy, instead of unemployment mounting rapidly, its effect is to produce considerable underemployment inside factories. This underemployment is, of course, perfectly obvious to those in the factories and gives them the correct impression that, if trade happens to get a little worse, quite a large number of them will inevitably be stood off. *In fine*, a low growth policy increases fears of redundancy and is therefore a great obstacle to getting the elimination of restrictive practices, the primary object of which is to prevent redundancy.

This gives another reason for linking a policy of higher growth closely to any serious attempt to get labour co-operation in a non-inflationary wages policy.

Although the present initiative (1962) for such a wages policy appears rather half-hearted, there is hope that, if preliminary discussions are initiated by the National Economic Development Council, or take place in other ways, real progress may be made. The fact that labour relations are, on the whole, good in the United Kingdom, and that there has always been an atmosphere of give and take, makes the country a good place for this kind of policy, which, if successful, would be a new departure in the history of capitalism. The need for it has come forward as the natural consequence of a policy for full employment and higher growth.

CHAPTER 8

Economic Policy

I. THEMES, METHODS AND AGENCIES

There is no doubt that central policy making plays a bigger part in the progress of the economy of the United Kingdom than it did before the war. In the last ten years the movement has not been towards greater state ownership or control of the means of production. In regard to nationalization, the pattern has been static; it may well remain more or less so, even if the Labour Party is returned to power. But in that event there might be a reactivation of some of the other ways in which the state influences economic life.

The main themes of economic policy in recent years have been as follows. The external balance-of-payments problem has been a recurrent preoccupation. The financial losses of the war left a vast gap, and it would hardly be reasonable to expect this to be filled by the ordinary automatic processes of a free economy. One might as well rely on those automatic processes to see a nation through a major war! This problem has not always been wisely handled, and there was some premature optimism in the late nineteen fifties. It is to be noted that the United States has recently had its balance-of-payments problem, which has, for the first time in its history, been having some influence on central policy making, notably on that of the Federal Reserve System. The American deficit has not, of course, had the same cause as the British; rather it has arisen largely from the statesmanlike generosity of the Americans in helping the developing countries of the world.

Another theme in the United Kingdom has been the recurrent tendency towards inflation. This has also been a problem for the United States, and each country should be able to learn much from the experience of the other.

There has also been the theme of maintaining a high and steady level of employment. This was recognized for the first time as being a specific duty of the central government in a White Paper on *Employment Policy*, published in 1943, to which the three principal Parties in the state, Conservative, Labour and Liberal, all subscribed. This theme, however, has given no worry to policy makers in the United Kingdom, since in this case the economic forces within the free enterprise economy have sufficed to sustain a high level of employment automatically. In the United States the case has been rather different in recent years.

Another theme has been the task of ironing out the business cycle. This objective has been pursued more faithfully in the United States than it has in the United Kingdom, where the other themes, notably the external balance of payments and inflation, have interfered more with what was required to be done from a pure business cycle point of view. This may have happened on occasion in the United States policy also; for instance, the view has been expressed that the Federal Reserve System made money tight a little too quickly during the recovery from the recession of 1958, in order to damp down wage demands and give the right background for those crucial discussions which led to the steel strike of 1959. But, by and large, the American authorities appear not to have deviated far from the policies that, in their own judgement—which may not always have been right—were best suited to smoothing out the business cycle. The deviations in the United Kingdom have been more serious.

Finally, there have been, in the very recent period, belated signs that the authorities were beginning to regard an adequate growth rate as a proper objective of governmental policy. Attention has been called to the rather low growth rate of the United Kingdom in recent years. Not much, one might almost say nothing, has so far been done about this. But the institution of the National Economic Development Council may be regarded as a sign that official thinking is beginning to take this matter seriously. There were great hopes in certain circles in the United Kingdom that an important new departure in policy, in the interests of growth, might result from the meeting of the British Prime Minister with Mr. Kennedy on his first accession to the Presidency. These hopes have been disappointed. Whereas that interview doubtless did not appear so important to Americans, one may be permitted to add that, considered objectively, the change of administration in the United

States has not appeared to tilt the economy so decidedly in the direction of greater growth as had been hoped.

The instruments for effectuating policy, in relation to the themes listed, are in part the same in the United Kingdom as they are in the United States. There are the two great weapons of monetary and fiscal policy. There are certain further weapons at the disposal of the British authorities. There is now a fairly well recognized procedure for varying the terms on which purchases on consumer credit are permitted. (Something similar was attempted in the earlier post-war days in the United States.) The legally required terms are stiffened when inflationary pressures appear to be developing, and relaxed in times of recession. Despite the fact that the nationalized industries are managed by independent corporations, the central government, which provides them with capital, can, and does, have influence on the pace at which capital projects for the extension of services or modernization of equipment are put into effect. The central government can also have influence on the pace of capital development by the local authorities, not only by varying interest rates, but also by direct advice. For a considerable period a body known as the Capital Issues Committee, which was a sort of offshoot of the Treasury, had the authority to control new capital issues, and could be more restrictive in times of inflationary pressure; however, its powers have been largely circumscribed since 1958. The British government also has some influence on the flow of capital funds into the outer Commonwealth. For instance, at the Montreal Conference in 1958 it was agreed to adopt various measures for expediting United Kingdom assistance to Commonwealth development.

While there are thus a number of different themes of policy and a number of different instruments for implementing them, there is usually a single integrated policy at any one time towards which the departments concerned co-operate. The only exception is that monetary policy may, at certain times, be somewhat independent, when it is specifically related to the external situation, particularly to short-term capital movements; at other times monetary policy may be regarded as part and parcel of the general policy.

Ultimately, policy springs from Cabinet decisions. There is the ancient

British doctrine of Cabinet unanimity. If there are strong differences of view as between important Ministers, these are kept unknown to the public to the greatest possible extent, and Cabinet Ministers speak with one voice. This element of secrecy extends to some extent through the whole machinery of government, so that it is difficult for an outsider to know in any given period where the true sources of influence are.

It may, however, be safe to state as a general rule that the influence of the Treasury is paramount in all economic matters. Its leadership is recognized by the whole Civil Service. It has various methods of co-ordinating policy, including membership of inter-departmental committees. The Head (since 1956 joint Head) of the Treasury is also Head of the whole Civil Service.

The leadership springs, not only from the essential nature of its work, but also from a certain intellectual eminence. All the different departments are manned by career civil servants, apart from two or three politicians (Members of Parliament), who occupy the political offices and change with changes of government, and at other times also. But apart from the chief Minister—in the case of the Treasury the Chancellor of the Exchequer—the more prominent civil servants, i.e., the career men, have greater influence in the formation of policy than the politicians. These careers begin at a very early age, normally immediately after men (or women) have taken their B.A. degrees at their universities, and admission is by examination. Because of the great traditions of the Treasury and the fact that it is known to occupy a predominant position, the most intellectual of the candidates give the Treasury their first option, and thus it may be able to recruit those at the top of the list in the examinations. Accordingly its intellectual eminence is perpetuated from generation to generation. Indeed the British Treasury may constitute one of the greatest concentrations of brain-power in the world.

The main historic role of the Treasury has been to be the watchdog over the taxpayer's purse. The importance of this role stems from the philosophy that dominated British public life, including both main political parties, for a number of generations, namely that it was the duty of the government to confine its activities to the bare minimum, and, above all, to let as much money as possible fructify in the pockets of the citizens, rather than to fritter it away on governmental activities not absolutely necessary. This put the Treasury, the main duty of which was to supervise and pare down the spendings of all other departments, into a pivotal position. The test of skill was how to run the machinery of government efficiently with the least possible expenditure. Of course that skill still has its place today. The traditions and deeply entrenched ways of thought of the Treasury may still be coloured somewhat by this historic role.

Some have thought that it may be unfortunate that an institution with these traditions continues to have a paramount influence on the shape of policy. When it comes to the wider issues of economic policy formation—ironing out the business cycle, maintaining full employment, securing a balance between consumption and investment, maintaining maximum growth—the tendency always to curb and curtail may not be salutary. The Treasury is no longer responsible only for the proceedings of one sector of the economy (the public sector), which in the old days was fairly small in relation to the totality; it has become responsible for balance in the economy as a whole. Some boosting is sometimes required. Of course the Treasury recognizes this, but its instincts may incline it too much in the deflationary direction. A very important example of this will be given presently.

During the war a group of economists was set up under a Minister without departmental duties, to give advice to the Cabinet as a whole on war-time economics and the mobilization of resources for the war effort; this was known as the Economic Section of the War Cabinet Secretariat. It was kept in being when the war was over. But before long it was gobbled up by the Treasury, although retaining some independence under it. Its Head was re-christened Economic Adviser to the Government. The section has not expanded greatly. While the Economic Adviser no doubt retains an influence in his own right—the position has always been occupied by an economist of distinction—that influence cannot be as independent as it might have been had the section remained directly responsible, under the aegis of some Minister not the Chancellor, to the Cabinet itself.

Some of us believe that, despite its high intellectual eminence, thinking in the Treasury is somewhat stale. There was a moment after the war and after the death of the late Lord Keynes, whose presence in the Treasury throughout the war doubtless had an enlivening influence there, when the Treasury seemed to have become more Keynesian than Keynes.[1] This may have been connected with the personal influence of Sir Richard Hopkins, who retired shortly afterwards. That influence seems to have worn off rather quickly. Secret from the general public and raised aloft in relation to the other departments of state, the Treasury can easily become complacent. To judge from its little monthly bulletin and the speeches that it allows successive Chancellors to make, it appears to continue to be guided by patterns of thought long since obsolete. Some of these will be referred to later.

While the Bank of England has an ancient tradition of independence, it began to have to maintain close liaison with the Treasury after the breakdown of the gold standard in 1931. This was presumably carried one stage further with the nationalization of the Bank of England in 1946. Despite this, it may be believed—although in this sphere also all is secret—that the Bank continues to exert an independent influence. Within the Bank a distinction must be drawn between the inner core, who continuously devote their thought to policy making, and the general run of directors, some of them part time. These are drawn from business life; in the old days they were mainly Merchant Bankers. The proceedings of the Tribunal appointed in 1957 to investigate an alleged "leak" about an impending change of the Bank Rate, while entirely vindicating the honourable conduct of the directors concerned, uncovered some of the most stupid statements about the condition of the economy that can ever have been expressed. It may be believed that these did not represent the thinking of the inner core.

By the academic training and record of its members, one might suppose that the Treasury would embody higher intellectual eminence than the Bank of England. But responsibility for day-to-day operations may have an enlivening effect upon the intelligence. It may stave off tendencies to staleness and complacency. The memoranda submitted by the Bank of England in 1957 to the Committee on the Working of the

[1] Cf. pages 50–1 above.

Monetary System (Radcliffe Committee) are remarkably alive, interesting and subtle.

There are great achievements in the post-war period which one believes to be attributable to the Bank of England—the transferable sterling account system, the monetary arrangements necessary for the re-opening of commodity markets in the United Kingdom, the revival of foreign exchange markets, including markets in forward exchange, the re-opening of the London Gold Bullion Market and, above all, the restoration of the *de facto* convertibility of sterling in 1955.

In the memoranda submitted to the Radcliffe Committee attention is paid to the multifarious and complicated influences operating upon the money market, and in all this field considerable intellectual grasp is shown. Too little attention is paid to the underlying "real" phenomena of production, investment and growth. It might be argued that this was not the business of the authority that is responsible first and foremost for monetary matters. But this in the modern situation is too narrow a view. One would suppose that the Board of Governors of the Federal Reserve System and the Federal Reserve Banks do pay greater attention to "real" phenomena.

Apart from the Treasury and the Bank of England, I believe that there is no agency exerting an influence of fundamental importance on economic policy formation, although doubtless the different Ministries have some weight in matters within their own sphere. They have their own interests and points of view. But they are probably less independent and, one may add, less conflicting in their policies than the equivalent Ministries in the United States. The British system is more unitary. The process of smoothing out and resolving conflicts has been carried further.

Owing to the British constitution and the relation of the Executive to the Legislature, Parliament probably has less influence on fundamental issues of economic policy than Congress. If the House of Commons refused to accept the line of the Cabinet on any important issue, the Prime Minister would simply dissolve it, there would be a General Election and harmony between the Executive and the Legislature would be restored.

II. DOCTRINES

After the war was over, it was believed that the jointly sponsored White Paper,[2] declaring that it was the duty of the government to maintain a high and steady level of employment, would have a far-reaching effect on governmental action. This assumption of responsibility for full employment was regarded as a great achievement, emanating from a war-time resolve never to go back to the grim inter-war conditions of heavy unemployment and slump. But, in fact, this brave resolve had no sooner been taken than it became obsolete. For at least six years after the war, and for the best part of ten, natural forces maintained the economy in very full activity, so that no special governmental measures were required to obtain this objective. And then another phenomenon began to appear, namely underemployment inside factories. Some reasons for this have already been stated.[3] The consequence was that unemployment ceased to give a reliable danger signal that the economy was going into recession.

There are two objectives in a policy for full employment.

The first one is to avoid the grave social evils of unemployment. That objective may be achieved to a considerable extent if employers refrain from dismissing workers when their business becomes slack. Thus one may think that employers, by their new attitude, have taken a difficult load of responsibility off the governmental authorities, and this is therefore to be welcomed. There is, indeed, another side to this. It is complained that the retentiveness of employers reduces the mobility of labour to an undesirable extent. The social benefit, however, of this new attitude must surely be taken to outweigh the disadvantage of diminishing mobility.

The second objective of a full employment policy is to get the economy to produce as much as it is capable of doing. One of the things that impressed one about the pre-war situation was the absurdity of having a mass of able-bodied people, only too ready to work, kept idle when they might be producing useful goods. It was a case of "poverty in the midst of plenty". This second objective, namely that of making full use of the available man-power of the country, is not

[2] Employment Policy, 1944, Cmd. 6527.

[3] Cf. page 179 above.

achieved if from time to time work goes slack inside the factories. Over a long haul this second objective may be just as important for the welfare of a country as the first. Failure to make full use of labour resources may diminish the incentive for fresh investment and thus have a cumulative effect, year by year, on the standard of living of the country. The trouble has been that by modern thinking there is a political edge to the first objective. In the United Kingdom a government could not retain power if visible unemployment began to grow substantially. But there is no political edge to the second objective; if it is pointed out that labour is underemployed inside factories, the politicians may feel that this is a point of merely academic interest. The fact does not impinge on their day-to-day activities that this same underemployment may, if it becomes endemic, cause a serious decline in the country's position over the years.

What is now needed to replace the full employment policy is a specific and declared policy for economic growth. So far this has hardly figured as an objective in the British scene. With the appointment of the National Economic Development Council it may now begin to do so; but the matter is not absolutely clear. Most other countries, especially the less developed, have been thinking rather actively about growth for some time now.

Growth has only just begun, if indeed it has begun, to figure as an objective in the United Kingdom. What has probably not come to birth yet at all in the minds of policy makers is any conception that the theory underlying growth economics is not just something that anyone of reasonable intelligence can deduce from the theories of static economics learned thirty years earlier. To understand how policy should be shaped towards promoting growth, a great revolution of fundamental thinking is required, and not in the Civil Service only.

Meanwhile we may revert to certain subjects that have been matters of discussion. I believe that the vital distinction, and in some respects contrast, between demand inflation and cost inflation is not fully recognized, and that, deep down, the Treasury still believes that inflation is unitary, and that this unitary inflation is in fact nothing else than demand inflation. Cure demand inflation, and the rest will look after itself. There have, we have seen, been occasions when a direct approach has been made to the wages problem, e.g., as early as Sir Stafford Cripps's wage restraint policy, and this may suggest that those concerned did *not* think that the wages problem could be solved by the simple recipe of eliminating demand inflation.

The recent stress placed by the (former) British Chancellor (Mr. Selwyn Lloyd) on an "incomes policy" may indicate a new enlightenment. But it does not do so clearly. The "incomes policy" may be thought of as something designed to check rising costs of production and keep the United Kingdom competitive. That is correct, and all to the good. But one has an uncomfortable feeling that this "incomes policy" is also, and simultaneously, thought of as a policy of demand deflation. Thus the "incomes policy" gives no clear evidence that the authorities have got away from the unitary concept of inflation. But this is quite inappropriate for the United Kingdom at the present time. I venture to suggest that conditions are largely similar in the United States, the adverse external balance of payments of which clearly points to the need for cost restraint, while demand requires some stimulus.

The condition of the United Kingdom in April 1962 certainly still required vigilant attention to the dangers of cost inflation. Export prices appeared to have been edging up more than those of some competitor countries. Furthermore there is that final one-sixth of the journey of post-war structural readjustment still to be achieved, by which exports have got to be raised further relatively to imports. This means that the United Kingdom has not only to keep as competitive as before, but to become still more competitive.

But demand is at the present time greatly insufficient, and industry is slack. Accordingly one needs both a policy for an abatement of cost increases and a policy for increasing demand. Raising wages in excess of productivity does not increase the demand for goods and services, since the excess incomes are merely absorbed in higher prices. The effective demand for goods and services can be increased, and can only be increased, by such measures as credit relaxation, reduction of the Budget surplus, a stimulus to investment and the reduction of restrictions on consumer credit. Does the Chancellor understand, and does the Treasury understand, that it is possible, and in certain circumstances desirable, to combine a policy in restraint of income distribution with a policy for increasing the demand for goods and services by measures in the monetary, fiscal and other fields? I have an uncomfortable feeling that the Treasury still adheres to the unitary view of inflation.

As well as having a case such as exists in the United Kingdom now, and probably in the United States also, in which cost deflation and demand expansion are simultaneously needed, one may have the opposite case, which was manifested for several years in Germany recently. There demand was too great for good health and led to demand-inflationary pressure, while, in relation anyhow to international equilibrium, costs were too low. Demand deflation and cost inflation were to be desired. Here we had a paradoxical case which brings out the point that cost inflation and demand inflation can work in opposite directions, in which the undue *lowness* of costs was causing a demand inflation. The lowness of costs, by encouraging high exports and discouraging imports, caused a favourable balance of payments, and the consequent inflow of funds more than offset the internal deflationary monetary policy and caused a net demand inflation inside the country.

The contrast between demand inflation and cost inflation is valid even within the well-worn territory of static economics. But when we come to growth (or dynamic) economics, further problems arise. It is right at the point of the interaction between static theory and growth theory that we may have the greatest confusion of thought. This, I feel sure, applies to the United States also. We may revert to the question of causal interaction. It is generally supposed that a demand inflation will normally tend to cause a cost inflation. And this doubtless does often happen, especially if the demand inflation is strong, as in wartime. If employment is very good, operatives will be more insistent in their wage claims. If the demand inflation causes a rise in prices, they will have a good arguing point; if the demand inflation causes high profit, employers will be easier in granting wage increases; if their markets are expanding, they will be more anxious to prevent stoppages, such as might result from refusals of wage demands; they will be easier with their money, in order to avoid trouble. All these phenomena lie within the realm of thought of traditional, i.e., static, economics.

It by no means follows from the above that a high growth rate is more likely to cause cost inflation than a low growth rate. That is the essential point to grasp. With a high growth rate all the various elements in the economy will be expanding simultaneously—output per head, industrial capacity, etc. Indeed a higher rate of growth may be an antidote to cost inflation. In economic text-books students learn about "diminishing returns" and about "increasing returns". When they read about modern industrial organization, they learn how widespread "increasing returns" are; but in the more theoretical part of their economic study, "increasing returns" are usually forgotten about. They are a more difficult morsel to assimilate into a smoooth and simple theoretical pattern. But when we are dealing with growth, we just cannot afford to forget about "increasing returns". With a higher growth rate "increasing returns" will be a more lively influence than with a lower growth rate. With a higher growth rate increasing returns will make it possible to absorb a *greater* rate of wage increases than it would be with a lower growth rate. Thus a higher growth rate may be cost deflationary, and that may be true, not only in the long-run, but in quite a short period also.

Now where what I have called the traditional theory and growth theory interact is right here. It may be impossible to get the higher growth rate going unless fairly full activity is established. If there is spare capacity, there will not be the motive to make increased investment. But it is the new investment that raises productivity and thereby makes growth possible. Growth and investment interact. The rising market gives the motive for extra investment, and the extra investment, by raising productivity, raises the market. Furthermore, full activity will stimulate the rate of replacement and modernization; and this in turn will stimulate growth.

And so we are left with this. It may be true that a high level of activity has a certain cost-inflationary effect. There are reasons for holding that a higher growth rate has a cost-deflationary effect. But it may be impossible to get the higher growth rate without first establishing a high level of activity. Therefore it may be necessary to accept such cost-inflationary tendency as accompanies a high level of activity in order to get the more lasting and important cost-deflationary effect caused by a higher level of growth. This is the problem that requires thinking through in the United States and the United Kingdom. I fear that the British Treasury is far indeed from applying its mind to it.

It is particularly since 1955 that attempts to combat cost inflation by demand deflation have had an unfortunate effect in causing under-employment and a low growth rate. During 1955 itself there was an investment boom and there were symptoms of demand-inflationary pressure. Reference has already been made in an earlier chapter to the difficulties encountered by the authorities in their attempts to implement a monetary disinflation by traditional methods. However, the authorities proceeded manfully along a number of different lines and met with success. This produced a slight recession in the United Kingdom for three years, in the first two of which most other industrial countries were experiencing a rather strong investment boom. Orders fell off in the winter of 1955–1956 and in the course of 1956 fell below completions. Meanwhile manufacturing production and productivity both fell. It is an age-old doctrine that monetary policy should react promptly to a changed situation. But in 1956 cost inflation was still proceeding. Wage inflation and ex-factory prices proceeded upwards as much as in the preceding year of boom. It was in consequence of this that damping measures were retained until mid-1958, and indeed intensified at the time of the bogus crisis in the summer of 1957. In the earlier period of 1957 there had been very faint signs of revival, but a marked recession occurred thereafter. This went to the extent of causing a noticeable increase in unemployment, and it was doubtless that increase that actuated the authorities to change course in the later part of 1958. Expansionist measures were then adopted over a wide field. The result was very good. Manufacturing output rose by 15 per cent in as many months, much the greater part of this being due to the increased output per person already employed. As there was no special cause operating in 1959 on the supply side, it becomes quite obvious in retrospect that, had enough demand been present, output per person could have pursued an upward course during the preceding three years. The reason why it did not do so was that demand deflation was kept on for too long with a view to combating the cost inflation.

A similar story has been repeated since then. It was just arguable in early 1960 that, if demand continued to increase at its recent pace for the rest of that year, inflationary pressures might begin to develop. There were not, however, any signs of inflationary pressures having already developed. Nonetheless it may have been sensible to introduce restraining measures, with a view to reversing them as soon as it became evident that the economy was not becoming over-heated. This was not done. The restraining measures have been maintained until the present time (1962), and were intensified in the summer of 1961. The consequence has been a fairly marked, and needless, recession. It is worth noting that cost-inflationary symptoms were rather slight during the period of strong growth, but became more marked again during the subsequent period of flatness. By 1961, however, the main preoccupation of the authorities was not cost inflation, but the deterioration in the balance of payments, the causes of which we discussed in Chapter 6.

This brings us to another aspect of traditional doctrine. The Treasury appears to take the view that damping down home demand is good for exports. The experience in the six years after the war may have made a deep impression on the minds of those concerned. In that period we need not doubt that damping down home demand helped exports, because for most of the time total demand was much greater than could be met and exporters had a sellers' market. If one made a gap in home demand, export orders flooded in and filled it. Whether this doctrine is valid in ordinary periods may be doubted. The argument is that, if producers are running slack on the side of home orders, they will look about more keenly for export opportunities and offer prompter delivery. This view of the matter cannot be entirely brushed aside; it may have a limited validity. But most producers are very doubtful of it. They argue that a decline of total turnover raises unit costs of production, makes it more difficult for producers to offer competitive prices in foreign markets, and thus on balance loses them foreign orders. It is possible that both views are correct, according to the particular circumstances of the case. I myself believe that what may be called the producers' view has a much greater scope of application than the Treasury view. The British experience in the last seven years does not provide a scrap of evidence for the idea that exports prosper when the home market is weak. On the contrary, the actual facts of the case are that export orders rose most in the periods when home orders were rising most. This does not by itself prove anything, since, anyhow in certain years, there was a consilience between world prosperity and domestic prosperity. But this was not so in all cases. For instance, 1956 was the year in which home demand was flat and world exports expanded more than they had in 1955. British exports, despite the flatness of home demand, did not do so. At least we can say that the facts give no support to the Treasury view. Nonetheless it appears to be held there as an unquestionable dogma. It is another case of the neglect of "increasing returns" in text-book teachings thirty years ago.

It is, of course, easy to get a short-run improvement in the balance of payments by damping the internal economy, via imports. This happened both in 1956 and in 1961. The decrease in demand for imported materials, owing to a lower factory turnover, is supplemented by a decrease of demand due to de-stocking; if prospects are poor, producers let their stocks run down temporarily. This is not a very fruitful approach to a balance-of-payments problem. Any saving on the import bill through de-stocking is subsequently offset, taking one year with another. As regards the saving through a lower rate of usage of materials, this will be a temporary gain only, if the economy is subsequently able to expand in accordance with its potential and to make good lost ground. It will be a permanent gain only if the economy is unable ever to regain the lost ground, owing to the loss of experience that would have been gained in the period of growth that has been missed out. This is a point that crops up again and again in growth theory. It often happens that the ground lost during two or three years of pause can never be regained because of the experience lost in those years. Thus the gain on the side of imports will be permanent only if a lasting damage has been inflicted on the economy and on exports. And that is not very nice.

There is a deeper problem that arises in relation to imports, which is on that same borderline between traditional theory and growth theory that has already been referred to in relation to cost inflation. It may be the case that if an economy is pushed up to full activity, its "marginal" rate of importation will be higher than its average; that may be because with full activity certain specific goods get into short supply and purchasers look around foreign markets to satisfy the needs that cannot be met at home. It does *not* follow from this that a higher rate of growth would entail a disproportionately high increase of imports. The Treasury has recently published a note[4] which seems to suggest that a given growth of output in the United Kingdom entails a disproportionately large growth of imports. There is not a shred of evidence in the post-war British history to support this view. Whether a high internal growth rate entails a disproportionately higher growth of imports or not depends on entirely different considerations from those affecting the relation between the level of activity at a given moment and the level of imports. The former depends on whether the sphere in which those improvements in production which make growth possible, or, one should more strictly say, which actually constitute growth, occur mainly in export industries or in import-competing industries or in the production of non-tradeable goods.

The same consideration arises here as in the case of a cost inflation. It may not be possible to get a good growth rate without first pushing the economy up to a fairly full level of activity. The latter process may cause a disproportionate increase of imports just as it may cause a disproportionate increase of cost inflation. That may have to be accepted as a once-over setback if one wants to get high growth. It by no means follows that high growth will in itself increase cost inflation—rather, I have argued, the other way round—or will itself increase the propensity to import.

A high growth rate may, however, adversely affect the balance in a different way, namely if growth rates in other countries are lower and there is a consequent difficulty in getting a proportionate expansion of exports.

A thorough university training on these relations should be required before people are admitted to those great centres of power where National Income policies are formed. Otherwise economic policies may be botched. And that does not augur well for the future of the free world, in its competition with an altogether different kind of economic system.

There has been much confusion of thought also on the relation between consumption and investment. There is no doubt that a high

[4] Treasury Bulletin, February 1962.

level of investment is an essential part of the process of a high rate of growth. But a high growth of consumption is also a necessary part of that pattern; and, under free enterprise, a high level of investment is not likely to be achieved unless there is a high growth of consumption. For it is the prospect of a rising market for end products that supplies the necessary motive for investment. It stands out clearly from the figures both in the United States and in the United Kingdom that in the earlier part of the post-war period when the demand for end products (including defence items) was increasing more rapidly, investment increased more than it did in the later period when the demand for end products was increasing less rapidly.

If the economic policy makers desire to see investment take a higher proportion of the National Product, they are not likely to have success by such measures as investment allowances, if the demand for end products is inadequate. If consumption rises and is expected to continue to do so, investment will look after itself; but if consumption is not expected to rise, then such special encouragements for investment are likely to have small effect.

The historic record shows that investment and consumption normally rise and fall together. An increase of consumption can, of course, in certain circumstances, be a rival to an increase of investment, if initially the economy is absolutely fully employed; but if it is, investment is likely to be running at a high level in any case. For considerable parts of the post-war period neither the United States nor the United Kingdom economy have been fully active, so that this rivalry should have been regarded as irrelevant. During the war there was, of course, such a rivalry, and in the United Kingdom for a fairly extended period after the war also, and in those circumstances it was perfectly sensible to reduce consumption with a view to increasing investment, although for reasons already explained I thought that the British authorities went too far in this direction in the post-war quinquennium.

A very interesting case arose in the United Kingdom in the winter of 1955–1956, when the economy was in fact fairly fully employed. There was an investment boom and investment orders were running far ahead of possible deliveries. It seemed, therefore, sensible to take monetary and other measures likely to reduce investment orders, so as to reduce the further piling up of backlogs and to help exports. But it seemed no less sensible to seek to reduce consumption, since aggregate demand was at that time excessive, in order to release man-power for investment. This was done. The experiment seemed sensible, and yet it failed. Investment was expanding rapidly at that time, and was presumably expanding as quickly as it could, given inevitable technical bottlenecks. The labour released from durable consumer goods in consequence of measures taken to reduce the demand for them, did not find its way into the investment goods industries, but filled vacancies in catering trades, etc., or went off the labour market. Thus, despite the full employment, the abatement in the demand for labour for consumer goods did not in fact help investment, although there may have been some release of steel at that time, which did. Meanwhile the damping of consumption caused investment orders to turn down fairly promptly, and this in turn led, after there had been time for factories to be completed and the backlog to be worked off, to a reduction of investment by manufacturing industry. I am confident that, if the damping of consumption had been less, or anyhow not so protracted, in 1956, there would have been more investment by manufacturing industry between 1957 and 1959.

It is desirable to have a level of investment sufficient to get a modernization of productive processes, in accordance with the most recent technological findings. If investment has been below the optimum level, this has doubtless been partly due to a too restrictive monetary policy, but it has also been partly due to the fact that the authorities have not perceived that a necessary condition for encouraging investment is to allow consumption to grow at an appropriate rate. They have also tended from time to time to underrate the amount of disguised unemployment inside factories. To this trend of policy, which may be said to arise from a fallacy, there has been added a recurrent propaganda on the part of the do-gooders. In earlier times economists found support among congenital Puritans. In those days the sovereign economic remedies were to work hard, save hard and live sparely; these maxims were naturally warmly welcomed by the Puritans. Then came the day when it was pointed out that these maxims were not alone enough, since they might lead to the total unemployment of the whole economy. Demand must be allowed to flourish within limits, in order that people should be given the incentive to produce and be kept at work. But the Puritans have been coming back into their own. "We quite understand", they say, "that some increase in demand must be allowed, and that will be all right by us so long as it is a demand for more investment." And since the ancient traditions of the British Treasury have their affinity with Puritanism, the investment doctrine is welcome in that quarter also. What must not be allowed is any idea that to increase consumption would be a good thing. I am not at all sure that it is not this old puritanical streak, operating doubtless at the level of the unconscious mind, that has caused the British authorities persistently to underestimate disguised unemployment. Only admit that that exists, and you might be forced to admit that people could be allowed to consume more, an admission that can never be dragged out by argument from those who disapprove of pleasure as such.

Actually the United Kingdom has not been doing badly in the matter of investment. Its annual rate of net investment (constant prices) rose nearly $2\frac{1}{2}$ times between 1948 and 1961. It is doubtful whether so great a further increase of investment in the next dozen years could be put to good use. Perhaps it could be. But it certainly will not occur unless consumption is allowed to rise much more quickly than it has been rising in the last decade.

Proposals for a tax credit on investment are at present before the American public. Since the war the British have had a system of accelerated allowances on capital consumption. More recently there has been introduced what is called an "investment allowance" which is in fact a subsidy. The accelerated allowances on capital consumption merely meant getting in advance tax relief that would be due to come in anyhow by the time that the equipment was finally written off; but the investment allowance is something in addition to the ordinary (or expedited) allowances for capital consumption. This investment allowance is presumably designed to encourage investment. It is therefore a curious thing that through most of the period interest rates have been kept at a high level by monetary policy. It seems odd to encourage investment by a subsidy at the cost of the taxpayer, while at the same time discouraging investment by a high rate of interest, which is also largely at the expense of the taxpayer owing to the high level of the

National Debt. We have seen that the war was successfully financed at 3 per cent. At March 1948 the total National Debt was £25.6 billion and the interest charge upon it was £500 million. In 1962 the total National Debt was £28 billion—not a very large increase—while the interest charge was £660 million. The main object of a high rate of interest is presumably to thin out investment projects. Thus we have two contradictory policies in simultaneous operation.

And this brings one to a centre of some very confused thinking, which has been detrimental to British policy. When one asks why the rate of interest has to be kept so high, it is stated that this is because of the high level of investment demand—more may be thrown in here about world-wide investment demand—in relation to available savings. It may even be suggested that the interest rate has not been "kept" high at all, but has just risen to its present height through the operation of market forces. Although it would be a very good thing if the United States and the United Kingdom did much more for the developing countries by way of investment, loans and aid—they might well double their existing contributions—these claims on investible funds are not large by comparison with the internal demands of the industrial countries themselves. Whatever the authorities may say, it is their own monetary policy that is clearly responsible for the increase of interest rates in the United Kingdom.

For a period after the war there may have been some deficiency in personal saving, but this was well covered by surpluses on government revenue account; and it was not in the earlier period that we had a high interest rate. The rise in the interest rate was notably in the later part of the period, when the ratio of personal savings to investment was growing. By the saving and investment doctrine the interest rate should have been falling at the very time that it was rising. This view about the necessity for a high interest rate because of the high level of investment in the modern world may be entirely dismissed; but it may be noted that it is not confined to the austere ranks of the British Treasury, but widely current among bankers and business men (and I have even seen it in United States publications), who are often unhappily prone to take up a saying of this sort, because it sounds plausible, without any reference to the facts of the case.

The second column of Table 43 is a statement of hard fact. The quantity of money component of the first column is also a statement of hard fact, but the figures in the column are subject to such minor errors as may arise in the compilation of National Income statistics. The third column is not so secure, since there may be a larger margin of error in the compilation of personal saving.

TABLE 43

DETERMINATION OF INTEREST RATE

1. Modern theory: as figures in Column (i) fall, the rate of interest should rise. (Broadly verified.)
2. Older so-called "orthodox" theory: as figures in column (iii) rise, the rate of interest should fall. (Not verified.)

Year	Quantity of money (Bank Deposits) divided by the money value of Gross Domestic Expenditure at market prices (1938=100)	Long-term rate of interest (percentage) (1938=3.38 per cent)	Personal and governmental savings divided by gross capital formation (1938=100)
	(i)	(ii)	(iii)
1946	151.4	2.60	37.33
1947	157.0	2.76	122.8
1948	133.8	3.21	126.1
1949	141.0	3.30	117.1
1950	120.8	3.54	107.1
1951	104.2	3.78	114.4
1952	100.5	4.23	99.10
1953	96.58	4.08	99.38
1954	94.95	3.75	95.83
1955	90.01	4.17	92.41
1956	79.68	4.73	113.2
1957	77.02	4.98	112.9
1958	73.41	4.98	109.2
1959	76.23	4.82	105.2
1960	74.13	5.42	115.4
1961	72.88	6.20	126.8

The post-war easy money period stands out clearly in the first column, with a substantial tightening up between 1949 and 1951; then the tightening proceeds more moderately until we come to the severe tightening between 1955 and 1956, after which again there is further tightening. Although there are minor deviations in particular years, since we are bound to allow for some other influences operating upon the interest rate, there is a general conformity of the interest rate figures with what the theory that the rate of interest is governed by the ratio of the quantity of money to the work that it has to do, would lead one to expect. First we have the rates in the immediate post-war period, which were below the 1938 level. There is an accelerated increase between 1949 and 1952, and again after 1955.

On the whole, personal and government savings together relative to investment requirements appear to have been in excess of the 1938 level for most of the time. It is to be noted that company saving is not included in the supply of saving since, if all saving were included, saving would always be equal to investment and the idea of a varying balance between supply and demand would be meaningless; company saving is the residual. A strong rise in the saving ratio is visible after 1955, a period in which the rate of interest was rising still more strongly. There was a particularly notable increase in saving in 1960 and 1961 and a particularly notable rise in the rate of interest. In both years the increase in personal saving *alone* was greater than the whole of the increase of investment.

Of course one reason why there is so high a rate of interest has been because of the British problem of the external balance of payments. The monetary authorities were having to tailor down the money supply in order to maintain the high interest rate. This keeps cropping up. A high rate of interest is required to attract capital, both short-term and long-term, from abroad, or to prevent it leaving these shores. There are all sorts of curious delicacies, complexes and inhibitions in the discussion of economic matters. While in one part of their mind the authorities may know quite well that we have to have a high interest rate because we are not willing to deal with the balance-of-payments problem in some other way, yet in another part of their mind they do not like to admit this. If they did, one would turn to them and say: "There you are, you are stunting the growth of the British economy by a high interest rate because of the external balance; that is something that we sincerely hoped had been outlawed as a measure of policy when the war was over; it seems to belong to the worst old days of the gold standard and deflation." But before replying to this they have taken refuge in the other part of their mind. "Oh, no," they say, "the high interest rate has nothing to do with that; it is simply an aspect of the world-wide shortage of investible funds." In fact, all rubbish.

I believe that the high rate of interest has been a very important factor holding down the British growth rate. Alongside this is the persistent policy of restraining consumption. The most fundamental objection to carrying out a given investment project is that the market is not large enough to absorb its output. If that obstacle is present, the project is ruled out of court. But there may be another obstacle, namely a financial limitation. This may tilt the balance against a project if there is any doubt about market expectations, and for a number of firms may make the project impossible. One should not ignore the financial side as a factor limiting growth. It is said that there are not many firms who are deterred by the rate of interest considered as an arithmetical quantity, the cost of which one works out and balances against the prospective returns of a project. Such arithmetical computation may weigh in certain cases and there have been well-known discussions about how important (or unimportant) this is. But, if the high interest rate is something that is being enforced by the authorities by monetary policy, as is the case in the United Kingdom at present, then it is bound to be accompanied by a general financial stringency. The capital market is an imperfect one. Firms have their customary channels for raising money, and if these are blocked they may look round somewhere else; and if, when they look round somewhere else, they find nothing that can be conveniently done, they have to give up their projects. Monetary tightness reduces the facility of raising money through all the different channels, including trade credit, an important element.

This discouragement of investment is undoubtedly bad for growth. It is on the occasion of investment that the firm tries out the latest kind of equipment, and it is the use of such equipment that is the source of growth in the economy. Furthermore, when there is financial stringency, the rate of replacement may be slowed down. Replacement gives another opportunity for introducing more modern and efficient methods of production. It may be that there are many giant businesses which are above financial considerations. But there are many medium-sized firms which are not; and for the growth of the economy as a whole we need these to be moving forward also, wherever progressive elements are to be found.

The question of the balance between personal savings and investment requirements is important also in relation to the Budget surplus. This brings us back to the problem that cropped up in relation to the nationalization of industry. The fact that the public have lost their taste for governmental stock and that the British government has to find large sums every year for the capital outlay of the nationalized industries, leads the authorities to hope that the Chancellor of the Exchequer may cover as much as he possibly can of the sums needed for this capital outlay out of the taxation that he imposes. The Bank of England knows that it will be difficult for it to keep its grip on the monetary situation if it has to arrange for funding a large amount of the National Debt all the time. It is perfectly right in wishing to keep its grip on the monetary situation. But the fact remains that, if the flow of personal savings is rising relatively to investment requirements, and if to those personal savings the Chancellor of the Exchequer adds a large block of compulsory saving in the form of an above-the-line surplus, this is bound to have a strongly deflationary effect on the economy as a whole. This tendency to have Budget surpluses, when from a business cycle point of view they are altogether inappropriate, has been another factor holding down the British growth rate.

The figures for 1960 and 1961 reflect the strong rise (in fact a doubling) of personal saving. The Chancellor of the Exchequer has, nonetheless, thought it expedient to maintain a large Budget surplus. The combined effect has been a squeeze on business profits. The view of the authorities that damping the home market encourages exports has already been discussed. Surely a severe squeeze on profits must be bad for exports, since in many cases it reduces the possibility of investment, which might in its turn reduce costs of production.

In the United States there has also been an upward tendency in personal saving in recent years, although not so strong a one as in the United Kingdom, and more spread out. It is probably the case that the rise in the saving–investment ratio has been responsible for the profit squeeze that has been occurring in the United States also. It is arguable that not enough purchasing power will be returned into the circuit in the demand for goods and services, unless the United States institutes a "Federal Capital Budget". This would entitle the Federal government to borrow. This procedure need not involve any increase in Federal government spending; indeed it would be quite consistent with a decrease. But the Capital Budget would make it possible, by the remission of taxation, to increase disposable personal incomes, and thus raise the demand for goods and services, both on consumer and investment account, and thereby also terminate the squeeze on corporate profits.

The foregoing has suggested that a rather considerable revision is needed in the fundamental economic theory that lies behind Treasury thinking and policy, if the United Kingdom is to succeed in achieving an adequate growth rate. New thinking is required about the relation of demand inflation to cost inflation; about the relation of both to growth, as distinguished from and contrasted with the high level of employment at a given moment of time; about the relation of growth to the external balance of payments; about the relation of the growth of consumption to that of investment; about the relation of the tendency towards personal saving to the Budget surplus; and about the deleterious effect of National Debt funding at times not appropriate from a business cycle point of view. It is my contention that wrong thinking about all these matters was the cause of the United Kingdom having had lower economic growth than the countries of Continental Europe in the last few years.

It is fair to add here that the best thinking in the world cannot promote growth, if there is an overriding imperative that activity must be damped by whatever amount is required to reduce the import of materials sufficiently to secure an even balance of payments. It is only fair, therefore, that I should disclose that in my opinion the United Kingdom should solve this problem by the temporary re-imposition of import restrictions. Incidentally it may be observed that the policy of damping home activity may not be effective in restoring the balance of payments, unless carried so far as to increase unemployment to a level that would be politically unacceptable. On principle I am strongly opposed to import restrictions, and in the past I have urged that the United Kingdom should push on to the greatest possible extent with import liberalization, even if this meant taking risks with the reserve. It is against the background of favouring a liberal commercial policy that I urge restrictions in this particular phase. It is for this reason that from time to time I have stressed the point that basically the British adverse balance is due to the *financial* losses owing to the war and its consequences; that these financial losses involved the need for a great structural readjustment, i.e., an increase of exports without a countervailing increase of imports; and that the United Kingdom has already achieved five-sixths of the task of this structural readjustment, which is of a size unparalleled in other countries since the war, and quite possibly in modern history. Import restriction should not normally be a part of a policy for balanced growth. But the correction of such a huge structural maladjustment is something that takes the British case outside these normal rules.

All import restriction is unneighbourly. But the formal import restriction of unneeded goods is likely to be less unneighbourly than the *de facto* reduction of imports consequential upon the damping of domestic activity. For the former are more likely to affect richer countries and the latter to affect poorer countries. This is a very fundamental point, one indeed affecting the viability of the free world as a whole; and men of goodwill should press hard for its incorporation in the code of conduct approved by the GATT. Already the free world has suffered substantially from the United Kingdom's having brought fewer materials than it would require, if fully active, in order to comply with the GATT's hostility to the imposition of formal restrictions on the import of junk.

To return to the changes in basic thinking that are required, one may wonder what will actuate these. The initiative can hardly be expected to come from the Cabinet. Can it come from the National Economic Development Council? Will its influence be strong enough to avail against the deeply entrenched position of the Treasury?

How might a change of thinking come in the Treasury itself? It may be difficult for very busy men, always burdened with great responsibilities, to refurbish their ideas in the light of new doctrines, which they have no time to study profoundly, which are often not presented in an assimilable form, and which quite sensible people, if laymen in economic matters, might find it hard to distinguish from airy fairy nothings. Looking at it in this way, one might despair of the needed change occurring.

The tragic thing is that if it does not occur, the United Kingdom may sink down and fail to play the part that could be so important for sustaining the strength and growth of the free world.

Might the influence come from the United States? Ideas from that source are always welcomed in the United Kingdom. I have already mentioned the meeting of President Kennedy with Prime Minister Macmillan, the outcome of which was so disappointing, because it failed to promote a joint policy of growth. One has to acknowledge the possibility that the ultimate policy makers in the United States itself are, despite its entirely different set up, and for different causes, also sunk to some extent in obsolescent economic theory. The challenge is to economists in both countries, not only to sharpen their thoughts, but also to translate them into language that is understandable by intelligent men of affairs.

CHAPTER 9

Outlook for the Future

I. GOVERNMENT WITH A "NEW LOOK"?

While the patient scholar is slogging away with his pen, political events may move more rapidly. The last chapter, which was written in April 1962, is rather pessimistic in regard to the possibility of a change of policy in the United Kingdom. Seeking round for some new source of inspiration, I wrote, "The initiative can hardly be expected to come from the Cabinet." And now (in July 1962) it appears that the Cabinet is, after all, in the process of initiating a new line of policy. There has been a change in the all-important office of Chancellor of the Exchequer. Since the previous Chancellor had been discharging his duties efficiently from a technical point of view and commanded the respect of his Party, one must believe that the cause of the change has been a realization that the previous policy was not achieving the results expected of it, and that something different is required. It would be premature to assume that all will now go forward quite differently. New men may come into office bringing fresh vision, but the remorseless persistency and the plausibility of the Treasury in bringing arguments against a change of course may succeed in quenching the ardour of the new Ministers. That has happened before.

The danger that the new initiative might peter out is made the greater by the fact that the problems involved are difficult and subtle, and that the implementation of a new policy may require more drastic decisions than the newcomers realize, before which they may in due course quail.

A few words must first be said about the scope of possible changes. There is no reason to suppose that any change will be, or ought to be, made in the general policy that has come to be called an "incomes policy", which may be said to have been set going by the former Chancellor, Mr. Selwyn Lloyd. On the contrary, if general policy becomes more expansionist, then an "incomes policy" will be more needed than it was before. The idea behind the incomes policy is that there is a specific factor causing inflation on the cost side, and that this cannot be eliminated merely by damping down the demand for goods and services. Accordingly it has seemed needful to approach the inflation problem at the grass roots by securing co-operation on the labour side in implementing a more rational wages policy. The existence of an incomes policy of this sort is tantamount to a repudiation of the view that, if you keep aggregate demand in balance with the supply potential of the economy, the problem of inflation will not arise.

It appeared at the time of the inception of his incomes policy that Mr. Selwyn Lloyd did not handle the matter altogether tactfully. A new Chancellor might repair mistakes that were made in this regard. As well as more tact, a much more far-flung initiative will be required, extending beyond the Trades Union Congress, and dealing with particular Unions, if a more rational wages policy is to be hammered out, as explained in an earlier chapter. It must be stressed that this is *not* the main significance of the recent Cabinet changes. It is hoped that the significance lies in a decision to adopt a more expansionist policy on the *demand* side.

Mr. Selwyn Lloyd will have lasting credit for having brought into being the National Economic Development Council, to assess, on a fairly long-term basis, the potentialities of the British economy for growth. It has already provided what it regards as a proper target for the growth in the National Income of 4 per cent a year over a five-year period. This is in line with the target set by the Council of Ministers of the OECD group of countries of a 4.1 per cent increase over a ten-year period, in its communiqué issued in November 1961.

While the government will doubtless rely much on the further assessments and recommendations of the National Economic Development Council, it is too much to hope that these can be forthcoming quickly, since it is desired that, when made, they should carry the weight that rather extensive research can alone give them. It is desirable, by contrast, that the switch to a more expansionist monetary and general economic policy should come quickly.

It is appropriate to ask what kind of programme an advocate of a policy of greater growth would recommend. Of prime importance are policies in the monetary and fiscal fields. The United Kingdom has the advantage of other possible weapons of policy (nationalized industries, consumer credit, etc.), but these are, in the last analysis, subsidiary to the monetary and fiscal weapons.

The long-term rate of interest is now (July 1962) running at about 6 per cent. This high rate is directly attributable to the curtailment of the money supply, as shown in Table 43 (p. 201). I myself believe that the United Kingdom should aim at moving towards the traditional 3 per cent which was shown to be compatible with the vast expansion of the British economy during most of the nineteenth century. This low rate did not lead to inflation; on the contrary, taking boom and recession years together, prices were falling on average in that century. Advocacy of 3 per cent might be taken to be an extreme view. It would be more in the spirit of caution and compromise—although these qualities are not always virtues in relation to the matter in hand—to set a 3½ per cent long-term interest rate as the target for the years ahead. This does not mean that we should seek to establish 3½ per cent immediately. It would probably be desirable for the change to come fairly gradually. (It may be noted, however, that the change from 5 per cent to 3 per cent came rather quickly, when it did at long last come, fourteen years after the First World War.)

The policy of reducing the long-term rate of interest can be carried out in a perfectly normal way by increasing the money supply, which is now so drastically restricted, by open-market operations on the part of the Bank of England. This would be entirely contrary to the policy of recent years of unloading government bonds on to the market at the greatest possible rate, whenever opportunity offered. The reasons for the anxious desire to unload were explained fully in Chapter 5. Thus the new policy would in existing circumstances be very much against the grain. And this is one of the many instances of the need that a new Chancellor, if he is genuinely bent on an expansionist policy, should be rather drastically resolute in refusing to accept the various counter arguments put up to him.

It is arguable that at an appropriate moment the Chancellor should announce on some important occasion, and with all the weight at his command, that in his considered view the United Kingdom long-term rate of interest should, in due course, fall to $3\frac{1}{2}$ per cent. If it was known that he was bent on an expansionist policy, a belief would be generated that he would succeed in due course in realizing his objective as regards the interest rate. This would at once give a strong lift to the prices of government bonds, and the authorities might be anxious, quite rightly, to prevent the upward movement proceeding too fast, in a way that might cause an unhealthy speculative boom. They could counter this by selling securities. A mere statement of this kind by the Chancellor would give them the opportunity of selling securities in far greater quantity and at higher prices than they have been able to do for many years past.

A paradox of a rather acute kind would then arise. Sales of bonds by the authorities on a large scale would inevitably reduce the "money supply", which on the surface would appear to be exactly the opposite of what one wanted to do in order to implement a more expansionist monetary policy. It is expedient at this point to remind the reader of the mechanics of the matter. If sales of government bonds are from the Banking Department of the Bank of England, this reduces the money supply directly (the normal effect of open market sales in any country). The reduction in the cash basis of the clearing banks then compels them to cut down their lendings of different kinds. Alternatively, government bonds may be sold from governmental capital funds, including that of the Issue Department of the Bank of England. In this case the gap made by the sales has to be filled in with Treasury Bills. This in turn must have the effect, until the next Budget, of restricting the flow of tender Treasury Bills into the market. This in turn will cause a squeeze on the liquidity of the clearing banks. Their "liquidity ratio" will tend to fall below 30 per cent, and for that reason they will be compelled to reduce their lending.

Nonetheless, despite all this, it is unlikely that the course of events outlined above would have a net deflationary effect. The expansion of the economy, which results from the increase in orders for goods and services placed, depends in the short period on two causes, namely (1) opinion about future demand and (2) the availability of finance. The knowledge that the government was bent on a more expansionist policy, together with a statement by the Chancellor about $3\frac{1}{2}$ per cent long-term interest, would convince people that demand was likely to expand. This new opinion about the future of demand might well have the consequence of a substantial and sufficient rate of increase of orders, even if, paradoxically, the money supply was at the same time becoming tighter. *In fine*, the expansionist forces released in (1) above would probably outweigh depressive forces (2) owing to a decrease in the money supply for the time being.

And then another factor would come into play. A rise in government bond prices, which would doubtless be accompanied or followed by a rise in other security prices also, would be a factor increasing overall liquidity in the manner correctly described by the Radcliffe Report (which was faulty in other respects), and this might well outweigh the decrease of liquidity due to a contraction in the money supply.

Accordingly I believe that a statement of this kind by the Chancellor would quickly cause an increase of orders, even during a period in which the money supply was falling. This is a paradox; but a paradox is often true. This pattern of phenomena would obtain for a short period only. The effect of the Chancellor's statement on bond prices would, in due course, tend to wear off, and at that point the authorities would have to be ready to buy in the open market. It might be at this very point that the sharp clash between deeply-ingrained instincts and a correct monetary policy of expansion would come. This is where the Chancellor would have to keep a vigilant eye and exert to the full and with drastic resolution the authority inherent in his position. The Bank of England would tend to feel that the economy had been expanding well and was even in danger—that constant bugbear—of becoming "overheated" and to think the moment most inappropriate for an increase in the money supply. Yet that would be the very point at which an increase would be essential, viz., after the immediate impact effect of the announcement of a more expansionist policy had worn off. In succession to the psychological booster provided by the Chancellor's statement, a real booster in the form of easier money would be required.

It is to be noted that the yield on government bonds, having for the first time in history fallen below a well-accredited index (*Financial Times*) of the yield on industrial common stock (equities) in the summer of 1959, regained the latter level on July 19, 1962. A welcome revival of "gilt-edged" stock has in fact been proceeding for some time. But both yields are much too high for a mature economy such as the British, with personal savings running at so high a level, as already noted.

Then there is the question of fiscal policy. A large "above-the-line" surplus (£433 million) was provided in the Budget of April 1962. Personal savings are contributing amply enough to finance those capital expenditures for which the government is responsible in its "below-the-line" Budget. To provide for them out of taxation is to cover the same items twice over, to cut down the expenditure flow progressively and to cause a squeeze on profit, which has been a marked feature of the British economy recently. It is needful to reduce this surplus to much more modest dimensions. This is, of course, subject to the behaviour of capital formation and personal saving in the near future. If other expansionist policies caused a spectacular upturn of investment without causing a much greater flow of personal savings, then it might turn out that a reduction of the Budget surplus ought to be delayed.

Per contra, it might be argued that, from the point of view of expansion, one should not wait to bring the over-balanced Budget to an end. This is analogous to the American problem in 1962 as to whether tax cuts should be introduced immediately, in order to prevent a recession, or could be allowed to wait. The British constitutional procedure being different, the reduction of taxes would require a "Special Budget". Hitherto Special Budgets have only been used to damp down the economy, when it was conceived to be getting overheated; it would be a splendid thing to have a Special Budget for the opposite purpose!

The pattern of correct policy may be summarized as follows. The monetary tap should be turned on at once, by the normal method of "open-market operations". This would cause a quick increase of orders and, one hopes, a fairly quick increase of orders on account of capital formation. This could be supplemented by a statement by the Chancellor, desiring a 3½ per cent interest rate in due course, which would by itself have a strongly expansionist effect. By contrast, a mere statement by the Chancellor that he was in favour of an expanding economy, without mentioning anything so specific as a 3½ per cent interest rate, would be of no effect at all. We have had statements like that before; in the United States also. A specific statement might, paradoxically, promote a fairly rapid forward movement of the economy in such wise that it could be accompanied, without injury, by a decrease in the money supply, while the authorities were seizing the opportunity of a favourable market for government bonds. That phase would be short-term only. After that the money supply would have to be increased. The authorities should be watching very carefully to see the effect of monetary easement and, if this seemed insufficient, be prepared to introduce a Special Budget, producing a fiscal easement. I have no doubt that under such influence the British economy could show a better record of growth than the economies of the Continental European countries.

Of course there would be a price to pay. I have already stated that, in order to prevent a cost-push inflation, an incomes policy must be pushed forward on a wider front and with more imagination.

And then there is the more serious question of the external balance. We may divide this into the fundamental balance and the question of short-term capital.

A. Fundamental Balance

The United Kingdom balance has been apparently satisfactory in the first quarter of 1962. This must again be subdivided into (1) the current and (2) the capital account.

1. The current account in the first quarter was slightly favourable. Unfortunately there may be factors in this situation that are transitory only. There was an upsurge on account of the balance on "services", not counting government expenditures. This was unexpected. Details are not yet available, but the increase was said to be mainly on the side of interest, dividends and profits remitted to the United Kingdom. This improvement constituted an increase of £44 million over the first quarter of 1961. This, if simply multiplied by 4, would give an annual rate of increase of £176 million, which, if sustained, would go far to rectify the British balance of payments. But such receipts are notoriously unpredictable and it would be most dangerous to rely on the level of the balance on "services" being sustained in line with that in the first quarter. There may have been something fortuitous about this sudden upsurge of receipts.

Next we have to take the fact that imports have been damped, both owing to the lower level of industrial put-through consequent upon the Chancellor's restraining measures of July 1961 and also owing to some de-stocking, also consequent upon those measures. A mere cessation of de-stocking, which is inevitable, will increase the import bill. It will be increased also if the United Kingdom does not remain for ever at its recent low level of activity. *A fortiori* the import bill will rise, if the economy becomes more expansionist. Here may be mentioned the point, referred to in Chapter 8,[1] that, although there is no evidence for the view, or reason to suppose, that a higher growth rate of the economy entails a disproportionately higher rate of increase of imports, there may be some reason to suppose that the jacking up of the economy from a slack level to a fully employed level does entail a once-over increase in the rate of importation. When the economy is fully active, buyers may find it more difficult to get their needs met from home sources and therefore look around more keenly among foreign sources of supply.

On the other hand, exports rose steadily in the first half of 1962, and many hope that this rise will be continued. While this is a favourable factor of some importance, it is to be feared that the results so far achieved are not sufficient to outweigh the adverse factors already referred to. In the second quarter of 1962 seasonally-adjusted exports were 4 per cent up on the 1961 average and 4.7 per cent up on the seasonally-adjusted exports of the second quarter of 1961. It is to be noted, however, that about 1 per cent of the increase was due to the unsatisfactory factor of higher prices charged. While this increase of exports probably exceeds any increase that would be required on the import side, with National Income growing at 4 per cent a year, it is not sufficient *also* to make good the losses on the total current account that will occur, when the temporary favourable factors affecting imports are removed.

2. The United Kingdom capital account has recently been roughly in balance. For many years the authorities argued, I would say correctly, that the current account should show a favourable balance of some £300 million or £400 million a year, as a minimum, to cover debt repayments due by the United Kingdom, and also grants, aid and investments in the developing countries. This implies that there would nor-

[1] Pages 195–6.

mally be a negative balance (£300 million or £400 million) in the capital account. The reason why this has not happened recently is the very large inflow of American capital into the United Kingdom. I regard this as an unhealthy situation as well as being precarious. As for unhealthiness, if one places the United Kingdom on the spectrum of countries in the free world, from richest to poorest, or from most mature in respect of existing capital formation and the level of personal savings to the least mature, I suggest that the United Kingdom should be a net exporter of capital. If the inflow of American capital is to be welcomed, that should only be on the basis that the United Kingdom is itself exporting a *larger* amount of capital. I cannot regard an equality of inflow and outflow as a satisfactory situation. Furthermore, since, for reasons already reiterated, the United Kingdom is destined to continue to have some balance-of-payments difficulties for some time, there is danger in acquiring a rising amount of commitments in respect of profit to be remitted home on foreign (presumably mainly American) capital. However high the rate of inflow of fresh capital, the profit that has to be remitted on the whole corpus of foreign capital invested in the country is bound to overtop the inflow within a fairly short period. It might be said that the British position would not deteriorate so long as its export of capital, with the consequent expectation of receipts of profit, matched the inflow. But it is to be remembered that part of the so-called outflow of capital from the United Kingdom consists of the repayment of loans at very low interest rates and another substantial part of the outflow (governmental loans, etc.) will also yield only low interest. It is to be feared that, if the inflow and outflow match, there will be a net burden on the United Kingdom balance of payments in the fairly near future.

Then there is the question of precariousness. Recent events in Wall Street (July 1962) cannot but cause anxiety. It is cordially hoped in the United Kingdom that the American authorities will pursue policies which will offset any tendency of the Wall Street declines to affect the United States economy as a whole, and will cause a stronger growth rate in that economy. But, if that should not happen, then there could easily be a rather quick drying up of the inflow of capital from the United States. If American business is being temporarily weakened at home, whether in respect of profit and loss or in respect of liquidity, there is bound to be a decline in projects for building factories or acquiring existing firms in such a country as the United Kingdom.

Putting these things together, I should suppose that the United Kingdom should not regard itself in proper external balance unless the balance on current account is running at plus £200 million per annum, as a minimum, taking good and bad years together.

The favourable events in the first quarter of 1962 do not yet incline me to reverse the view expressed earlier in this book, that the United Kingdom still has about one-sixth of the journey to go, to complete its structural readjustments in relation to exports and imports as required by the external losses on the financial side due to the Second World War.

Some might take this situation as rightfully inhibiting the pursuit of any growth policy by the United Kingdom. No economist who believes in growth would agree to that. I submit that growth should be the first priority. While everything should be done, including a daring policy in relation to the depletion of reserves, to avoid having to reimpose temporary import restrictions, nonetheless I submit that such restrictions are preferable to a renewed damping of the economy. Let us suppose that a vigorous policy for growth is pursued, stopping only at the point at which demand-inflationary pressure begins to arise, and that the consequent increase of import requirements, together with the cessation of some transitory favourable factors, uncovers once again a weak external balance. What do the authorities then do? Do they once again, in line with numerous precedents during the last ten years, reimpose damping measures? Of course they should do that if the economy has really become subject to an excessive internal demand for goods and services. But, supposing that this situation has not arisen and that the only trouble is that a weak external balance is uncovered. I submit that no growth economist would vote in favour of damping measures merely to avoid the unpleasant necessity of having to impose import restrictions. The United States has shown a marvellous example in refraining from import restrictions during years of heavy external deficit. But it must be remembered that, for reasons connected with two world wars, the United States had a much larger margin of spare reserve.

It would perhaps be vexatious for the United Kingdom to impose import restrictions at once, since the external weakness has been temporarily covered up. But the machinery for imposing such restrictions should be created at once. There would have been difficulty in the recent period in imposing import restrictions owing to a lack of administrative machinery, even if at the top level the decision had been taken to do so; that defect should be remedied now. The United Kingdom should refrain as long as possible from imposing these restrictions, but at the same time should have it clearly in mind that such restrictions are to be preferred to holding the economy down below its potential growth rate. That is a point at which an expansionist Cabinet might come into conflict with the entrenched views of the Civil Service.

One of the things that has to be considered in this connection is the bad-neighbourliness of imposing import restrictions. There has been some most confused thinking on this point. To put the matter in the simplest terms, when a critical external situation arises there are two alternatives. One may reduce the import bill by damping down domestic activity and, by consequence, import requirements; or one may impose direct import restrictions on some finished manufactures that are not strictly necessary. The point that is overlooked is that *both* these ways of restoring the external balance are unneighbourly. If there is an imperative necessity for cutting down the import bill by, say, £300 million a year, foreigners are hurt, at this stage we may say equally, whether £300 million is knocked off the import bill by slack working and diminished import requirements for materials or components, or £300 million is knocked off the import bill by direct import restriction on unneeded finished goods. But in fact, from the point of view of good-neighbourliness, the former policy, i.e., damping home activity, is much more destructive. For the victims of that policy are mainly primary producers, often developing countries, often poor countries, while the victims of the latter policy, i.e., direct restriction, are much more likely to be rich countries. Furthermore, the reduction of imports of materials is more likely to have an effect on world prices, and therefore, while hitting the primary producers directly, will hit the industrial countries also, indirectly. Primary producers have been having rather a bad time in recent years; I believe that a careful analysis would show that the United Kingdom policy alone (of frequently damping down its own activity) has had a substantial effect on the prosperity of primary producers round the world.

I do not believe that the principles of the GATT, whether according to the intentions in the original agreement or otherwise, make it mandatory upon a country to reduce its own activity below the optimum level before seeking to rectify its external balance by import restrictions. The latter are allowed to meet the case of an adverse balance of payments.

The GATT naturally frowns upon any import restrictions. It has in mind that these are not the right answer to inflationary pressure; deflationary measures should be adopted to counter that, and these might make the import restrictions unnecessary. Or the GATT may fear that some balance-of-payments difficulty, which could be overcome in other ways, might be used as a mere excuse for the imposition of import restrictions, which might really be desired for protectionist reasons or for other reasons tending to frustrate the purposes of the GATT. All this plays upon the tender consciences of the British authorities; it makes them particularly reluctant to go to the GATT, and they are also reluctant, of course, to take action that would be a bad example to the rest of the world. It has for long been British policy to encourage the greatest amount of freedom of trade, both in their own interest and for ideological reasons. All this is quite praiseworthy so long as it does not have the result, when the crunch comes, of the authorities preferring to damp down the economy rather than impose import restrictions. I am convinced that, from the wider point of view of the free world as a whole, it is less harmful for the United Kingdom to impose import restrictions on unneeded manufactures than to damp down its economy, thereby inflicting direct injury on primary producers, tending to reduce primary product prices, and so inflicting indirect injury on the industrial countries also.

B. Short-Term Capital

From 1960 to 1962 the United Kingdom attracted much short-term capital by having a high Bank Rate. This was needed to offset the deficit in the fundamental balance. If an easier money policy is introduced, aiming at a reduction in the long-term rate of interest, it will be difficult to hold short-term rates at a high level. Furthermore it has appeared recently that what is in essence short-term capital, that is, capital liable to quick withdrawal, has been moving under the influence of long-term rates as well as short-term rates; one may seek to get the benefit of the high yield of bonds for a short period, when it is thought that the bonds are not likely to fall in capital value. *In fine*, some apparently long-term capital is in fact short-term.

A reduction of rates in the United Kingdom, whether long-term or short-term, might cause a withdrawal of short-term capital on a substantial scale. This could cause the authorities alarm and make them agitate with the Chancellor to revert to a tighter money policy; thus the whole growth policy could be frustrated. This is yet another crucial point at which the Chancellor might have to present a very firm front. He should be prepared to let the gold reserve run down to a low level and exert full drawing rights on the International Monetary Fund. The spectacle of falling reserves might give rise to a "critical" situation and lead to a further outflow of capital.

However, such an exodus, although it causes a great scare when it occurs, can be of a finite amount only, and the potential drain should be capable of being met. The existing United Kingdom gold reserves substantially exceed the liabilities constituted by sterling balances held in countries outside the sterling area, and there need be no fear that these would be drawn down to zero. Furthermore there are unexhausted drawing rights on the International Monetary Fund, together with possible assistance from the "Paris Club".

It has to be admitted that the outflow might be rather large. It appears that much more short-term money has come in than is represented by the sterling balances held abroad, as recorded. During 1961 and 1962 there were large favourable items for "Unrecorded Transactions" in the balance of payments accounts. While some part of these may represent genuine favourable items that escape the statistical net, the greater part may be presumed to consist of capital temporarily lodged and invested in securities of some sort. The statisticians have recently felt justified in reallocating some part of the Unrecorded Transactions; to the extent that this involved the inclusion of foreign purchases of United Kingdom bonds under the head of long-term capital movement, it may be misleading. If an exodus of capital due to the reduction of interest rates in the United Kingdom and a consequent gold outflow led to any lack of confidence in sterling, there could be an additional outward movement of short-term capital of important size constituted by "leads and lags" in trade payments. These various factors could create a situation in which the Chancellor had to be not merely firm, but adamantine. If a growth policy is to be carried through, it will have to have top priority. While these pages have been critical of the "stop and go" policy of the United Kingdom authorities during the last seven years, it must not be supposed that they did not have, from time to time, quite serious anxieties, which seemed to them to make it indispensable to put on the brake.

The awkward situation that now obtains in relation to short-term capital is due to the authorities being prepared to deal with a rather serious deficit by a high Bank Rate without imposing import restrictions. I myself hold, and have continued to argue, that this policy was foolhardy. The deficit could not be regarded as a short-term affair only, but represented the final one-sixth of the journey towards the structural readjustments required by war-time losses. Although this should by no means be taken too tragically, it represented a more serious gap than could wisely be papered over by the attraction of short-term capital. Of course, if one has at the back of one's mind the view that one can always in the last resort rectify the situation by damping down the domestic economy still further, one could have a feeling of relative security. But if damping measures are disallowed on principle, except such as may be required to reduce demand-inflationary pressure, which has not existed in the period in question, one has to be a little more careful about the basic balance of payments. The attitude of the British authorities was a manifestation of a general point of view, shared by Americans, that one should do one's utmost to promote greater freedom of international trade. So far so good. But it has to be recognized that in the last resort there can be a basic conflict between the requirements of growth policy and the requirement for the removal of all restrictions on foreign trade. I fear that so long as growth policy is given second priority, the free world will show a lower rate of progress than the Communist world.

In relation to the British dilemma as regards short-term capital outlined above, it would be helpful if the Americans also established lower internal interest rates. And this, I venture to suggest, they need to do if they are themselves to establish a growth rate in the United States commensurate with the intrinsic energy of the American people, and to reduce unemployment to a lower level. Unfortunately at this juncture the Americans are also embarrassed by a balance of payments problem. Right thinking shows clearly that the problems of growth in the various countries of the free world are interlocked, and that an effort of collective thinking is called for.

The most important thing that the Americans could do to ease the situation would be to double the dollar price of gold. All the countries of the free world are now living on too short a shoe-string, as regards reserves. The value of the dollar in terms of goods has fallen to less than half its pre-war level; that of other currencies has fallen likewise, and by more in the case of those that have since been devalued against the dollar. The consequence of this is that, in spite of the supplementation provided by the holding of key currencies as reserves and the drawing rights on the International Monetary Fund, the aggregate value of available reserves for international settlement has fallen to not much more than half its previous level relatively to the value of the international commitments, for meeting the oscillations in which reserves are held. The result is that temporary balance-of-payments deficits have to be taken more seriously than they were in the old days, and give rise to damping policies that hinder growth. If reserves had been larger, in relation to the value of international trade, deficits such as those sustained by both the United States and the United Kingdom recently, would not have given rise to so much anxiety. In the longer run "natural forces" come in to correct those deficits. It is impossible to combine (1) adequate growth rates in the free enterprise countries, (2) non-discriminatory multilateral international trade without import restrictions and (3) very narrow reserves for international settlement. One or other has to give way. In the recent period it is growth that has been sacrificed. It would have been better to proceed more cautiously as regards the second objective. The obvious solution is to alter the third condition and to enlarge the amount of reserves available for international settlement. If that were done, the seeming conflict between growth and unrestricted international trade might largely disappear.

The Americans have been very reluctant to make a change in the dollar price of gold. Fundamentally this appears to be a prestige point. But, I submit, it is a mistaken one. The dollar has in fact long since lost half its value owing to the events of the Second World War, and the Americans have lost no credit in the eyes of the world because of that fact. It is generally recognized that that is the sort of thing that has to happen if one has a war of the magnitude of the Second World War. To double the dollar price of gold would be merely to give recognition to an existing fact. The Americans would not really lose credit for doing so; on the contrary, the rest of the world would be delighted and give them good marks for their courage and common sense. One might accordingly be inclined to describe the unwillingness to alter the dollar price of gold not as a "prestige point" but as a "non-recognition complex".

Apart from the prestige point, there may be a consideration of "honour" in the minds of the Americans. They may feel that foreign holders of dollars would be justified in expecting some compensation in the event of the dollar price of gold being marked up, and that this would be a severe burden upon the Americans. This point should be looked at very carefully and precisely; so long as there is vagueness about it, the point of honour might be a major obstacle to re-valuation, since a liability of unspecified magnitude may seem much more formidable than it really is.

No consideration at all need be paid to non-official holders of dollars. They hold them for their own convenience and at their own risk. The point of honour could only be held to arise in the case of the central banks, etc., which have held dollars out of consideration for American embarrassments during a period when they were legally entitled to ask for their encashment into gold at the rate of 35 dollars an ounce. But by no means all the central bank dollar holdings should be regarded as compensation-worthy. The greater part of these holdings have been for routine convenience, viz., to meet oscillations in the prospective net dollar liabilities of their respective countries, or, alternatively, to have the advantage of interest, which gold does not yield. To take the former point, no detriment would be caused by a change in the dollar price of gold, since the dollar reserves would remain available to meet the purpose for which they were held, namely, oscillations in dollar liabilities; they would not have lost any value in relation to these. As regards the second point, the holders have had the advantage of earning interest during the period. That interest was presumably a mark of the inferior liquidity of the dollar, which was due precisely because there was always the possibility that the value of the dollar relative to gold might be altered. In this world one cannot have something for nothing. The central bank holders have had their interest and they have taken their risk; if a halving of the gold value of the dollar was a little more than they anticipated, well, that is of the essence of taking a risk.

But a question of honour does arise in relation to those dollars which have been held, in excess of normal need, entirely to relieve the Americans of embarrassments. This factor has been operating only in the very recent period. We may probably take the central bank holdings of dollars at the end of 1959 as quite free of any motive of trying to help the Americans. Between the end of 1959 and the latest quotation, the central bank dollar holdings rose by about $2 billion. This gives the order of magnitude of the amount on which there would be an equitable case for compensation. It has to be set against a profit of about $16 billion. This would be no great burden to the Americans.

Being trained to believe that money is an important factor governing economic trends, I hold that, so far as economics are concerned, the success of free enterprise in competition with the system of Communist planning depends more than anything else on whether the free-enterprise countries have the good sense to raise the currency value of gold.

II. THE COMMON MARKET.

At the time of writing there is still much doubt whether the United Kingdom will gain admission to the European Common Market on acceptable terms. In the recent period there has been a good deal of unthinking enthusiasm in favour of the United Kingdom entry into the Common Market, especially in metropolitan circles. It has become a fashion and a talking point, like a good play or novel, of which it is bad form not to express admiration.

There is said to be a grave political question involved, which is somewhat obscure to an economist. There is, of course, the all-important question of the defence of the free world. But it would seem that institutions already exist that ought to be able to handle this efficiently. There is NATO. For a closer co-ordination of European efforts in relation to matters which NATO is for any reason not competent to handle, there is the Western European Union. It may be recalled that when the project for a European Defence Community broke down, owing to the final decision by the French that they could not agree to it (1954), the American spokesman declared that the Americans might have to have an "agonizing reappraisal" of their whole policy of commitment for the defence of Europe. At this point Sir Anthony Eden (Lord Avon), then British Foreign Secretary, made hurried journeys from capital to capital, and, by making certain British commitments, via the Western European Union, was thought to have brought into existence something so nearly resembling what the European Defence Community might have been, that the Americans no longer deemed the "agonizing reappraisal" necessary.

I would suggest that, if NATO and the Western European Union between them have in any degree failed to do a perfectly satisfactory job as regards defence, that is not for lack of an institutional set-up but because the countries involved are unwilling to make the necessary sacrifices. One cannot have strong defence without the residents of the countries concerned feeling it in their own pockets. It may be that the British have not made enough sacrifices; but their devotion of 6.3 per cent of their National Income[2] for that purpose, compared with 8.8 per cent for the United States, is not perhaps too bad. It is puzzling why a further organization (European Economic Community) is required to handle this vital question of defence.

In regard to other "political" aspects, there is great obscurity about what is demanded. If it is a question of the details of national government, there is no doubt that the British would be unwilling to surrender power over those questions commonly dealt with in the Parliament at

[2] Cf. page 18.

Westminster to a bureaucracy in Brussels. The line in the popular poem, "Britons never will be slaves", may be in point here.

But I am concerned only with the economic issue. In 1948 Western Europe as a whole was very weak in economic terms. It was rightly thought that, considering its resources in manpower, skill, technology and science, it was all wrong that it should be apparently so weak compared, for instance, with Russia, and that this was partly due to the barriers to intra-European trade. Since 1948 vast progress has been made. Much credit must be given to the magnificent generosity and statesmanship of the Americans in carrying out the project for "Marshall Aid"; without that assistance the Europeans might have continued to languish for a much longer period. Apart from the large provision of goods gratis, Marshall Aid helped by adding to European reserves and enabling the countries of Europe to break down the barriers to intra-European trade, by arranging for a multilateral settlement through the European Payments Union and by the trade liberalization sponsored by the OEEC.

The nineteen fifties have been a period of notable growth by the countries of Continental Europe, and especially by those now forming the European Economic Community. It must be observed, however, that this economic expansion cannot be attributed to the formation of that Community. To quote the figures provided by OECD, the annual rate of increase of industrial production between 1953 and 1957 was 8.7 per cent a year. The year 1958 was one of pause, coinciding with recessions in the United States and the United Kingdom and with a general world recession. Between 1958 and 1961 the annual rate of growth in the European Economic Community countries was 8.1 per cent. Not much need be made of the point that the rate of increase since the formation of the Common Market was fractionally lower; but there is clearly no evidence from the figures that its formation has had a stimulating effect.

On general grounds there is a great deal to be said for the creation of a Free Trade Area in the whole of Europe, so as to provide a sufficiently large market for mass production and specialization. The latter is perhaps the more important point. With the progress of science and technology, the whole of Europe is by no means too large an area to have complete specialization in laboratory research and the production of the more sophisticated products, with complete freedom of trade, so that each requirement can be met from whatever is the point in Europe at which the specialist producer is located. If this was all that was to be said about the matter, the economic case in favour of entry by the United Kingdom into the Common Market would be overwhelming.

Unfortunately there are certain other aspects. Professor Viner has analysed the question of Customs Unions from the theoretical point of view, and given good marks to a Customs Union to the extent that it is trade "creating", and bad marks to the extent that it is trade "diverting". A Customs Union is trade creating to the extent that it causes one member, say France, to switch its purchases from its own high cost producers on to lower cost producers in another country, say Germany. It is trade diverting if it causes the French to switch their custom from a low-cost producer, say in the United States, to a higher-cost producer, say in Germany. It is to be noted that the latter effect can occur even if the French tariff on American goods is not raised at all. In the new situation German goods come in duty free, while American goods are still subject to the old tariff; that may cause a switch of custom away from the United States to Germany, even if the German quoted price is higher than the American price.

Doubtless entry by the United Kingdom into the Common Market would cause a certain amount of trade creation. But it is to be feared that the trade-diverting effects might be very much larger. This is due to the position of the United Kingdom of being, owing to its island status and its history, so very large a purchaser from overseas.

It has been said that during the consideration of greater European economic integration, the United Kingdom at one point dragged its feet. This may be true. The question came to the fore immediately after the matter of the European Defence Community had been settled. It was during the last six months of the Prime Ministership of Sir Winston Churchill; there was a General Election at this time and other distracting events. Had the British entered into intimate conversations at once, it is thought that they could easily have secured "terms" for some kind of Free Trade Area, which would have safeguarded their overseas trade. The European conversations that took place at the Messina meeting at this time led to the drafting of the Treaty of Rome, which gave the European Economic Community the form of a Customs Union and not a Free Trade Area. The European countries concerned took the view that they had made sacrifices in order to get this agreement and were disinclined for further sacrifices. Thus the Treaty of Rome has assumed a certain rigidity. While it would be unthinkable for the United Kingdom to sign it without some modification, it is doubtful if sufficient modifications can be obtained to prevent the Treaty of Rome being seriously trade diverting, in a way that would be injurious both to the United Kingdom and to the free world as a whole.

The importance of the United Kingdom as a purchaser from overseas may be illustrated by the fact that in 1960 its imports, excluding those from Western Europe and the United States, were about two-thirds of the United States imports from outside Western Europe. If we omit the Western Hemisphere, the United Kingdom was a greater importer from countries other than Europe than the United States itself. A switch of important magnitude in its custom away from the overseas world towards Europe would have a very bad effect on the fortunes of developing countries overseas, many of them very poor.

If we consider the matter from a world point of view, much attention ought to be paid to the plight of developing countries. It is generally agreed that the gap between the standard of living in these and the standard of living in the mature countries should not be allowed to continue to widen. If the mature countries of the free world turn their backs on the developing countries, the latter are bound to be more inclined to look favourably on specious offers coming from other quarters. If the developing countries are to raise themselves out of their present poverty, it is absolutely essential that their imports should grow on a rising curve. They will need capital goods and materials that they cannot produce themselves; and they will need increased imports of consumer goods also if they are to provide any incentive, as they must, to those who are expected to switch their efforts from primitive processes to the more complicated tasks required in modern industrial production.

Part of this problem may be solved by the provision of aid or of loans below commercial rates; it is certainly expedient that some of the load should be taken off the United States, which has hitherto been so much in the forefront; or, to put it better, it is expedient that the countries of Europe should *supplement* what it is hoped the Americans will continue to do, by providing much larger amounts than heretofore. But the problems of the developing countries cannot be solved by charity alone. The scale of charity could not be sufficiently great without becoming unhealthy; and indeed the citizens of the mature countries would not be willing to grant so much. Nor can the problem be solved mainly by direct capital investment in the developing countries. If this were attempted, profits remitted home would soon overtop the annual rate of fresh capital investment, and be an insupportable burden on the balances of payments of the developing countries.

The main solution to the problem of the need of the developing countries to have rising imports is that the mature countries should give them increasing export outlets for what they are able to produce, whether in the way of primary products or traditional manufactures. This is in accordance with the excellent paper on *Trends in International Trade*, published by the GATT in 1958. What the mature countries can best do to help developing countries is to maintain expansion at home, avoid recessions, and be hospitable to imports from developing countries. The Treaty of Rome goes dead against this doctrine.

One may give an example. The British have allowed duty-free imports of textile products from the Commonwealth. For such countries as India, Pakistan and Hong Kong these revenues have been a life-line. It is true that Lancashire has been severely hit, and there has been in operation a gentleman's agreement limiting the rate of increase of these imports, to give time for further readjustments in the United Kingdom. Nothing could be more retrograde than for the United Kingdom to allow duty-free imports of textiles from the Continent of Europe while imposing the common European tariff on such imports from the developing countries of the Commonwealth. Yet this would be the requirement of the Treaty of Rome. At the time of writing it is to be feared that no sufficient concession can be secured under this head.

In this connection it is most important that Americans should understand that the main issue at stake here is not the existence of Commonwealth "preferences". What the Treaty of Rome requires is the imposition by the United Kingdom of *dis*-preferences, often heavy *dis*-preferences, against goods from overseas, including those from its Commonwealth, with which it has historic connections, and including those from developing countries, for which the British market has been a valuable asset. Thus the United Kingdom's signature of the Treaty of Rome would be bad not only by Viner's criterion of trade diversion (switching from low-cost to high-cost producers), but also by a "welfare" criterion, viz., switching custom from developing countries which need it badly to mature countries which need it much less.

Agricultural production has hitherto been somewhat backward on the Continent of Europe, by American, or indeed by British, standards. There is little doubt that this position is in the course of being rectified. There may be, as agricultural productivity rises, some consequent movement of population away from agriculture; but this is not likely to be great enough to prevent the production of substantial agricultural surpluses on the European continent. It is well known that there is a limit to the rate at which one can expect a population to move out of agriculture and that in every country agricultural interests are able to organize strong pressure groups. The United Kingdom is not likely to get into such a position in the foreseeable future, owing to the very low proportion of the population there engaged in agriculture. The United Kingdom will continue to depend in large measure on the imports of agricultural produce. Under the Treaty of Rome, the United Kingdom would have to satisfy a declining proportion of its food needs from overseas and a rising proportion from the Continent of Europe. Indeed it is said that one of the main factors favourable to the United Kingdom entry in France, which tends in general to look askance at it, is the feeling among its agricultural population that they will have a satisfactory vent for their surpluses in the United Kingdom. The general tendency of the Treaty of Rome is to take from the poorer countries and give to the richer.

It may be objected that not all Commonwealth countries, in whose interests the United Kingdom has been pleading, are poor. But those that are not poor are nonetheless not yet mature countries, and they need the assistance of rising export revenues. Such countries as

Australia and New Zealand have formidable problems ahead, if they are to develop themselves further and reach maturity. They will need not only their existing vents for agricultural output, but also vents for some of their manufactured products, if they are to balance their external accounts. But by the Treaty of Rome their manufactured exports to the United Kingdom would be subject to tariff, while imports from the European continent would be duty free.

The British have been labouring hard in negotiations to get the most they can for the Commonwealth. It does not appear that they could get nearly enough to meet the needs of the Commonwealth or to satisfy the dictum of Professor Viner, which looks to the general good, that the entry by the United Kingdom into the Common Market should not be trade diverting. In sustaining their arguments, the British negotiators have to rely heavily on the existence of the Commonwealth as a historic fact and on the moral obligations arising therefrom. The United Kingdom is also an important purchaser of produce from Latin America, and, if most of this trade were diverted to Europe, this would be quite a substantial setback for certain Latin-American countries (notably the Argentine and Uruguay). Those are developing countries, and such a switch would be retrograde. It is to be feared that the British have no leverage for arguing on behalf of Latin America in the negotiations. That is regrettable, but inevitable.

A large switch of purchases from the overseas world to Continental European sources would not only be damaging to the free world as a whole, but also be contrary to British interests, a point that the United Kingdom is bound to take into account. On the whole the switch would be from low-cost to high-cost producers and thus injure the British balance of payments at a time when, for reasons already explained, this is likely to continue precarious.

There is a quite different matter that would cause embarrassment if the United Kingdom joined the European Economic Community. It is not likely that British agriculture would suffer much injury, apart from horticulture, which is at present protected by import duties from continental competition. But the general method by which British agriculture is protected would be changed. At present food prices in the United Kingdom are based on world prices and British farmers are helped by subsidies ("deficiency payments", etc.). Food prices within the EEC are raised above world level by tariff protection; they are probably rendered sufficiently high by this method to suit British farmers. If the United Kingdom joined the Common Market, it would be expected to adopt the continental system, namely abandon its subsidies to farming and establish a higher price level for food. This would have a most adverse effect on the endeavours to prevent a wage-cost spiral, which have already been referred to. Wage-earners would insist on an increase of wages to meet the higher cost of living as caused by higher food prices. This could easily lead to a renewed wage-price spiral. Furthermore it would injure British competitiveness in export markets. It has been suggested that any increase in the cost of living due to higher food prices could be offset by reducing taxes that now bear on wage-earners, since the government would be saving money now paid out in subsidies. It is a misconception to suppose that the problem can be fully solved in this way. The fact of the matter is that, to the extent that food imports cost more than before, as they would if there was a switch from overseas to Continental Europe, the British would have to suffer some deterioration in their standard of living, or at least an abatement in the rate of increase to which they have been accustomed over the last decade. While this will be inevitable, the wage-earners will not readily acquiesce in it; they will consequently make a special push to restore their previous position and, since in the nature of the case they will not be able to do so, this must lead to renewed wage-price spiralling.

Opinion in the United Kingdom has recently been hardening against the idea of entry, and, with the passage of time, views outside the metropolis come to have greater weight.

Throughout the negotiations it has been supposed that American influence has been exerted in favour of the United Kingdom joining the Common Market. The reasons for this are somewhat mysterious to the British mind. It would seem to be contrary to American interests. It would appear to be in the American interest, especially having regard to recent balance-of-payments difficulties, that the Common Market tariffs against the outside world should be as low as possible, and it is presumed that they will use all their influence to secure this result; such influence would be strengthened by the powers recently granted to

Mr. Kennedy to make mutual tariff concessions. If the United Kingdom does not enter, it would be on the same side of the bargaining table as the United States in this matter, and it must be presumed that their combined influence in securing a more outward-looking attitude on the part of the European Economic Community would be greater, even if only a little greater, than the United States influence alone. Thus the United States would have an ally in the United Kingdom in relation to its proper objectives of policy. But if the United Kingdom entered the Common Market, it would be on the other side of the bargaining table, and that would presumably cause a deterioration in the bargaining power of the United States of substantial amount. When a member of a party leaves it to join the opposite party, there is a deterioration in the position of the former not by one vote, but by two votes.

The only rationalization of the American attitude that readily comes to mind is that it would simplify the world-wide diplomacy of the United States if the whole of Europe spoke with one voice, instead of only a politically integrated European Economic Community speaking with one voice and the tiresome British weighing in with another point of view. There are fewer parties to be "squared" in relation to any grand design that is an objective of American policy. This, considered by itself, is a perfectly reasonable attitude. But the benefits to be derived from such a simplification are not sufficient to outweigh the grievous detriment to the economic viability of the whole free world, should the United Kingdom enter the Common Market on such terms as at present appear to be the best obtainable.

Any prediction at present of the outcome of the negotiations is likely to be overtaken by events. It does not appear probable that the British will obtain acceptable economic terms. That being so, it is quite probable that the Prime Minister will be unwilling to recommend entry. On the other hand, it is possible that some political motive might cause him to persist in the project, even if the economic terms are not good. In that case it is probable that there would be a General Election and that the Labour Party would be returned to power.

III. WIDER PROSPECT

It is exceedingly difficult for anyone to assess the quality of the British achievement in the last eighteen years. In many fields of industry great progress has been made. At the same time there has been much criticism of backwardness and inefficiency in other fields. The problem of the structural readjustment, so often referred to in this book, has been an exceedingly formidable one, and critics do not always make allowance for its large dimensions. The United Kingdom has also been hampered by the "stop-and-go" policy, itself a by-product of the balance-of-payments problem. This has undoubtedly checked investment and been an obstacle to the modernization of industry. A firm that has a radical programme of reconstruction needs to hope that its markets will expand for a number of years ahead; if it knows that there is a greater probability that a damping policy will be reintroduced after a year or two, it may well be unwilling to take the necessary risks.

The United Kingdom has suffered from a scarcity of good engineers and other technologists. Great efforts are being made to remedy this defect by an expansion of university facilities and technological institutes. These cannot yield immediate fruits, but it is hoped that great changes in the availability of highly qualified personnel will occur in the twenty years ahead.

There is an important basic factor in the situation which is favourable. The population is likely to remain relatively stationary. Import requirements are mainly for food and basic materials. With a stationary population, requirements for these are not likely to rise as rapidly as National Income. On the other hand the outside world is likely to have a steeply rising demand for the kind of products in which the United Kingdom has a comparative advantage. Even if it does not retain its present share of world markets, the amount that it is able to sell is still likely to rise at a greater rate than its requirements for food and materials. This is basically a strong position.

Index

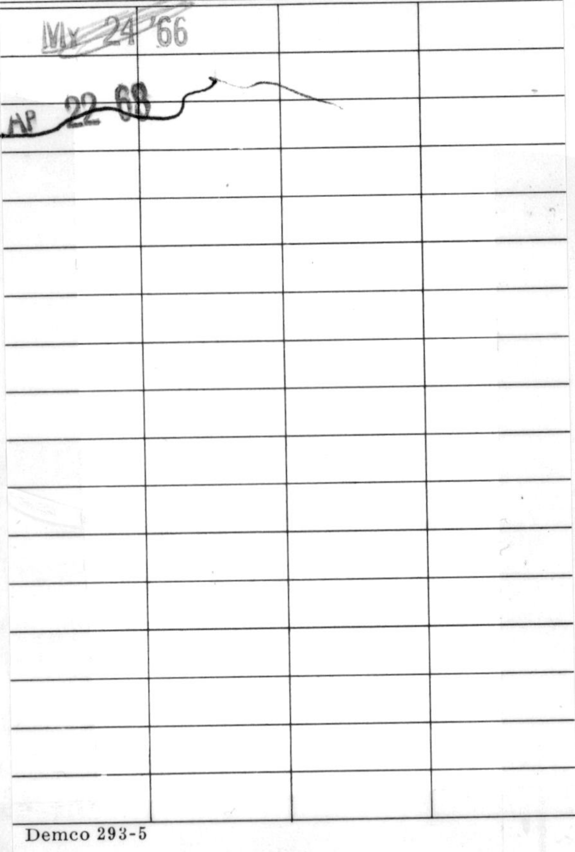